SUICIDE

Studies in Pure Sociology

DONALD BLACK, EDITOR

SUICIDE
The Social Causes of Self-Destruction

JASON MANNING

University of Virginia Press
Charlottesville and London

University of Virginia Press
© 2020 by the Rector and Visitors of the University of Virginia
All rights reserved
Printed in the United States of America on acid-free paper

First published 2020

ISBN 978-0-8139-4434-0 (hardcover)
ISBN 978-0-8139-4439-5 (paper)
ISBN 978-0-8139-4435-7 (ebook)

1 3 5 7 9 8 6 4 2

Library of Congress Cataloging-in-Publication Data is available for this title.

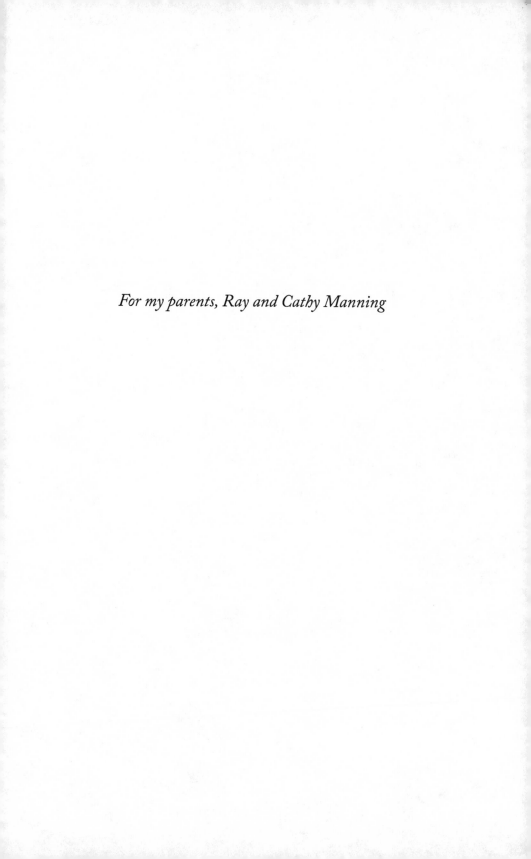

For my parents, Ray and Cathy Manning

Contents

Preface

Suicide is one of sociology's oldest subjects. Emile Durkheim's famous *Suicide: A Study in Sociology*, is revered as a classic, and its ideas are often featured in introductory sociology courses. It is renowned partly for being counterintuitive. People in the modern West tend to think of suicide as a profoundly individualistic action, something firmly rooted in the internal drama of the human mind. Durkheim forcefully argued that suicide varied predictably from one society to another and was thus something explicable with external social conditions. First hearing of these ideas as an undergraduate student, I was immediately intrigued. It was fascinating to think that this seemingly personal decision was predictably shaped by impersonal, external forces. I checked out a copy of Durkheim's book from the campus library, found a quiet corner, and began to read.

The spirit of this book harkens back to Durkheim's foundational work and to the optimism and confidence it displayed. It reflects my position that suicide is a social behavior and one that we can explain both sociologically and scientifically. Though a psychiatric model currently dominates public discourse on suicide, sociology still has important contributions to make toward understanding this topic. And these contributions go beyond uncritically clinging to the ideas of the field's revered founder. Thus this book takes up Durkheim's spirit but also departs from his substance. While my work incorporates ideas from his classic theory, it utilizes a relatively new kind of approach to sociology—an innovative theoretical strategy called *pure sociology*, first developed by sociologist Donald Black in the 1970s. In doing so, it also draws upon a body of work concerned with something other than suicide as such—conflict, and all the myriad ways that people handle it. The result is that many of my ideas treat suicide as a variable aspect of conflict, asking why some conflicts are more likely than others to drive people to self-destruction. Though this approach might seem narrow—people kill themselves for many reasons besides conflict—I argue that it shows a new path for the sociology of suicide, one in which we shift our focus away from comparing the suicide rates of groups to comparing the likelihood of suicide across different social situations.

I explain all this in more detail in the following chapters. For now, I ask readers who might be more comfortable with the traditional Durkheimian approach to keep an open mind about the potential of this new strategy. And I invite readers unfamiliar with sociology altogether to learn about all the strange ways that suicide, or any other human behavior, can vary across different social environments.

I should, however, give a small warning. Suicide is a form of violence that hits close to home for many readers. In modern America, as well as many other countries, suicide is both more frequent than homicide and more widely distributed across regions, ethnic groups, and social classes. It is likely that many of my readers will know someone who has died by suicide and may be interested in the topic exactly because of this. If so, my condolences. I am aware that suicide often produces a special sort of grief and can be a particularly difficult kind of bereavement to deal with. But beware that the remainder of this book approaches suicide with scientific detachment, as a strange phenomenon in need of explaining. I believe this the proper attitude for the sociologist to take, as moralizing can get in the way of describing and explaining, but some may be put off by it. So too for many of the cases I describe in the following pages, which readers may find disturbing. Perhaps even some of the theoretical ideas I advance might cause offense. For instance, the idea that suicide can be a weapon of social conflict, or that it is ever anything other than a symptom of uncontrollable illness, might be unwelcome. If you object that a deceased love one would never have meant to hurt anyone left behind, you are likely right—the patterns I describe in these chapters are not the only patterns that exist and are perhaps not the pattern that best matches the cases in your own life. But the reverse is also true, and there is value in considering patterns of behavior that may at first seem alien.

Should you dislike the book, the blame is mine. But if you find it valuable, I must share credit with a great many people who helped it come to be. I first studied sociology, including the topic of suicide, as an undergraduate at Christopher Newport University, where I was inspired by professors Bob Durrell, Joseph F. Healy, Lea Pellet, and Virginia Purtle. My sociological education continued as a graduate student at the University of Virginia, a department filled with outstanding intellects. I learned a great deal from the faculty there, including Rae Lesser Blumberg, Stephan Fuchs, Paul Kingston, Krishan Kumar, Jeffrey Olick, and the late Steven Nock. I also learned a great deal from my fellow graduate students, most especially Bradley Campbell, Laura Holian, and Justin Snyder. Their friendship and colleagueship were a boon beyond all measure.

The same can be said for the opportunity to work with Donald Black, under whose guidance I completed my doctoral studies and whose own highly innovative work provides most of the foundation for all that I have done since. I first read his *Social Structure of Right and Wrong* shortly before arriving at the University of Virginia and understood right away that I had discovered something new and exciting. I am grateful I was able to take his courses and learn from him in person. This book would be impossible without the theories, concepts, and perspective that he developed over many years in his unending quest to advance scientific sociology. He also read and commented on several earlier phases of the work. Aside from my intellectual debt, I owe him many thanks for his advice, support, and the occasional beer. It has truly been a privilege to know him.

Given the influence of my time at Virginia, I must also thank the University's Bayly-Tiffany Scholarship for generously funding much of my graduate study.

As a faculty member at West Virginia University, work on this book was facilitated by having welcoming and supportive colleagues, including especially Corey Colyer and Rachel Stein. In addition, Rae Lesser Blumberg, Bradley Campbell, Mark Cooney, Joseph E. Davis, Elizabeth Nalepa, Larry Nichols, and James Tucker deserve thanks for commenting on earlier phases of this work. Richard Holway, history and social sciences editor at University of Virginia Press, also deserves thanks for his helpful comments and suggestions regarding the book manuscript. So too do managing editor Ellen Satrom, who provided additional feedback prior to publication, and manuscript editor George Roupe, whose attention to detail was crucial for sanding and polishing the final product.

Some of the data cited in this book come from a study of coroners' files, which would not have been possible without the cooperation and assistance of Dr. Ronald Holmes and the wonderful, friendly, and professional investigators and staff at the Jefferson County Coroner's Office. I owe similar thanks to Patricia McCay, coordinator of the West Virginia Domestic Violence Fatality Review Team, for facilitating my study of domestic homicide-suicide cases. I also owe a special debt to Gage Donahue and the members of the Louisville Survivors of Suicide support group for inviting me into their midst and reminding me that suicide is not just a scientific curiosity but a human tragedy with great costs for those left behind.

Material from previous scholarly publications is incorporated in this book, though with substantial alteration and reorganization. Parts of my 2012 article "Suicide as Social Control," published in *Sociological Forum*, are visible in chapters 1–4 and in the conclusion. My 2015 article "Aggressive Suicide," published in the *International Journal of Law Crime and Justice*, contributes material to chapters 1 and 3. Parts of my 2015 article "Suicide and Social Time," published in *Dilemas: Revistas de Estudos de Conflicto e Controle Social*, are modified to make up large sections of chapters 2 and 3 and a small part of the conclusion. I thank these journals and their publishers for permission to use this material.

During the later stages of the book, as I worried about deadlines and revisions, I was extremely grateful for the encouragement and understanding of my wise and beautiful wife, Kirsten Youngee Song. I cannot imagine a better partner.

Finally, the biggest debt is to my parents, Ray and Cathy Manning. They fed and sheltered me, trained and taught me, loved and encouraged me. They always provided unwavering support, even when their kid decided to spend eight years in graduate school studying strange and morbid topics. And they always set a good example, one that I can only hope to live up to. They have always worked hard and have learned to do many different things. They are wise and thoughtful. They are kind and generous to everyone they meet. They are the best parents a son could ask for, and this book is dedicated to them.

SUICIDE

The Death of Mohamed Bouazizi

Mohamed Bouazizi rose on the morning of December 17, 2010, and set off for work. He left his modest stucco home in the Tunisian town of Sidi Bouzid and headed for the town center, where by eight o'clock he was pushing along a wheelbarrow full of fruits and vegetables. The night before, he had acquired about $200 worth of produce on credit. He was the breadwinner for a family of eight, and with luck, he would make enough selling the produce to continue supporting his mother, brother, and younger siblings.

The local police arrived around 10:30 to find the street vendor busy at work. They confronted him about the fact that he was vending without a permit. Mohamed and other local vendors often experienced such harassment and understood that the intent was to shake them down for a bribe (Fahim 2011). But Mohamed did not have enough money to bribe the officers, nor did he have any personal connections that would give him leverage with the corrupt local government.

Eyewitnesses disagree on the exact details of Mohamed's encounter with the police. Some say he was beaten, slapped, and spat upon by a policewoman—something that would have greatly shamed Mohamed. "She humiliated him," his sister later said. "Everyone was watching" (quoted in Fahim 2011). All agree he was publicly chastised and that the police confiscated his wheelbarrow, produce, and electronic scale. The incident left Mohamed humiliated, angered, and deprived of his only means of making a living and providing for his family (Abouzeid 2011; Fahim 2011; Ryan 2011; Sengupta 2011).

Mohamed immediately went to the governor's office to lodge a complaint and to demand the return of his costly electronic scale. The governor, however, refused to see or listen to him. At one point, a desperate Mohamed threatened that he would burn himself if the governor would not hear his case. Still the governor refused.

It had not been an idle threat. Mohamed left the office, went to a nearby petrol station, and acquired a can of gasoline. He returned and stood in the middle of the street, facing the governor's office. He shouted, "How do you expect me to make a living?" Then he poured the gasoline over himself and struck a match (Simon 2011).

Mohamed was engulfed in flame. Bystanders rushed to his aid and eventually succeed in putting out the fire. Mohamed, severely burned, was taken to a hospital, where he eventually succumbed to his injuries.

The story of his suicide by fire quickly spread throughout the country. Many sympathizers blamed the corrupt government for driving him to such a desperate act, and within hours the first protestors took to the streets. His friends and relatives gathered outside the governor's office, throwing coins at the gate and shouting, "Here is your bribe!" (Fahim 2011). When Mohamed died in the hospital a month after the incident, thousands participated in his funeral procession, during which they chanted, "We will avenge you . . . we will make those who caused your death weep" (Falk 2011; Sengupta 2011).

The protests grew larger, more widespread, and more violent. Attempts to suppress them were ineffective and counterproductive. Fearing for his safety, Tunisia's autocratic president fled into exile, ending his twenty-three-year rule (Noueihed 2011). And still the effects of Mohamed's death continued to radiate outward. Over a dozen aggrieved citizens in Algeria, Egypt, and elsewhere followed his example by lighting themselves on fire as similar waves of protest, riot, and revolution swept through the Arab world (Abouzeid 2011). The Arab Spring uprisings, as they are now known, led to regime change, civil war, and the mass migration of refugees—a cascade of geopolitical changes triggered by the suicide of one enraged and desperate street vendor.

In some ways, the suicide of Mohamed Bouazizi is unusual: most who commit suicide do not publicly burn themselves, and most deaths do not have such widespread impact on society. But his story does illustrate some much more common features of suicide.

First, his suicide was sparked by social causes. Legal officials had left him humiliated and suffering from a major financial blow. Whether or not psychological factors predisposed him to such a reaction, the fact remains that he killed himself when and where he did because of his interactions with other people—people who exerted social dominance over him, humiliated him, and took his property. We can observe similar social causes in many cases of suicide. For example, Aaron Swartz, an American inventor and copyright activist, hanged himself when faced with the threat of prolonged imprisonment and massive fines for allegedly illegally downloading academic papers from an online database (Dean 2013; Kemp, Trapasso, and McShane 2013). Prior to asphyxiating herself in a gas oven, poet Sylvia Plath suffered a devastating abandonment when her husband left her for another woman (Becker 2003). And near the end of World War II, Adolf Hitler shot himself in the head as Allied forces closed in on his headquarters, assuring the final defeat of his Nazi regime and his fall from power.

Mohamed's suicide also had social consequences. The typical suicide differs from his only in that its consequences play out on a smaller scale. While few suicides result in political upheaval, suicide often has tremendous consequences for the family, friends, and acquaintances of the deceased. Rock musician Dave Grohl described the suicide of his Nirvana bandmate Kurt Cobain as "probably the worst thing that has happened to me in my life" (Fullerton 2009). When Rutgers University student Tyler Clementi committed suicide in 2010, his roommate—who had previously used a web camera to spy on Clementi during a homosexual encounter—was publicly blamed for the suicide and sentenced by a federal court to thirty days in jail, three hundred hours of community service, mandatory counseling, and a $10,000 fine (Demarco and Friedman 2012). And in 2013 American country singer Mindy McCready, devastated by the suicide of her boyfriend and "soul mate" David Wilson, shot herself on the spot where he had killed himself one month earlier (Red 2013; Red and Beekman 2013). Suicide destroys relationships, alters reputations, and can lead to grief, guilt, blame, shame, sympathy, therapy, vengeance, and more suicide.

Finally, Mohamed's death was a social behavior in and of itself. He first threatened suicide in an attempt to obtain redress and then followed through on his threat as a way of expressing grievances against the corrupt officials who had wronged him. His suicide was an act of protest, carried out using a dramatic means of death also found in other widely publicized cases of political protest. The suicide was no less social than the mass demonstrations it inspired.

Other suicides are also social acts. Some are instances of altruistic self-sacrifice. Thus English explorer Lawrence Oates, seeing that his failing health was slowing his party's trek back from the South Pole in 1912, chose to end his life by walking out into a blizzard rather than continue to delay his companions on their way to much-needed supplies.[1] Or suicide might be a ritualized way of displaying loyalty or reverence. For example, when

Japanese shogun Tokugawa Iemitsu died in 1651, thirteen of his closest advisors ritualistically disemboweled themselves in a final demonstration of fealty (Rankin 2012:99). Still other suicides are, like Mohamed's fiery death, a way of handling conflict—a means of expressing grievances, seeking justice, or getting even.

We see in Mohamed's story that suicide is a form of social behavior sparked by social causes. It thus requires sociological explanation. This book presents such an explanation—a purely sociological theory of suicide. It addresses the kinds of social conditions that make people more or less likely to kill themselves. To do so, it focuses on cases, like that of Mohamed, where suicide is a way of expressing grievances or otherwise handling conflict. It may seem counterintuitive, but narrowing our focus in this way allows for much broader insights and helps us understand both conflict and suicide more generally. Thus this book not only addresses the question of when conflict leads to suicide, but the broader question of why different conflicts produce different outcomes—why fight rather than flight, why avoidance rather than negotiation, why capitulation rather than resistance. And my theory about why conflict leads to suicide also help us understand suicides that occur for other reasons, in other contexts. The theory helps us understand self-destructive behavior of all kinds. As we shall see, there is much that sociology can teach us about suicide.

1

Suicide and Conflict

I felt like I was up against a brick wall again! I was angry. I was furious at them for not taking this seriously and at myself for being a victim again. I was gonna show them. My husband took my daughters and said, "Come on, Mom's gonna off herself," and left. . . . I was gonna show them how much I was hurting, and I was gonna make him sorry that he said that to my daughters. (quoted in Heckler 1994:116)

Suicide is found in almost every human society, and is one of the most common forms of violence in the modern world. In the contemporary United States, the rate of suicide is about double the rate of homicide. And while criminal homicide in modern wealthy countries tends to be concentrated in a handful of high-poverty neighborhoods, suicide has a much wider distribution, touching the lives of a large swathe of the population.

But what exactly is suicide? The answer is not necessarily obvious. People engage in a wide variety of self-destructive behavior. Much of it is nonfatal, but sometimes the difference between death and survival is largely a matter of luck.[1] Scholars of suicide differ on whether to limit the term to fatalities or to also include unsuccessful attempts. They might also disagree on whether a particular mental state is necessary for an act of self-destruction to be considered a suicide. For instance, some might argue that if a young child of nine years old were to hang himself to death, it should not count as a suicide because the child did not understand the permanence of death.[2]

In this book we will use a broad definition: *suicide is the self-application of lethal violence.* "Lethal" means violence that is life threatening, as when someone is shot, stabbed, or hanged. Lethality is a continuum, a sliding scale of destructiveness or likelihood of causing death. The question of where exactly to draw the line between suicide and some lesser form of self-destruction need not concern us, as long as our definition focuses our attention on a family of similar acts. While the puzzle of why some suicide attempts are more lethal than others is important, for now it is enough to note that the topic of suicide includes all relatively lethal violence people inflict on themselves, even if they ultimately survive the attempt and regardless of whether they "truly" wanted to die.[3]

We can take a similar approach to the criterion of self-infliction, for this too can be a matter of degree. For instance, consider that people who inflict violence on themselves sometimes have assistance in doing so. American pathologist Jack Kevorkian, for example, assisted as many as 130 terminally ill patients in committing suicide by supplying them with and instructing them in how to use a device for injecting lethal chemicals into their body (Davey 2007; Jackson 2011). Some who wish to die even manipulate other people into acting as their executioners. The Bible describes how the Israelite King Saul, after being defeated in battle, ordered his own shield bearer to slay him with a sword (1 Samuel 31:4). In modern times, citizens in the United States and elsewhere might commit "suicide by cop"—goading police officers into shooting them through such actions as brandishing unloaded weapons (Mohandie, Meloy, and Collins 2009; Patton and Fremouw 2016). Again we have a continuum—the extent to which people are the sole and direct agent of their own demise varies, from pure suicide to cases that might better be classified as extreme risk taking or as voluntary execution. And again it is worthwhile to ask what explains this variation. But for the time being, we can simply consider all these cases as belonging to the same broad family, while focusing our attention on the cases in which people are most active in bringing about their own demise.

These considerations show that suicide is not a homogeneous category, and when we examine this category closely, we see many other kinds of variation as well. For instance, while many individuals make the decision to die completely on their own, others might be pressured or even ordered to kill themselves. When the Greek philosopher Socrates was found guilty of corrupting the youth of Athens, he was sentenced to act as his own executioner by drinking hemlock—and he chose to carry out the sentence, despite having an opportunity to flee into exile (Duff 1982–83). Suicide can be public, like the fiery death of Mohamed Bouazizi, or private, as when renowned art photographer Diane Arbus, long prone to bouts of severe depression, lay undiscovered for two days after fatally slitting her wrists in her New York City apartment (Bosworth 1984:320).[4] Some suicides are impulsive, occurring with at most a few moments of planning, while others are highly premeditated. Japanese author Yukio Mishima had been planning his death for a year when he and several conspirators stormed and occupied the office of a Japanese military official, from which Mishima broadcast a political manifesto before ceremonially stabbing himself with a sword (Flanagan 2014:190–243). Some suicides involve only the death of a single individual, while others involve suicide pacts between two or more people who vow to end their lives together. Adolf Hitler died alongside his wife, Eva, who took a lethal dose of cyanide after the couple had said their final goodbyes to Hitler's inner circle (Linge 2009). Suicide may even be a group project, as when thirty-nine members of the Heaven's Gate religious group ingested a fatal mixture of phenobarbital and vodka in 1997 in an effort to shed their earthly bodies and rendezvous with an alien spaceship (Lalich 2004).

Suicide, one can see, occurs in different forms and varieties. It might be collective or individual, voluntary or coercive, public or private, assisted or resisted, certainly fatal or a risky gamble with death. It might also arise from a variety of causes or contexts, such as depression, terminal illness, political struggle, or religious fervor. One major context for suicide is conflict, and it is this context that will be the main focus of this book.

Conflict, as defined by sociologist Donald Black, is "a clash of right and wrong" that occurs "whenever anyone provokes or expresses a grievance" (Black 1998:xiii; see also Black 2011:3). People might condemn others for arrogance, greed, sloth, impatience, or stupidity. We might criticize someone for not showing enough interest in us or for prying too deeply into our affairs, for having bad taste or for aping our own style, for failing to offer praise or for being a sycophant. We complain about being slighted and insulted, betrayed and abandoned, overworked and underpaid. Conflict is as ubiquitous as it is inescapable.[5]

People handle conflict in a staggering variety of ways. We might shun or avoid those who offend us—we give them the cold shoulder, force them to resign from the organization, or boycott their business. We might resort to aggression and violence—getting into fistfights, spanking misbehaving children, executing convicted criminals, or assassinating political opponents. We might talk things out and negotiate some solution to the problem, seeking compromise, repair, and peace. Or we might complain to a third party such as a legal official or workplace supervisor, and depend on this figure to find a solution and right the wrong. All these behaviors are, in sociological parlance, forms of *conflict management* or *social control*—ways of expressing and handling grievances, defining and responding to deviance, or otherwise handling conflict (Black 1976:105; Black 1998:3, 74–90). Conflict thus produces a plethora of behaviors, including gossip, feuds, lawsuits, arrests, divorce, terrorism, rioting, sit-ins, strikes, and genocide. It should come as no surprise, then, that it also produces suicide. Conflicts cause suicide, and much suicide is a way of handling or responding to conflict. That is, suicide can be a form of conflict management or social control (Baumgartner 1984; Black 1998:66, 72n2; Manning 2012). Indeed, any particular act of suicide might belong to one or more broader categories of conflict management, such as escape, protest, or punishment (compare Douglas 1967:299–334; Baechler 1975:55–199; Taylor 1982:140–93; Maris 1981:291).[6]

Suicide as Escape

In many cases, self-destruction is a means of fleeing from one's enemies—a kind of escape of last resort. The Roman politician Brutus—who famously betrayed and helped assassinate the dictator Julius Caesar—thus turned to suicide when defeated by his rivals at the Battle of Philippi in 42 BCE. Having fled into the hills with his surviving men, he knew that his eventual capture was inevitable. He therefore ran himself through with his own sword after telling his men, "By all means we must fly; not with our feet, however, but with our hands" (Plutarch 1918:245). Defeated warriors throughout history have made a similar choice.[7] Slaves might turn to suicide to escape from the abuse and punishment of their masters. African slaves on Cuban plantations sometimes killed themselves in the belief that they would be resurrected in their homeland, hanging themselves next to bundles of belongings and food that they believed would accompany them on their supernatural flight from bondage (Peréz 2005:38). And suspected criminals in modern America might kill themselves to escape from the legal authorities. The coroners' records of Louisville, Kentucky, describe the case of a young black man who was pulled over by the police in what they describe as a routine traffic stop.[8] Upon stopping his vehicle he jumped out and fled the scene on foot. The police pursued him, and after a short chase he ran into the yard behind a house and unsuccessfully attempted to break into the resident's garage. The resident then saw the man shoot himself in the head. According to police, the man was wanted on an outstanding charge.

In other cases suicide is not only a matter of escape but a way of expressing one's moral disapproval by withdrawing from the situation. For instance, after a military victory cemented Julius Caesar's hold on power, it appeared likely he would pardon his political opponent Cato, as he had done with other defeated adversaries. But Cato, loyal to the ideals of the Republic, refused to live under Caesar's authority or cooperate with the new dictator's display of mercy. Instead he stabbed himself in the abdomen and, when others attempted to save him, hastened death by plucking out his own bowels (Griffin 1986b; Plutarch 1919; Zadorojnyl 2007). The defiant nature of his act suggests not just flight from suffering but an act of moralistic avoidance—handling a grievance by breaking off contact with the offending party (Black 1998:79). People in daily life often express their grievances by cutting off ties and refusing to interact or cooperate, whether by ceasing to speak to an offensive acquaintance, walking out on an unfaithful spouse, or resigning from a corrupt organization. Suicide may be, in the words of anthropologist Klaus-Friedrich Koch, "the most extreme manifestation of avoidance" (Koch 1974:75). But suicide does much more than remove the self-killer from conflict—it may drastically alter its course.

Suicide as Protest

Suicide can be a tactic of protest or appeal, a means to seek redress by drawing attention to injustice, communicating the severity of grievances, and convincing others to rectify the situation (Douglas 1967:308–9). Perhaps the most famous case in modern times occurred in Vietnam in 1963. At the time, the government of Vietnam was headed by Catholic president Ngo Dinh Diem, whose policies discriminated against the Buddhist majority, making it difficult for Buddhists to gain government employment and forbidding public expressions of Buddhist culture. This led to an escalating cycle of conflicts between the government and activist groups led by Buddhist monks. Activists would stage marches and demonstrations, while government forces would arrest protestors and raid Buddhist monasteries. Against this backdrop an older monk, Thich Quang Duc, volunteered to burn himself on behalf of the Buddhist cause. Though initially skeptical, his monastic superiors eventually agreed to the idea and helped plan and organize the event (Chanoff and Van Toai 1986:141–43). On June 11, 1963, a progression of monks escorted Quang Duc to a busy Saigon intersection, where they announced his intentions to the assembled crowd. Quang Duc then soaked himself in gasoline, sat in lotus position, and set himself ablaze. Before his death, he left a note addressed to the president, which read, "I have the honour to present my words to President Diem, asking him to be kind and tolerant towards his people and enforce a policy of religious equality" (quoted in Biggs 2005:172). The words apparently had little direct effect on President Diem, but the act succeeded in shocking bystanders and in winning widespread sympathy for the Buddhist cause. Not long after photos of Quang Duc's self-immolation appeared in US newspapers, the US government withdrew its support for President Diem, leaving him vulnerable to the coup that eventually removed him from power (Biggs 2005; LePoer 1989).

Thich Quang Duc was far from the first person to kill himself on behalf of a political cause. In 1905, for example, a Korean official named Min Yong-hwan cut his own throat to protest his country's annexation by Japan, making his intentions known in letters addressed to the Western powers and to the Korean people (Biggs 2008:23). And in Japan in the 1880s, demonstrations aimed at convincing the imperial government to create a parliament sometimes involved suicide. One protestor disemboweled himself at the front gate of the imperial residence, leaving a letter stating his intentions: "These days, those who follow the Imperial instructions are anxious about the situation that prevails in our country. They come to Tokyo to appeal to the government for the establishment of a parliament. The government should consider their supplications. . . . I have decided to encourage these supplicants by sacrificing my own self" (quoted in Seward 1968:97).

But though not the first protest suicide, Quang Duc's death was highly influential. According to sociologist Michael Biggs (2008), Quang Duc's suicide quickly inspired imitators and led to public self-burning becoming a widespread tactic of political protest around the globe. One early example of this diffusion was the 1965 suicide of Norman Morrison, an American Quaker who burned himself outside of the office the US secretary of defense as an act of protest against the Vietnam War (King 2000:127; Biggs 2005:181). Mohamed Bouazizi might have had such cases in mind when he chose burning as a method of suicide. Still more recently, in 2017, a young Tibetan monk named Jamyang Losal set himself on fire to protest China's control of Tibet, becoming the 150th Tibetan to do so since 2009 (Gyatso 2017).

Self-burnings often occur in conjunction with other kinds of collective protest activity, such as marches, strikes, and sit-ins (Biggs 2005; Kim 2008).[9] But suicide as protest does not only occur in large-scale political conflicts. People sometimes turn to self-destruction to protest their own individual circumstances or appeal to a personal acquaintance to change his or her errant ways. In a famous case from the history of Japan, a loyal retainer killed himself to convince his young lord to abandon a pattern of irresponsible and reckless behavior that threatened to undermine the feudal house (Seward

1968:38). In modern times, people who survive suicide attempts sometimes say that their behavior was less about a desire to die and more a matter of risking death in order to appeal to a friend or relative (Baechler 1975:132–34; Firth 1967; Taylor 1982:179–84; Schnyder et al. 1999). For example:

> A 19-year-old girl became very distressed when a married man with whom she had been having an affair returned to his pregnant wife. She bombarded the man with letters, telephone calls, and visits until finally, a court order was placed on her. The following day she took a substantial overdose of barbiturates before wandering into the street, collapsing and being taken to the hospital. Upon being asked whether she intended to kill herself she said, "I don't know. . . . Not really I suppose . . . but I couldn't see any other way of getting through to him. (quoted in Taylor 1982:183)

This young woman is not unique: a survey of over a thousand suicide attempters from several European countries revealed that about 14 percent cited wanting someone else to change their mind as a "major influence" on their decision (Hjelmeland et al. 2002:385). Some who survive suicide attempts of this kind report to interviewers that their attempt resulted in having their demands met (Michel and Valach 1997). In one case, a woman overdosed on aspirin after her lover refused to leave his family and live with her. The act apparently succeeded in altering the behavior of the lover, who then began living with her and was still living with her six years later. According to the victim, her suicide attempt "had brought him to his senses" (quoted in Douglas 1967:278). In another case, a young French woman wanted her mother to divorce her stepfather, who was strict, demanding, and possessive. After the young woman survived taking an overdose of pills, her mother finally began to consider divorce (Baechler 1975:134). In modern America, many recognize that suicide attempts can be a "cry for help," and surely many of these are cries for help with or from specific people. Of course not everyone survives self-destructive appeals. In contemporary rural North China, locals understand that those who kill themselves in the context of family disputes were "gambling for *qi*," meaning they made an angry and reckless attempt to gain leverage in interpersonal politics: "When wronged too much, one is likely to set life as a trump card to win one's qi" (Fei 2005:10).

Used as a tactic of protest or appeal, suicide draws attention to grievances, wins sympathy, and perhaps shames or frightens others into ceasing obnoxious conduct or otherwise helping remedy the situation. But sometimes suicide is less about seeking recompense than about seeking vengeance.

Suicide as Punishment

Suicide can be an act of a punishment aimed at those left behind. Anthropologist M. D. W. Jeffreys (1952) identified two means by which suicide can act as a form of vengeance against the living: supernatural sanctions and social sanctions. Though Jeffreys was writing mainly about patterns he observed in African societies, we can see examples of these punitive forms of suicide in many societies around the world and throughout history.

SUPERNATURAL SANCTIONS

People in many cultures believe that suicide is a source of supernatural pollution, placing a curse upon anything or anyone closely connected to the death. The home in which a man hanged himself might have to be abandoned; a tree from which he hanged himself might need to be uprooted and burned. In some cultures, people believe that suicide unleashes supernatural forces that punish anyone whose conduct was responsible for driving the deceased to take his or her own life. The result is that some aggrieved individuals in these cultures turn to suicide specifically because they want to put such a curse upon an enemy. For example, in colonial Tanganyika (now part of Tanzania), "When a man has a grievance, and receives no redress, he will, as a final resort, go before the wrongdoer and say, 'I shall commit suicide, and rise up as an evil spirit to torment you'" (Gouldsbury and Sheane 1911, quoted in Jeffreys 1952:119). The same practice was found in traditional India, where members of the priestly Brahman caste might use suicide to avenge an injury—for "it was generally believed that the ghost of such deceased would harass and prosecute the offender" (Thakur 1963:63). Thus "when one of the Rajput rājās once levied a war-subsidy on the Brāhmanas, 'some of the wealthiest, having expostulated in vain, poniarded themselves in his presence, pouring maledictions on his head with their last breath'" (Thakur 1963:64). Similarly, an ethnographer studying Taiwanese farmers during the mid-twentieth century reports that "the ghost of a suicide is believed to be particularly powerful and absolutely determined to bring tragedy to the people responsible" (Wolf 1972:163).

Posthumous supernatural vengeance is likewise prominent among the Maroon tribes of Suriname and French Guiana.[10] These peoples, the descendants of escaped African slaves, share a belief in vengeful spirits called *kunu*, "the spirit of a person or god who was wronged during his lifetime, which dedicates itself to tormenting eternally the matrilineal descendants and the close matrilineal kinsmen of the offender" (Price 1973:87). One way of initiating a *kunu* is self-destruction. For example, in one case among the Aluku Maroons, "a man of the Awara Bakka lineage . . . committed suicide two or three generations ago when he was unjustly accused of a crime by a man of the Dju lineage. Since then, [his spirit] has been exterminating the Dju lineage little by little" (Hurault 1961:345). Another man "committed suicide when accused of sorcery by the people of his lineage. Since then, his [spirit] has caused sickness and deaths in his own village" (Hurault 1961:345). In Maroon societies, supernatural aggression lies behind most suicides, and threats of suicide are a common feature of disputes (Lenoir 1973:105; Price 1975:36; Bilby 1990:46).

The reader may not believe in the efficacy of supernatural curses, but clearly many people in the world do. Wherever there is a strong fear of the supernatural threat posed by suicide, there will be individuals tempted to use it as a weapon. Even when such beliefs are absent, however, suicide can still pose a threat against those left behind.

SOCIAL SANCTIONS

Sometimes suicide leads to "societal reprisals" against the deceased's adversary (Jeffreys 1952:120–21). Here, the social consequences of suicide spell trouble for someone who wronged the self-killer. A common pattern is for a member of Clan A to commit suicide in response to an offense by a member of Clan B, prompting other members of Clan A to hold the offender liable for the death. These aggrieved kin may then demand compensation for the death or even take bloody vengeance. Among the Lusi of Papua New Guinea, for example, battered wives sometimes commit suicide to mobilize their kinsmen against an abusive husband. These suicides involve specific behaviors that ensure they will be recognized as moralistic acts and produce the desired response: by dressing in her finest, killing herself in front of a witness, and sending a message to identify the cause of her death, "a suicidal woman can reasonably expect her kin and friends to consider her to have been a victim of homicide—to have been killed by shameful slander and abuse" (Counts 1987:196). The guilty party must then pay restitution to the family or else face vengeance. Even if the offender pays restitution, it will not guarantee his safety: one self-killer's father accepted compensation from her husband and then contracted a sorcerer to kill him anyway (Counts 1987:199). In another incident, a New Guinea Highlander named Ethel hanged herself after being beaten by her husband, Raphael: "Raphael's kin paid a large compensation payment to Ethel's relatives. In spite of this, Ethel's kinsmen met Raphael's plane when he returned to the Highlands [from working in nearby New Britain] and hacked him to pieces with axes as he stepped off the airplane" (Counts 1987:199). Though rarely this extreme, similar patterns of third-party sanctions are found throughout New Guinea (e.g., Johnson 1981; Stewart and Strathern 2003). They are found in other times and places as well. In older times, the Iroquois of North America considered suicide an act of vengeance and treated the victim's adversary "much in the same light as a murderer" (quoted in Fenton 1986:449). Among the Aguaruna Jívaro, a tribal people of Peru, the family of a suicide victim will "attempt to exact compensation in goods or cash" from whoever drove their kinsman to self-destruction; failing compensation, "they may assume a warlike posture" (Brown 1986:321).[11] And among the Ovimbundu of Angola, family vengeance occurs alongside a supernatural curse: the suicide victim's relatives "must avenge the death by action against the person who caused the suicide," and in addition "it is believed that the ghost of a suicide will return to haunt and punish those against whom the suicide has been committed" (quoted in Ennis and Lord 1962:159, 177; see also Edwards 1962:132,142).

Kin are not the only ones who might punish an offender on behalf of the suicide victim. Among the Cheyenne of the North American Great Plains, self-destruction would mobilize the community as a whole to banish the victim's adversary from the community (Hoebel 1976:159). In other settings, it is the government that steps in and levies sanctions against the victim's adversaries. Such was the case in China during the time of the Qing dynasty, where the legal code specified that driving another to suicide was a criminal offense.[12] The result, according to one missionary, was "that if you wish to be revenged on an enemy you have only to kill yourself to be sure of getting him into horrible trouble; for he falls into the hand of *justice,* and will certainly be tortured and ruined, if not deprived of life" (quoted in Pérez 2005:62; see also Meijer 1981). In these settings, such widely known and predictable third-party reactions make suicide an effective act of retaliation, and reports suggest that it is knowingly used as such.

In the modern United States, driving another to suicide is not officially recognized as a crime, but it might result in civil litigation or other legal problems for anyone thought to have done so (Knuth 1978). For example, consider the case of Tyler Clementi described above—his roommate was subject to jail time and hefty criminal fines for actions that allegedly contributed to Clementi's suicide. Still, such sanctions are presently rare and unpredictable enough that few people appear to count on them as a way of punishing those who have wronged them. But that does not mean that suicide in modern America is never a matter of hurting others.

PSYCHOLOGICAL SANCTIONS

A third major way suicide can be used as a punitive tactic is by inflicting psychological harm—such as trauma, guilt, and grief—upon those left behind.[13] Like any death, suicide is likely to cause suffering and grief for the friends and family of the deceased. Suicide also commonly inspires tremendous guilt among those left behind, who are prone to question whether they contributed to the act or could have done more to prevent it.[14] Most suicidal people surely did not want to leave behind such pain, and some actively take steps to prevent it by leaving notes that absolve others from blame. But some certainly appear to count on their death making another feel bad. In a survey of sixteen hundred Europeans who attempted suicide, 12 percent said a major influence on their attempt was wanting another to feel guilty (Hjelmeland et al. 2002:385). And there are clearly cases where individuals take steps to maximize the guilt and shame of their survivors, often in the form of harsh statements left behind before death. Among the Tikopia, an island people of Polynesia, suicide frequently occurs when "the person feels himself or herself offended and frustrated, and flounces off in a rage, often hurling back some pointed 'last words' to make the survivors regretful" (Firth 1967:128). A study of suicide notes in Louisville, Kentucky, revealed that about 22 percent of notes implicated another person's actions as the cause for the suicide, at least implicitly blaming them for the death, and about 9 percent expressed blame in an overt and hostile fashion (Manning 2015a). For example, an abusive husband left the following note to his recently estranged wife:

> Katie,
>
> Maybe you are happy now. I thought about taking you [i.e., killing her as well] but I don't think its worthwhile for I don't believe God will let you live to [*sic*] long. For you no good as they come. Take care of that doll [their daughter] I don't see how she could ever love you again. I can't understand why you left for there sure wasn't any one else if there was I wouldn't do this. Tell that doll I love her and to always be good. I wanted to talk to her but you made me so mad and I new [*sic*] I would cry. I have set [*sic*] here and cryed [*sic*] for an hour now. I hope you are happy. I don't see how you can stand to live. . . . You should frame this where you can read it wonse [*sic*] and a while you no good bitch. (quoted in Manning 2015a:332)

In another case, a young man who killed himself by driving his car off the road at a high rate of speed told his former girlfriend that "every time you hear the word suicide or car wreck I hope it reminds you of me, every time you cut yourself from now on I hope it reminds you of my face" (quoted in Manning 2015a:332). Yet another note read: "If you are reading this something has happened, you should have took my calls. All we needed to do was talk. You have always had a problem dealing [with] things. Now how are you going to deal [with] this. You should have kept your legs closed. . . . I don't care if you hate me now [because] each time you see our children you will see me. . . . What are you going to do? I hope you feel as bad as I have the past 4 weeks" (quoted in Manning 2015a:332). Another strategy for inflicting psychological harm is to force someone else to witness the suicide or its aftermath. One way of doing this is to ensure that the target of aggression will be the one to find the body.[15] Some who kill themselves take steps to prevent such discoveries, such as leaving their homes and traveling elsewhere to commit the act or posting notes outside locked rooms warning loved ones not to enter. Others, however, engage in the opposite behavior, making it more likely that another will find their body, sometimes in the most disturbing fashion possible. This may involve someone killing himself or herself at another person's dwelling or place of work. For example, one young man was involved in a dispute with his girlfriend at his own residence. Later that evening he went to his girlfriend's home (while she was elsewhere) and hanged himself from the roof of the front porch (Manning 2015a:333). Similarly, while some who use particularly gory methods of dispatch—such as shooting themselves in the head with powerful firearms—go outside to prevent making a grotesque mess in shared living quarters, others, either thoughtless or hostile, do not. In one case, an aggrieved man took gruesome steps to expose his estranged wife to the physical evidence of his death. According to the coroner's report,

> The 45-year-old had escaped from a mental hospital and had been searching for his wife, whom he had previously threatened to kill. The wife, who was in hiding elsewhere, summoned police to their home. After their arrival the officers found him barricaded inside. They heard a noise, and heard him yell. . . . One of the decedent's sons accompanied them as they broke the window and forced entry. They found the decedent lying in the middle room of the house with a shotgun wound to the stomach. The home was covered in blood—it looked as if he had smeared it on everything with his hands. Officers thought that

he touched everything his wife would use to remind her of his death. (quoted in Manning 2015a:333)

Another way in which persons expose others to their deaths is by forcing them to witness it at close range. For example, one forty-year-old man's girlfriend "had broken up with him about a week prior because he was an alcoholic and he had threatened her and her family." On the night of his death he was drinking with another man, during which time he repeatedly unloaded and reloaded a gun before declaring that "he was going over to his ex's house to kick the door in and blow his brains out in front of her"—which he soon did (quoted in Manning 2015a:334). It would not be surprising if the targets of such confrontational suicides suffered nightmares and other trauma symptoms in addition to whatever other psychological burdens arise from being implicated in another person's suicide.

Suicide, then, is often a way of protesting, punishing, or otherwise expressing grievances against other people. Whether as an act of avoidance, appeal, or aggression, such suicides are a kind of social control—a way of responding to conduct the perpetrator sees as unjust or offensive (Baumgartner 1984:328–29; Black 1976:2–5; Black 1998:xxiii). To the extent that self-destruction is social control, concerned with responding to perceived wrongs, it is a moralistic behavior—what we might call *moralistic suicide*.[16] Of course not all suicides are moralistic or otherwise caused by conflict. Statistics from the US Centers for Disease Control suggest that conflict causes around a third of all suicides in the contemporary United States (e.g., Centers for Disease Control 2006; Zwillich 2006). My own study of coroners' records in Louisville found about the same proportion, though only about a quarter of these (and thus about 8 percent of all suicides) involved such overt moralism as leaving blame-filled notes or committing confrontational suicide. A study of European suicide attempters asked them to rate whether various motives had a minor or major influence on their act: about 12 percent chose "I wanted to make others pay for the way they treated me" as a major influence, with a similar percentage picking it as a minor influence (Hjelmeland et al. 2002). Others picked less aggressive reasons that nonetheless suggest a kind of protest or appeal: we have already seen that about 14 percent picked "I wanted to persuade someone to change his/her mind" as a major influence (Hjelmeland et al. 2002). The proportion of suicides that are moralistic will also vary across locales and across categories of people. Because suicide among the old is more likely caused by such things as declining health and bereavement, conflict causes proportionally more among the young (Rich, Young, and Fowler

1986; Marttunen, Aro, and Lönnqvist 1993; Mościcki 2001).[17] It will also vary across societies and historical periods. While it may account for a minority of suicides in the contemporary West, there are several tribal and traditional societies where conflict is easily the dominant reason for suicide, and the typical suicide is an explicitly moralistic act. From a practical as well as a scientific standpoint, this form of behavior is far from trivial. And that is before we even consider a second sense in which suicide can arise from conflict and act as social control: the act of self-execution.

Suicide as Self-Execution

Not all moralistic suicides handle grievances toward other people. In some cases, suicidal people have grievances against themselves. Black (1998:65–72) argues that just as persons and groups engage in social control against others—protesting, punishing, or otherwise responding to their offensive behavior—so too they apply social control to themselves. They can unilaterally define their own conduct as deviant or offensive or agree when someone else complains about them. And even in situations where they could have done otherwise, people will sometimes voluntarily confess, apologize, pay compensation, or engage in some other act of atonement for their own wrongdoings. In extreme cases, Black proposes, they may even execute themselves (Black 1998:66).

It certainly appears that some who kill themselves are doing so in response to their own deviance. Consider a case from Victorian England in which a woman killed herself for being unfaithful to her husband: "Mary Renton, aged 25, the wife of a fisherman who was at sea, was found drowned in March 1894. The letter to her husband declared: 'I have deceived you ever since Friday night and I cannot bear to think of it again. . . . Tell Mother and brothers that I cannot disgrace them any longer'" (Bailey 1998:261). A suicidal person in modern Los Angeles likewise left a note expressing her self-complaints: "I've proved to be a miserable wife, mother, and homemaker—not even a decent companion" (quoted in Farberow and Schneidman 1957:43–44).

Suicide may follow a specific offense against another party. For example, those who kill others sometimes kill themselves in turn, possibly expressing guilt or remorse for the killing before doing so. In a case occurring among the Netsilik Eskimo,

> Oaniuk was killed accidentally during a hunt. Okoktok, a poor hunter, shot him during a caribou chase. Our informant is specific about the

unintentional character of this tragedy: "It is certain that Okoktok didn't want to kill Oaniuk, because the latter was a very excellent hunter." As he died, Oaniuk shouted for his gun in order to shoot back at Okoktok, but did not get the chance. Okoktok felt terribly guilty and later, visiting his neighbors, he declared himself ready to be killed. He was told: "You are not good game; if you want to kill yourself, go out and do it yourself." That is precisely what Okoktok did. (Balikci 1970:165)

A study of parent killing in nineteenth-century New York suggests that suicide following the killing of a parent was often a spontaneous, hot-blooded act that was followed by suicidal regret: "Offenders engaged in postoffense behaviors consistent with feelings of 'guilt and remorse' that were brought on by becoming cognizant of their violent actions. That is, these offenders did not flee, but stayed at the scene. . . . Some committed suicide; others ran to fetch medical assistance. . . . Some parricide offenders attempted to give cardiopulmonary resuscitation (CPR) to their dying parents" (Shon and Roberts 2010:52). Similarly, in twentieth-century Baltimore, a man who killed his wife cried out, "Oh my God, what did I do?" before committing suicide (Berman 1979).

This is not to say that all who kill themselves after killing another are executing themselves for the crime of murder. Many give no indication of guilt, shame, or regret, and studies of homicide-suicide in the United States, Canada, and elsewhere suggest that the typical case in these settings involves a perpetrator who planned in advance to kill himself along with his victim. Rather than a post hoc reaction to guilt, these cases have the character of suicide in which another person is "taken with" the killer (Milroy 1998; Dawson 2005; Manning 2015b). Pure self-execution is more often found in cases where a killing was impulsive or accidental, as in the examples above, or as in the case of an elderly New Orleans man who mistook his nurse for a burglar, fatally shot her, and then killed himself after realizing his mistake (Harper and Voigt 2007:308–9). People might also punish themselves for accidental deaths even if they were only indirectly responsible for them. For instance, in 1971, tragedy struck a French village when a floor collapsed during a wedding party, sending thirteen people plummeting to their deaths in a well shaft below. The owner of the room in which the party was held blamed himself for the deaths, telling townsfolk, "I shall never forgive myself," and committing suicide with a revolver soon after (Baechler 1975:98–99). More recently, when sixteen people were killed by the collapse of a metal grate at a

South Korean pop concert in 2014, the government official in charge of the venue's safety measures left a note reading, "I am sorry for the dead victims," before jumping to his death from a ten-story building (Kreps 2014).

In some conflicts, the offended party may even suggest or demand that the offender commit suicide. Again, consider the case of the Greek philosopher Socrates, who carried out his own death sentence by drinking hemlock. The Roman philosopher Seneca the Younger was likewise sentenced to die by his own hand when accused of conspiring against Emperor Nero. Though he denied the charge and may have been innocent, Seneca complied with the order, drinking hemlock and opening his veins in a hot bath (Griffin 1986a). And in premodern Japan, members of the samurai warrior class and, later, officers in the imperial military could also be ordered to commit suicide as punishment for crime, disobedience, and failure. Here self-execution took the form of seppuku, a ritualized act in which the offender disemboweled himself with a short sword (Pinguet 1993:129–35). One of the last cases of state-imposed seppuku occurred in 1868, when the Emperor Meiji sentenced a military officer to death for wrongly ordering his troops to fire on a foreign settlement. On the day of his death the officer confessed: "I, and I alone, unwarrantably gave the order to fire on the foreigners at Kobe. . . . For this crime I disembowel myself, and I beg you who are present to do me the honor of witnessing the act" (quoted in Pinguet 1993:152). He then stripped to the waist, knelt, and plunged a sword into his abdomen, drawing it all the way across his belly before making a slight upward cut at the end. Having fatally wounded himself in an extraordinarily painful fashion, the officer withdrew the sword, leaned forward, and extended his neck so that an assistant could deliver a coup de grace by severing his head (Pinguet 1993:152).

Suicide as a Psychological Problem

Why would anyone handle a conflict by committing suicide? Why do protestors who burn themselves not burn down the homes of their enemies instead? When will an aggrieved person try to hurt another by hurting herself? Under what conditions do offenders turn into their own executioners? What causes suicidal conflicts to erupt in the first place? And does understanding this tell us anything about what causes other types and patterns of suicide?

There are many ways to try to answer such questions. My goal here is to answer them sociologically—to address conflict and suicide as forms of social life that arise from social causes and that are shaped by social relationships.

Such an approach might seem strange to many readers. In the modern world, both professionals and the public commonly treat suicide as a medical or mental problem—the province of psychiatry and psychology, not sociology. Ask ordinary Americans what causes suicide, and they will likely answer by naming a form of mental illness: depression. Depression, in a psychiatric sense, refers to a state of prolonged, persistent, and intense sadness or low mood. It is often associated with a lack of motivation, inability to enjoy life, and low self-esteem. It is a painful state of mind that can lead to suicide as a means of ending mental suffering. Consider the following description of one depressed person's experience:

> Her youth contained no traumas; her adult life, as she describes it, was blessed. . . . But in the last months of 2000, apropos of nothing—no life changes, no losses—she slid into a depression of extraordinary depth and duration.
>
> "It began with a feeling of not really feeling as connected to things as usual," she told me one evening at the family's dining-room table. "Then it was like this wall fell around me. I felt sadder and sadder and then just numb."
>
> Her doctor prescribed progressively stronger antidepressants, but they scarcely touched her. A couple of weeks before Christmas, she stopped going to work. The simplest acts—deciding what to wear, making breakfast—required immense will. Then one day, alone in the house after Gary had taken the kids to school and gone to work, she felt so desperate to escape her pain that she drove to her doctor's office and told him that she didn't think she could go on anymore. (Dobbs 2006, quoted in Horwitz and Wakefield 2007:12)

Such depression is by definition distinct from the normal sadness everyone experiences following losses such as the death of a loved one.[18] That it can come out of the blue suggests that it is caused less by external conditions than by some internal disorder of the mind and body. One especially well-known theory is that depression stems from a malfunction in the brain's ability to produce and use the neurotransmitter serotonin. This belief has been the basis for many chemical medications marketed as treatments for depression—including such widely used drugs as Prozac, Paxil, and Zoloft—and their apparent effectiveness suggests it has some validity. On the other hand, more recent research fails to support the serotonin theory (Lacasse and Leo 2005). There is also research suggesting other physiological and chemical causes (such as inflammation and folate deficiency) and that other treatments (such as electroconvulsive therapy and ketamine) are also effective (see, e.g., Dantzer et al. 2008; Fava and Mischoulon 2009). A more recent theory is that the root cause of depression is a decreased rate of synaptic growth, and that all other purported causes and treatments have some relationship to this (Duman 2014). Another theory suggests abandoning the quest for a root cause altogether and viewing depression (and other mental illnesses) as a network of overlapping and mutually reinforcing symptoms, each of which might have its own cause or causes (Nuijten et al. 2016).[19] Whatever the truth of the matter, the notion that depression and suicide arise from a "chemical imbalance" is common in the United States and elsewhere, and for both professionals and laypeople it is often the first explanation of suicide that comes to mind.

Whatever its physiological basis, depression is a mental state that increases the risk of suicide, and other common explanations of suicide also focus on mental states. Psychologist Edwin Shneidman argues that almost all suicides are caused by psychological pain, including not only depression but also "shame, guilt, fear, anxiety, loneliness, angst, [and] dread of growing old or of dying badly" (Shneidman 1996:13). Psychologist Aaron T. Beck proposes that suicide is not due to pain itself so much as to hopelessness—a subjective belief that the pain will never end and one's situation will never improve. In one study, for instance, Beck and colleagues (1989) gave a large sample of psychotherapy outpatients a questionnaire meant to measure the degree to which they felt hopeless and found that those with high scores on this hopelessness measure were much more likely to kill themselves within the next ten years. And according to psychologist Thomas Joiner (2005), suicide occurs when hopelessness coincides with both a subjective perception that one's existence is a burden on others and a learned capacity to inflict violence on oneself, including habituation to physical pain.[20]

Suicide as a Sociological Problem

A sociological approach to suicide need not deny the validity of any of these psychological and psychiatric ideas. Mental pain, hopelessness, and perceived burdensomeness can indeed make people more likely to take their lives, and suicidal people often display deep sorrow prior to ending themselves. Genetics and body chemistry certainly influence human behavior, and the brain and mind are complex systems whose internal dynamics can produce change even when external input is fairly constant. Some individuals do apparently suffer from prolonged sadness without a clear external cause or else have extremely and unusually severe reactions to external stressors.

But we also know that the human organism does not operate in a vacuum and that the external environment can have a powerful influence. While it may be true that depressed people are more likely to commit suicide, it is also true that many people who kill themselves are not depressed in the psychiatric sense of the term. We might describe them as "depressed over" something—a lost job, broken relationship, public humiliation, or debilitating injury—but we need not appeal to a mysterious mental condition to identify the source of their suffering.[21] The same can be said for any other mental states associated with suicide, which are surely influenced by external as well as internal factors. Furthermore, just as not all who kill themselves are depressed, not all who suffer from depression kill themselves—indeed, the large majority do not. Rather, most find alternative ways of handling the situation, including possibly turning to others for help. Even those who try to commit suicide may find themselves prevented by others who restrain or rescue them. Finally, even if some people suffer from mental conditions that might predispose them to suicide, it is often some social event—such as a conflict—that ultimately triggers the act. Whatever its biological or psychological correlates, suicide clearly varies with its social environment as well.

Of course, no psychologist or psychiatrist would claim otherwise, and to varying extents prominent psychological theories of suicide have addressed the life events of those who kill themselves. Shneidman (1996), for instance, addresses some of the types of situations that thwart people's needs and give rise to psychological pain, while Joiner (2005) addresses experiences through which people might acquire the tolerance of pain and fear he claims are necessary for suicide. Still, scholars of the mind naturally focus on their area of expertise and give little systematic attention to social factors. Thus a 2010 article in *Psychology Today* entitled "The Six Reasons People Attempt Suicide" presents readers with the answers like "they're depressed," "they're psychotic," and "they're impulsive" (Lickerman 2010). Such answers tell us little about the social causes of suicide, the myriad ways in in which suicide can be a social behavior, and why suicide varies across social and cultural conditions.

Sociologists, on the other hand, focus on exactly these sorts of puzzles. Writing in the late nineteenth century, sociologist Emile Durkheim ([1897] 1951) famously observed consistent differences in suicide rates across countries and other geographic areas. Year after year, he noted, the suicide rates of some places were predictably higher than the rates of others. The suicide rates in England, for instance, were nearly double those in Italy, and the suicide rates in France were nearly double those in England (Durkheim [1897] 1951:50).[22] Surely, he argued, there must be some property of these societies that accounted for stable differences in their suicide rates. Furthermore, changes in suicide rates over time coincided with financial and political upheavals, such as economic depressions and wars. And he also observed that suicide rates varied across types of person—for example, single people had higher rates than married people, and soldiers had higher rates than civilians. These differences too suggested we can predict and explain suicide with social conditions, whether of countries or of individuals.

Durkheim's own explanation, which we will discuss in more detail in later chapters, was that suicide arises from extremes of social cohesion and moral regulation. In short, where people are too tightly bound to others, or not bound tightly enough, they are more likely to commit suicide. The same is true when they are given no social norms for how to live their lives or for when their lives are too restricted. While this theory is a classic in the field, it is not the last word on the topic. Some scholars criticize elements of the theory as vague and difficult to test, and researchers have found that the data support some of its claims better than others (see, e.g., Danigelis and Pope 1979; Gibbs and Martin 1964; Johnson 1965). More to the point, focused as he was either on societies (such as different countries) or individuals (such as different types of people), Durkheim did not adequately address a crucial level of social reality: that of relationships and interactions. When will conflict erupt in a human relationship? And why do some conflicts result in suicide while others do not? Exactly when and where will an instance of moralism or altruism or anything else become self-destructive? Who takes suicidal action toward whom?

Durkheim's theory is an important starting point, and we will draw on some of his insights in the coming chapters. But it is merely a first step in the sociology of suicide, and one that does not answer many questions we might have about suicide as a form of social behavior. What we will also need is a theory of conflict and social control and a strategy for explaining where and when these things will result in suicide rather than some alternative. Fortunately, there is already a body of theory aimed at explaining conflict, and it illustrates a strategy that is perfectly suited to the task of explaining the situational and interactive aspects of suicide. The strategy is a new and distinctive approach to sociology: pure sociology. Since even many sociologists are unfamiliar with this particular approach, let us address it in more detail.

Suicide and Pure Sociology

Pure sociology is a novel and distinctively sociological strategy of explanation developed by sociologist Donald Black. It is a framework, or paradigm, that can be used to develop theories of human behavior. Like more familiar sociological paradigms—such as the rational choice, conflict, or functionalist approaches—it is potentially applicable to any topic, from religious belief to financial altruism to predatory crime (Black 1995, 2000; Michalski 2003; Cooney 2006:59). Thus far, however, most pure sociological work deals with conflict and social control. Black first developed pure sociology in his theory of law, a set of principles that explain how legal cases are handled and why some conflicts involve more legal intervention than others (Black 1976; see also Cooney 2009). He and his students have since expanded this work to address many forms of conflict management, including avoidance, negotiation, therapy, and various forms of violence (Baumgartner 1988; Black 1998, 2004b; Horwitz 1984; Senechal de la Roche 1996; Campbell 2015b). More recently, Black even extended pure sociology to explain the origin of conflict itself (Black 2011).

As the name implies, pure sociology focuses exclusively on the social aspects of human behavior, ignoring psychology and biology (Black 1995). Indeed, pure sociology does not look at the behavior of individuals as such but at the behavior of forms of social life, such as law or altruism or science (e.g., Black 1976; Black 2000; Michalski 2003). For example, rather than asking what makes individual crime victims more likely to call the police or individual police officers more likely to make an arrest or individual judges and jurors more likely to convict a defendant, Black's theory of law simply asks what conditions lead a conflict to attract a greater quantity of law— that is, a greater amount of governmental social control brought to bear against the alleged offender. This way of looking at things allows us to skip over the myriad decisions of multiple individuals and to avoid the need to know about their different motives and beliefs. All that is necessary is to explain what social factors are conducive to a greater or lesser quantity of law, and we can predict the behavior of all the individuals involved in the case. Beyond law, Black and his students ask what makes a conflict more likely to produce other forms of social control, such as lynching or shunning or genocide (Black 1998; Campbell 2015b; Senechal de la Roche 1997). And using pure sociology, they answer these questions not with the motives, perceptions, and proclivities of individuals but with the structure and motion of social space.

SOCIAL SPACE

Social space refers to the different ways people and groups can be related to one another. They may be relationally close to one another, bound by strong ties of intimacy, or relationally distant, with little or no prior interaction. They might be culturally close, members of the same religious and ethnic group, or culturally distant, sharing few cultural practices of any kind. The degree of relational and cultural distance varies across relationships and across interactions. So too does the degree of vertical distance, or inequality: some are social elites, people whose wealth and power put them at higher social elevations relative to everyone else, while the poor and powerless occupy lower elevations. Relationships and interactions might be more or less unequal, and behavior might be directed upward toward higher elevations or downward toward lower ones.

Each instance of human behavior occurs in a particular configuration of social space, known as its *social structure* or *social geometry* (Black 1995). This structure is defined by the characteristics and relationships of everyone involved in the behavior, such as the various kinds of social distance between them, and by who is acting toward whom. Different structures tend to produce different behaviors, and so social geometry explains variation in social life. Each conflict, for example, has its own social structure, depending on whether it occurs between intimates or strangers, the culturally homogeneous or the culturally diverse, social equals or people of different rank. And this structure predicts how the conflict is likely to be handled.

For example, Black's theory of law proposes that law increases with relational distance (Black 1976:40–42). What this means is that, holding constant the nature of the grievance, such as whether it is a complaint about theft or about murder, it will tend to result in more legal intervention when the offender is someone more distant (such as a stranger) than if the offender is someone close (such as family member). People are thus more likely to call the police if they are victimized by strangers than if they are victimized by acquaintances and more likely to call the police if they are victimized by an acquaintance than if they are victimized by an intimate such as a spouse or boyfriend (see, e.g., Williams 1984; Fisher et al. 2003). And if the law does get involved, cases involving closer parties tend to get handled more leniently, meaning they are less likely to result in a conviction, and they tend to result in less severe sentences for those who are convicted (see, e.g., Cooney 2009:156–70). The same offense is therefore likely to be handled quite differently depending on the relational distance it spans.

The way a case is handled will also vary with the degree of inequality between victim and offender, as well was with the vertical direction of the complaint. According to Black's theory, law is greater in a downward direction than in an upward direction. This means that there is more legal intervention when the case involves a complaint by a social superior against a social inferior than if the case were reversed. For example, the theory would predict that in cases where an employer calls the police against her employee, there is a greater likelihood of the police making an arrest than in cases where an employee calls the police against her employer. And more punishment is likely when someone of low status victimizes someone of high status than when someone of high status victimizes someone of low status (see, e.g., Cooney 2009:36–62).

SOCIAL TIME

The structure of social space helps explain the form and quantity of behaviors and thus explains why conflicts get handled in different ways. But the social world is not static, and so this structure frequently changes. Relationships begin and end. People abandon old customs and adopt new ones. The humble rise and the mighty fall. Black refers to these fluctuations in social space as *social time* (Black 2011).[23] Just as the structure of social space explains human behavior, so too does its movement. Change is the basis of causality, with one event sparking another (Bohm 1959:1). So whereas social structure shapes conflict in predictable ways, social time is what causes conflicts to erupt in the first place. In his book *Moral Time,* Black proposes that "the greater and faster the movement of social time, the greater is the likelihood of conflict and the greater the conflict is likely to be" (Black 2011:6). For example, every change in intimacy has the potential to spark conflict, be it a guest who overstays his welcome or a friend who fails to keep in touch. But the greater and faster the change in intimacy, the more likely it is to give offense, and the more severe the offense is likely to be. A slight reduction in contact is less likely to cause grievances than suddenly terminating the relationship altogether, and falling out of touch with an acquaintance will not provoke nearly so severe a reaction as cutting off ties to a spouse. The same is true for changes in status inequality or cultural diversity: the greater and faster the fluctuation in social space, the more likely and severe the conflict.

Social space and social time are ubiquitous features of human life, defined by the patterning and tempo of our relationships and interactions, and there is much they can explain about human behavior. Here, then, is a framework that can be used to examine suicidal conflicts. Using Black's pure sociology, and building on previous theories of conflict and social control, we can ask which movements of social time are most likely to cause suicidal conflict and which conflict structures are most likely to produce suicide. Beyond this, we can ask which social changes are most likely to cause suicide in general. And we can ask which structures encourage behaviors like altruism or ritual to take suicidal forms, or how social structure effects behaviors like therapy and rescue that might prevent suicide.

The rest of this book is devoted to exploring these questions. Its goal is to outline a general theory that explains when and where suicidal conflict will occur and therefore contribute to theories of both suicide and conflict. To develop and illustrate this theory I rely on evidence from a variety of sources, including historical accounts, psychiatric case studies, police and coroners' reports, large-sample statistical studies, and ethnographic observations. Most of the cited information is secondary, culled from the extensive literature on suicide compiled by anthropologists, historians, medical researchers, psychologists, and sociologists. Some evidence also comes from my own studies of coroners' records in Kentucky and West Virginia. More details about methodology are available in appendix A. For now, note that this variety of sources from different disciplines is what allows us to examine suicide up close, to see how it varies across a wide range of social circumstances, and to find patterns that hold true across many different types of society.

Suicide is no less social than any other human behavior. It varies across societies and across social locations within societies. It comes in different forms and varieties and is often rooted in some larger category of social life. As this chapter has emphasized, suicide frequently occurs in the course of conflict, whether in the private conflicts of individuals or large-scale political struggles. It can even act as a form of social control, a moralistic behavior aimed at righting wrongs and punishing offenses. It might be protest or punishment, avoidance or appeal, escape or revenge. As such, it also varies across relationships and situations. It varies from one conflict to another. Most of all, it varies with the structure and motion of social space, and this is our key to explaining it.

2

Suicide and Inequality

The critical turning point came when the Korea Electric Power, formally privatized but still government managed, brought suit, claiming damages caused by a strike, and took provisional seizure against staff and common members in the spring of 2002. The companies temporarily seized 14 billion won ($11.7 million) from the union staff; 14.5 billion won ($12.1 million) from the union's fund; and 18.2 billion won ($15.2 million) from 3,172 members. . . . [Union leader] Kim Joo-ik, was receiving at most 130,000 won ($108) a month at the time of his suicide of a monthly salary of about 1.5 million won ($1,250). . . . The company also laid many laborers off to frighten the workers into ending the strike. Many union members abandoned the strike in the face of these threats. These conditions compelled Kim Joo-ik to commit suicide. (Jang 2004:275)

In most societies we can see distinctions between high class and low class, dominant and subordinate, those who are looked up to and those who are looked down upon. This is social inequality, also called stratification, and it comprises the vertical dimension of social space.

Stratification, and thus vertical space, is defined by differences in social status. For many readers, wealth is probably the most obvious kind of social status and differences in wealth the most obvious kind of social inequality. Wealth is an economic status determined by the possession of material goods such as food, shelter, productive property, or the currency with which to buy such things (Black 1976:11). Differences in wealth are easy to observe in contemporary societies and attract a lot of attention in everyday life. But there are also other forms of status and thus other kinds of inequality (see generally Black 1976). Authority, for example, is a hierarchical status, defined by the ability to successfully give orders and by one's rank within a chain of command. Within organizations, greater rank often goes along with greater wealth, but the two forms of status are not identical. A police officer, for instance, might be less wealthy than you but can still order you to pull over and stop your car. Another form of status is respectability, a moral status arising from one's reputation for deviant or virtuous conduct (Black 1976:111–12). Some people are praised, admired, and respected for their good behavior, while others have much worse reputations. Someone with a lengthy criminal record or notoriety for past misdeeds has low respectability, regardless of his or her wealth.

Each type of status has similar effects, generally producing various advantages for those who have them relative to those who lack them. The same goes for other types, such as education, organization, and conventionality (Black 1976:61–99).[1] Each may also act as a kind of capital that makes it easier to gain the others, as when wealth is used to purchase education or to enhance one's reputation through charity. Thus while they can and do vary independently, these subdimensions of inequality also tend to cluster together. And while we can consider each type of status in isolation, we can also take account of all of them at once to assess someone's overall social standing. Whether we look at one kind of status or all of them together, in Black's conceptual language we are measuring someone's *social elevation*, or location along the vertical dimension of social space.

Suicide and Social Elevation

We can observe the social elevation of any person or group and so compare behaviors that occur at high elevations, between those of high status, to those that occur at low elevations, between those of low status. Many studies examine how the overall probability of suicide varies according to elevation, though sometimes with contradictory results. Writing in the late nineteenth century, Durkheim ([1897] 1951:245) suggested that poverty was a "protective factor" against suicide, citing the lower suicide rates in poorer nations (such as Ireland) compared to wealthier ones (such as France). A half century later, sociologists Andrew Henry and James Short (1954) likewise proposed that suicide was greater at higher elevations, citing as evidence the fact that white Americans have higher suicide rates than black Americans.[2] And using data from London in the early 1930s, psychiatrist Peter Sainsbury (1955) found that suicide victims were more likely to live on streets with higher average wealth and to belong to higher occupational classes, such as educated professionals or business owners (Sainsbury 1955:72–73).

Others, however, find that suicide is greater at lower elevations (Baudelot and Establet 2008:141–59). For example, a study of suicide in Australia between 1973 and 2003 found higher suicide rates in areas with lower income, education, and home ownership (Page et al. 2006). A study of the Chicago area between 1953 and 1963 found that suicide rates were higher for those in lower-status occupations—for instance, unskilled manual laborers had higher rates than professionals and craftsmen (Maris 1969:124–34). A recent meta-analysis of thirty-four published studies also found that low-skilled, low-income occupations have higher rates of suicide (Milner et al. 2013). And multicountry study of thousands of suicide attempters in Europe during the 1990s found that rates were greater among those with less education and home ownership (Lorant et al. 2005b; see also Schmidtke et al. 1996).

It appears more common for studies to find higher risk of suicide at low elevations, particularly if the studies directly examine the status characteristics of suicidal people rather than inferring them from, say, the average wealth of people in their geographic area. (In sociology, the former is considered stronger evidence than the latter—after all, just because a suicidal person belongs to a group with more wealthy people does not mean that he or she personally is wealthy.)[3] But the relationship does not seem as clear as others we will consider in this chapter, and most studies fail to account for the difference between being poor or unemployed and *becoming* poor or unemployed. As we discussed in the previous chapter, causality is by nature dynamic—cause and effect, stimulus and response, action and reaction (Black 2011:5; Bohm 1959:1). It is a relationship between events, with one change leading to another. While it's not clear if social elevation has an effect, changes in social elevation certainly do.

Suicide and Vertical Mobility

Social status is always subject to change. Someone might accumulate wealth or squander it, find a job or lose one, win praise or provoke condemnation. They thus move upward or downward in the status structure—that is, they experience vertical mobility. And observers have long known that vertical mobility can prompt suicide.

Writing in the late 1800s, Durkheim said it was already a "well-known fact that economic crises have an aggravating effect on the suicidal tendency" (Durkheim [1897] 1951:241). In Austria and France, for instance, market crashes corresponded to spikes in the suicide rate, as did yearly spikes in the number of bankruptcies (Durkheim [1897] 1951:241–42). He argued that such crises disrupted the "equilibrium" between people's desires and their means of satisfying them, producing a state of unhappiness. Every individual, he claimed, needs a moral force to regulate his or her desires, and this force can only come from society. Norms about the appropriate lifestyle for different social classes or occupations serve this function: public opinion mandates a certain lifestyle for laborers, another for businessmen, and so forth, and people are criticized for aspiring to too much or for living too far below their means. "Under this pressure," Durkheim writes, "each in his sphere vaguely realizes the extreme limit set to his ambition and aspires to nothing beyond" (Durkheim [1897] 1951:250). Economic depressions are dangerous, he argued, because they "suddenly [cast] certain individuals into a lower state than their previous one," and since "they are not adjusted" to the condition, they "find it intolerable" (Durkheim [1897] 1951:252).

Durkheim's social psychology seems intuitive so far, but he also made a less intuitive claim: that upward mobility produces exactly the same effect. "With increased prosperity desires increase," he argued, and so "the richer prize offered these appetites stimulates them and makes them more exigent and impatient of control," leading to frustration and unhappiness. "How," Durkheim asks, "could the desire to live not be weakened under such conditions?" (Durkheim [1897] 1951:253). Thus he claimed that both upward and downward mobility lead to suicide. He referred to suicide caused by these effects as "anomic suicide," believing they stemmed from anomie, a condition that arises when people lack social norms to regulate their conduct (Durkheim [1897] 1951:258).

From a purely sociological perspective, it is not necessary to know the accuracy of Durkheim's ideas about the psychology of desire and unhappiness. What matters is the actual relationship between vertical mobility and suicide. As it turns out, Durkheim was only partially correct. Across time and place, downward mobility is indeed a common and powerful cause of suicide. Upward mobility, on the other hand, is not.

Before considering the evidence, note that downward mobility is a matter of degree: the loss might be smaller or greater, and it might happen gradually or suddenly. Black's theory of conflict proposes that the greater and faster the social change, the more likely it is to cause conflict. We can apply a similar logic here: the greater and faster the downward mobility, the more likely it is trigger suicide. In other words, suicide varies directly with downward mobility. Note also that social status is relative, and any instance of vertical mobility alters the degree of inequality in various relationships. "If we are equals," Black writes, "you become my inferior if I rise and my superior if I fall. If you are my superior, I lose some of my inferiority if you fall and you lose some of your superiority if I rise" (Black 2011:59). Viewed in this light, vertical mobility is a change in vertical space itself, one that causes stratification to increase or decrease. It is thus an instance of what Black calls *social time,* and comes in two types: *understratification* is when inequality declines, while *overstratification* is when inequality increases (Black 2011:59, 82). Both changes can produce conflict: people express grievances when those below them rise (perhaps condemning them as uppity or rebellious) and also when others rise above them (perhaps calling them greedy or domineering). But it appears suicidal conflict, and indeed suicide in general, is mostly due to overstratification, which occurs when people fall below others. We might thus say that suicide varies directly with overstratification. But when stratification increases, suicide occurs among those who are falling, being dominated, or being left behind, not among those who are rising or exercising domination. Suicide concentrates among those who experience an increase in their social inferiority—something Black (2011:71) calls *overinferiority.* Therefore it would be more precise to say: *suicide varies directly with overinferiority* (Manning 2015d). Calling it "overinferiority" might not sound terribly different from calling it "downward mobility," and indeed I will use the two terms interchangeably unless noted otherwise. But the concept of overinferiority helps draw our attention to the relative nature of social status and also to the fact that one's social status can change even within the context of a particular relationship or social network. Also recall that, since there are several types or dimensions of social status, there can be several sources of overinferiority. Perhaps the most obvious is the loss of wealth.

THE LOSS OF WEALTH

In over a century of research since Durkheim published his theory of suicide, little evidence has supported his claim that suicide rates increase during economic booms as well as during busts. One of the first to question the notion was another French sociologist named Maurice Halbwachs. Tracing yearly suicide rates in Germany from the mid-1800s to the early 1900s, Halbwachs ([1930] 1978:231–44) concluded that suicide did indeed tend to rise during downturns in the economy, as measured by falling prices and rising bankruptcies, but that it did not rise during periods of growth. Halbwachs noted that one apparent exception, a sudden spike in suicide rates that Durkheim drew attention to when arguing that sudden growth leads to suicide, coincided with changes in record keeping that would have led to more suicides being officially recognized and recorded (Halbwachs [1930] 1978:236). This would mean a sudden increase in the official suicide rate even if the number of actual suicides was stable or declining. This, he suggests, gave Durkheim an inaccurate view of the broader pattern.

Regardless of the source of the error, several other studies confirm that suicide rates rise during economic recessions and depressions—times of greater downward mobility—but not during periods of rising prosperity. Such was the case for the United States throughout the twentieth century (e.g., Henry and Short 1954:23–44; Yang 1992; Luo et al. 2011; but compare Pierce 1967). During the Great Depression, for instance, US suicide deaths increased even as mortality from other causes declined (Granados and Roux 2009). One analysis of 115 US cities in thirty-six states found that suicide mortality rose with the number of banks that temporarily or permanently suspended activities, something that would have led to sudden economic hardship for their customers (Stuckler et al. 2012). With few exceptions, similar patterns have been found for other countries, such as Australia, Korea, and Japan (Araki and Murata 1987; Chang et al. 2009; Morrell et al. 1993; but compare Hintikka, Saarinen, and Viinamäki 1999). And they continue to be found in more recent times. For example, using a method known as time-series analysis that measures how suicide rates deviate from previous trends, researchers have found that the global economic crisis of 2008—often called the Great Recession—led to rising suicide rates throughout Europe and the Americas, including such diverse countries as Chile, Mexico, and Norway (Chang et al. 2013; Reeves et al. 2012; Barr et al. 2012).

Sociologists know that relationships found at the level of the nation, state, or city do not always apply to the individuals within those groupings. Perhaps individuals who experience downward mobility are not actually more likely to kill themselves, and there is some other reason why economic shocks raise a society's overall suicide rate. Yet when we look to case studies of individual suicides, they confirm the lethal role of downward mobility. Consider some cases that occurred during the Great Depression:

> Ignatz Engel was a retired cigar maker in the Bronx who invested in the market in time to be wiped out by the Crash. On Nov.13, depressed over his losses, he lay down on a blanket in his kitchen and opened all the jets of the gas range. The next day, the president of the Rochester Gas and Electric Corp., no longer able to endure his loss of more than $1,200,000, ended his own life. . . . Confirming the international

implications of Wall Street's debacle, there were suicides by a broker in Chile and another in Cuba, the latter found hanged in the Members' Room of the Havana Exchange. In Philadelphia, one broker shot himself at the Penn Athletic Club and another was hauled out of the Schuylkill after "the cold water had changed his mind." The retrieval of Julius Umbach from the Hudson was less auspicious. His suicide was explained by notes in his pocket calling for more margin. . . . A young man named Lytle shot and killed himself in a hotel in Milwaukee, leaving behind four cents and a suicide note directing that "my body should go to science, my soul to Andrew W. Mellon and sympathy to my creditors." The note also asked that his body not be removed from the room until the rent was up. (Lowenthal 1987)

One study in New Orleans, based on interviews with the family and neighbors of men who committed suicide, found that the a majority of self-killers had recently lost a job, suffered a reduction in pay, or experienced some other form of economic decline, and that they were more likely than their neighbors to have experienced such a loss (Breed 1963).[4] A study of suicides in Chicago similarly found that 37 percent of male victims had retired or become disabled just prior to their suicide and that only about 23 percent were working full time (Maris 1981:137). Another analysis of coroners' records in another US city found that economic strains such as the loss of a car or home were a contributing factor in nearly two-thirds of suicides (Stack and Wasserman 2007). And a "sociological autopsy" of one hundred suicides in a UK city reveals that coroners' files cited the role of unemployment in 20 percent of cases and the role of debt in another 10 percent of cases (Fincham et al. 2011).

Researchers using larger samples find similar patterns. A census-based study of all Finnish men between 1981 and 1985 found that those who lost their jobs were nearly twice as likely to commit suicide by the end of the study period. Notably, this study controlled for several background factors such as age, marital status, mental health, physical health, and socioeconomic status prior to unemployment, providing evidence that the relationship is not simply a matter of those factors predisposing people to be both suicidal and unemployable (Martikainen 1990; see also Moser, Fox, and Jones 1984). A longitudinal study of over 400,000 individuals in the United States revealed a similar relationship: among both men and women, those who lost jobs were more likely to kill themselves in the subsequent year than those who had not lost jobs. The effect was particularly strong for men: those who lost jobs were two to three times more likely to have killed themselves by the two-year follow-up survey (Kposowa 2001). The effect was also stronger immediately after the loss, suggesting that downward mobility is more dangerous than simply having a low social elevation. A cohort study of over two million New Zealanders likewise found that unemployment more than doubled the risk of suicide (Blakely, Collings, and Atkinson 2003; compare Fergusson, Boden, and Horwood 2007).

Of course, unemployment is not the only indicator of economic loss. Losing one's home is also a severe economic blow. Researchers in Sweden compared a sample of over 21,000 evicted persons to an over 700,000-person random sample of the general population and found that, controlling for factors like education, employment, and mental health diagnosis, those who were evicted were four times more likely to kill themselves within the year (Rojas and Stenberg 2016:410–11). Nor is the relationship between economic loss and suicide limited to Western nations. Consider a case from early twentieth-century China: "Mr. Lee was a clerk in a store in [Yangzhou]. He was 29 years old and had four children, although his wages were only $10.00 per month, out of which he had to support his aged parents in addition to his wife and children. . . . He fell heavily into debt. The high rates of interest charged made it impossible to repay the loans and he went even more deeply into debt. . . . After several months, to cap his misfortunes, the store in which he was employed failed and he was thrown out of work. . . . Finally in despair he jumped into the Grand Canal and was drowned" (quoted in Baechler 1975:69). More recently, in Hong Kong, a comparison of 150 suicide victims to 150 nonsuicidal controls found that those who killed themselves were more likely to have had work and financial problems in recent months, including unemployment and unmanageable debt (Chen et al. 2006; see also Chan et al. 2007). In India in recent times the economic effects of globalization have rendered the owners of small farms much more vulnerable to mounting debt culminating in foreclosure. The suicide rates of farmers have thus increased, with many farmers killing themselves due to crop failures and indebtedness (Mohanty 2005; Mishra 2006; Vasavi 2009). Wealthier farmers have the advantage of a greater economic cushion and better ability to diversify their crops and so are less likely to suffer the catastrophic loss of their entire farm. Suicide is thus concentrated among the poorer farmers and tends to occur in harvest season—the time when they find out whether they will pay their debts or lose their farm (Mohanty 2005:256–57). But though less vulnerable, wealthier farmers are not entirely immune: one wealthy farmer "advanced more than two hundred thousand rupees" to poorer growers and killed himself when crop failures made him lose hope of recovering his investment (Mohanty 2005:264).

The role of downward mobility can also be seen in historical records. For instance, in Worcestershire in 1293 "a free tennant of the Count of Glocester, Adam le Yep, was forced by poverty to receive servile tennancy, which would make him a villein; he had often sworn to kill himself rather than accept such a fate; in fact he drowned himself in the Severn" (Baechler 1975:84). In the eighteenth century, English aristocrats became fond of gambling in elaborate card games, and many upper-class suicides followed massive gambling losses (MacDonald and Murphy 1990:278–80). A study of coroners' records from nineteenth-century England shows that unemployment and financial ruin were among the most common reasons given for suicide (Anderson 1987:117–19). And in eighteenth-century Geneva, technological changes led to high unemployment among watchmakers, causing them to have the highest suicide rate of any occupational group (Watt 2001:180–82). One watchmaker killed himself with arsenic after finding his skills rendered obsolete: "According to his employer, Jean Pierre Rivoire, Delaine had showed considerable talent and had made a decent living when he worked in the manufacture of 'the old style' of watches. With the introduction of new styles and techniques, however, Delaine found himself compelled to come work for Rivoire to learn the new methods. This was almost as if he were beginning a second apprenticeship, and Rivoire attested that Delaine was upset about the considerable loss in income that he suffered as a result of technological change" (Watt 2001:180–82).[5]

So far we have considered such widely recognized forms of wealth as homes, land, money, and sources of income. But if we define wealth as the material means of existence, it includes something more: our physical capacity to make a living and to care for ourselves and our loved ones. Thus Black (2011:76) considers the human body "the most fundamental means of production" and our physical health to be the most fundamental form of wealth. We can therefore consider illness and injury a form of downward mobility, one that is often particularly devastating and likely to cause suicide.

In my study of 260 coroners' records from Louisville, physical illness was cited as a reason for suicide in 32 percent of the cases. Chronic, debilitating, and terminal illnesses were common. For example, one foreman's severe arthritis had led to an inability to use his hands, and "he had told several family members he was 'ready to go'" shortly before killing himself. A Swedish study found physical illness and disability played a role in about 17 percent of four hundred cases (Stensman and Sundqvist-Stensman 1988). Other research finds that being diagnosed with cancer doubles the risk of suicide (Misono et al. 2008; Robinson et al. 2009). Disabled persons generally have higher rates of suicide, and the rate of suicide increases with the degree of disability (Hopkins 1971; Giannini et al. 2010). Among the elderly, visual impairment is associated with higher risk of suicide (Waern et al. 2002). Old age in general involves an irreversible physical decline, and the general pattern throughout most of the world is for suicide rates to increase with age (World Health Organization 2002:191). Studies of coroners' records confirm that declining health often plays a role in the suicide of the aged (Fincham et al. 2011:157; Rubenowitz et al. 2001).[6]

Of course injury and illness are physically painful and exhausting, as are many treatments for them. It is no surprise that many would like to escape from such suffering, and this surely accounts for much of the association between disease and suicide.[7] But even with little or no physical pain, or when such pain can be controlled by medication, declining health is still a loss of stature that many find intolerable. As Black comments, "Sickness . . . not only incapacitates and kills but frequently leads to a condition of social dependency similar to a child's" (Black 2011:79). Note that disability also deprives one of the ability to engage in a variety of tasks and so reduces the kind of stature that comes from performing well. This sort of stature, which Black (2000) calls *functional status,* is what elevates star athletes over benchwarmers, even among unpaid amateurs. Unemployment too might be understood not just as the loss of income and the economic stature it provides but also as failure in one's social role. Where men are expected to act as providers for their spouses and children, for instance, unemployment can be especially damaging for them. In Ghana, when a man is unable to fulfill his economic role as breadwinner, others will dismiss him as "a useless man" (Adinkrah 2012). Studies in the United Kingdom and United States suggest that men—particularly middle-aged men, who are likely to be most enmeshed in the breadwinner role—are more likely than women to kill themselves over unemployment and other economic failures (e.g., Rich et al. 1988; Fincham et al. 2011:154–56). Thus, while social welfare might mitigate the economic effects of losing a job or becoming disabled, and so prevent many suicides (see, e.g., Hosaka 2009), it will not completely erase the impact of these losses. For example, one young New Zealander—who killed himself after being dismissed for "a work-related infraction"—said that "he never wanted to be without work again; he hated feeling worthless, useless, and powerless. He experienced these empty feelings on the dole" (Weaver and

Munro 2013:15). And even in societies with generous welfare states, such as Denmark, retirement brings increased risk of suicide (Qin et al. 2000).

THE LOSS OF RESPECT

Damage to one's reputation—what we might call respectability, prestige, or moral status—is another form of downward mobility that causes suicide (on the concept of respectability, see Black 1976:111). Sometimes the loss of respectability might stem from other kinds of loss, such as unemployment or disability, and so compound their effects. In the words of one unemployed American interviewed by psychologists during the 1930s, "When I go out, I cast down my eyes because I feel myself wholly inferior. . . . Former acquaintances and friends of better times are no longer so cordial. . . . Their eyes seem to say, 'You are not worth it, you don't work'" (quoted in Goffman 1974:17). The shame and stigma of failure is one source of reputational damage. Another is being publicly accused of committing a crime or engaging in other sorts of serious wrongdoing. Many kill themselves after such accusations. For example, in South Korea in 2009, former president Roh Moo-hyun killed himself after becoming embroiled in a corruption investigation. Following allegations that he accepted $6 million in bribes during his 2003–8 presidency, he jumped to his death from a cliff (Sohn 2009). In China in 2015, after Chinese authorities blamed a disastrous waste dump landslide on the violation of safety regulations, the official in charge of regulating the dump hanged himself (Hunt and Lu 2015). And in 2017, the day after a news story accused him of sexual misconduct, a Republican member of Kentucky's House of Representatives shot himself in the head (Novelly 2017).

In some settings the loss of respect might be the most drastic kind of downward mobility that ever occurs. In tribal and peasant societies with little stored wealth of any kind, drastic gains and losses of wealth are comparatively rare. But word travels fast in the village, and reputations are permanent. For the Nivkh (or Gilyak), a hunter-gatherer group in western Russia, "disgrace and shame are a great punishment. . . . The Gilyak who is convicted of doing something shameful goes out into the taiga and . . . hangs himself" (Shternberg 1933). An ethnographic study of suicide in a Serbian village reports that male suicides tend to occur "in response to or fear of social disapproval, such as destruction of reputation or loss of prestige in society" (Filipovic 1982:194). In Southern Africa, a Zulu informant states that "when I am found to have done a bad thing I have [shame] because now everyone knows what I did. . . . A man has [shame] when he has committed rape;

he feels shy when walking in the neighborhood of the woman; he feels disgraced when discovered. There is no way of 'cleansing' himself, except a man may kill himself. Many men commit suicide in such as a situation" (quoted in Raum 1973:452). Among the Lepcha villagers of the Himalayas, most suicide follows a public rebuke: "There have been six suicides in Lingthem and the neighbouring smaller villages in the last twenty years, and in every case the suicide has been immediately subsequent to a public reproof. . . . Chélé's father killed himself because his wife and her family publicly blamed him for neglecting her and his work while she was ill. Kurma's uncle killed himself because he was blamed for not keeping his wife in order, and Kurma's brother because he was blamed for his uncle's suicide" (Gorer 1967:269). Similarly, suicide among the Trobriand islanders of Melanesia often follows a public accusation of deviant conduct, as when one young man jumped to his death from a palm tree after being accused of incest (Malinowski [1926] 1976:77–79). Shame and humiliation cause suicide among the Toraja of Indonesia as well: one man killed himself "because of the shame he felt for having physically abused his children," while a woman "killed herself because she was pregnant while still unmarried" (Hollan 1990:370). And villagers in nineteenth-century Sussex, England, killed themselves due to "humiliation and loss of neighbourly or family esteem" (Anderson 1987:156).

Individuals vary in their sensitivity to sociological variables, and so do cultures. Some societies place a greater value on reputation and breed a greater sensitivity to shame. In contemporary Ghana, "a number of . . . proverbs and maxims suggest suicide is preferable to enduring shame," and public disgrace is perhaps the most common reason for suicide (Adinkrah 2012:478). In one case "a 32-year-old man killed himself after witnesses discovered him copulating with a sheep. He immediately fled his village and was found dead several miles away from the scene, having drunk pesticide" (Adinkrah 2012:478). Others Ghanians kill themselves when being investigated for theft or fraud. Sexual impotency is considered shameful for a man, and this too causes suicide, particularly when it becomes public knowledge (Adinkrah 2012). Compared to Western societies, East Asian societies tend to have a greater concern with saving face, and so shame likely plays a relatively greater role in Asian suicide than in Western suicide (Cain 2014; Leung and Cohen 2011; see also, e.g., Iga 1986). Reputation also has an exaggerated importance in what social scientists call "honor cultures," where people place a high value on physical strength and bravery. In such settings, respectability depends on the ability to retaliate violently against slights, insults, and other offenses, and whoever fails to retaliate suffers dishonor

(Black 2011:71–74; see also Cohen et al. 1996; Cooney 1998:107–32). Given their aggressiveness, the honorable are less prone to harm themselves than they are to attack their adversary, but should they fail to defend their honor in this way they will turn to suicide. Such was the case among eighteenth-century English aristocrats who were unable to avenge insults by fighting a duel (MacDonald and Murphy 1990:276). For example, "In 1741 a gamester named Nourse fell into a violent argument with Lord Windsor at a fashionable London casino, and challenged the peer to a duel. Windsor refused, and Nourse, knowing that he could not have refused to fight an equal, was so enraged and humiliated by the insult that he went home and cut his throat" (MacDonald and Murphy 1990:279).

Whether the issue is honor or not, being the target of insults, accusations, and punishments can trigger self-destruction, as can all manner of shame and humiliation. Some kinds of deviance are especially odious to most people, and those accused of them suffer an especially drastic loss of respectability. Those accused of sexual crimes against children, for instance, seem especially prone to kill themselves, and accusations of child molestation lead to a drastically elevated rate of suicide (Walter and Pridmore 2012; Hoffer et al. 2010). In 2018, for instance, actor Mark Salling, known for his role on the television program *Glee*, killed himself after pleading guilty to possession of child pornography (Dillon and Desantis 2018). Of course, those convicted of such crimes face not only the loss of social esteem: they also face incarceration or other punishment, which means their suicides are partly an escape from being dominated.

DOMINATION AND SUBJUGATION

Sometimes an increase in social inferiority stems from a person's losses. But sometimes it stems from other people's gains. This is especially so in hierarchical relationships, where domination by one party means subordination for another. Any act of domination—giving an order, coercing with threats, or inflicting punishment—lowers the status of the recipient. Each instance of domination increases someone's social inferiority, and so coercion and punishment often cause suicide. The conquest of one society by another can subjugate millions and sometimes produces mass suicide. During the Spanish conquest of Cuba, for example, native Cubans hanged and poisoned themselves in large numbers to avoid "serving such and so many ferocious tyrants" (Peréz 2005:4). Africans captured for slavery in the Americas also killed themselves in large numbers, sometimes individually and sometimes in groups (Piersen 1977; Peréz 2005:35). Sources suggest that slaves who had

been social or political elites in their homeland—and consequently experienced the greatest loss of stature—were particularly likely to choose death
over bondage (Piersen 1977:151–52). For conquered elites, the loss of wealth
and authority is often compounded by the loss of honor, and so "the stage
of history is full of princes and generals who fall on their sword" rather
than face the humiliation of defeat (Van Hooff 1990:109; see also Murray
1998:48–58). This is so even when they might be spared the extreme depriva-
tions—such as slavery or execution—faced by commoners. In nineteenth-
century Ibadan (in present-day Nigeria), for instance, deposed military
chieftains sometimes chose suicide over a shameful exile; one chief, finding
himself on the losing side of a succession dispute, "chose death by ripping
his bowels open with a jack knife" (Adeboye 2006:9).

Though elites may have been especially likely to kill themselves following defeat, ancient battles and sieges sometimes caused mass suicides that
included generals, soldiers, and noncombatants alike. Through this means
they avoided enslavement, rape, destitution, and dishonor. When Alexander the Great invaded India, for example, residents of various conquered
towns and cities turned to mass suicide by fire (Thakur 1963:165). When the
Romans captured the Jewish fortress of Masada in 74 CE, they found all of
its defenders already dead by their own hands. European Jewish communities in the Middle Ages also responded to anti-Jewish pogroms with mass
suicide (Baechler 1975:93). In seventeenth- and eighteenth-century Russia,
members of the persecuted "Old Believer" sect sometimes committed mass
suicides after being besieged by government forces (Robbins 1986). Political
repression in modern society can also lead to widespread suicide, particularly if it involves losses across multiple dimensions of status. Thus when the
Nazis stripped German Jews of their livelihoods, property, and virtually all
other forms of social stature, the suicide rate of German Jews skyrocketed
(Goeschel 2009:96–117). The same was true for Jews in Nazi-occupied countries. After Germany annexed Austria in 1938, "Austrian Nazis humiliated
Jews in public, forcing them to kneel on the streets and clean the pave-
ments. . . . Hundreds of Austrian Jews committed suicide amidst the open
Nazi violence against Jews. . . . In ten days, from 12 to 22 March, at least
96 Viennese Jews committed suicide, including the cultural historian Egon
Friedell who jumped to his death out a window on March 16 when storm
troopers tried to arrest someone else in his house" (Goeschel 2009:98). One
resident of Amsterdam later recalled that "immediately after the German
invasion of Holland about 250 suicides were registered among the Jews of
Amsterdam in a few days" (Dublin 1963:77). Not long after, a similar wave

of suicide swept over non-Jewish Germans as the country sank into defeat at the hands of the Allies toward the end of World War II. Much of the Nazi leadership died this way, including Adolf Hitler, Joseph Goebbels, and Heinrich Himmler, as well as "53 out of 554 army generals, 14 out of 98 Luftwaffe generals, and 11 out of 53 admirals" (Goeschel 2009:151). Nor was it only the country's leadership. In areas facing the brutal Soviet occupation, "suicide occurred on a mass scale" with hundreds of suicides per village per month (Goeschel 2009:160).

DOWNWARD MOBILITY AS OVERINFERIORITY

Throughout this discussion I have used Black's (2011:71) term *overinferiority*—an increase in social inferiority—interchangeably with *downward mobility*. At the outset I even noted that the former might seem like just a newfangled way of talking about the latter. It is thus fair to ask whether the two propositions—*suicide varies directly with downward mobility* and *suicide varies directly with overinferiority*—are merely different ways of stating the same thing.

There are indeed many cases where they are functionally equivalent, in that they would make the same predictions about the risk or frequency of suicide. But one can yield hypotheses that the other does not. The proposition about overinferiority involves a conception of social status as both relative and zero sum (Black 2011:59). One implication is that the absolute magnitude of a loss will be less important than its effect on someone's position in a network of relationships. Where entire networks share similar degrees of downward mobility, then, their individual suicide risk should be lower than that of those who suffered comparable losses while their associates did not. There are presently little data that bear on this hypothesis, but it is possible to test by gathering data on social networks of suicide victims. Such a relationship would also be consistent with research (e.g., Chang et al. 2013; Mäki and Martikainen 2012) finding that the impact of unemployment on suicide varies inversely with the overall unemployment rate.[8]

Another implication of the idea that overinferiority causes suicide is that suicide is encouraged not just by falling but by falling behind: those who remain in place while their associates rise in wealth, respect, or other kinds of status should react in much the same way as those who suffer a loss, and so suicide risk should increase among those whose associates gain wealth, education, or promotions while they do not. Falling behind is therefore most likely to cause suicide in contexts where advancement is normal, as when students are held back in school or young men cannot find employment as their friends and age-mates move into the workforce. For instance, a study of 103 male self-killers among the Bimin-Kuskusmin of Papua New Guinea reveals that "all were between 23 and 34 years of age, a time in the Bimin-Kuskusmin social life-course when men have recently completed initiation, have married and are beginning to start families, and are launching careers in the linked domains of ritual and politics. . . . None of these men had ever become any kind of 'ritual leader' or 'man of political-economic importance'" (Poole 1985:160). And when someone falls while their close associates are rising, it should make the fall all the more dangerous. For example, one young New Zealander's failures were apparently magnified by his brother's success: "At sixteen Scott Bernard decided that he could never achieve his school certification. A friend noticed his sagging confidence on the two fronts that mattered: school and sports. 'His older brother achieved really well in marks plus sport at school. Scott was sensitive to this and also felt pressured to perform in Rugby which he eventually gave away this year'" (Weaver and Munro 2013:776).

Suicide and Vertical Direction

Downward mobility is a common cause of suicide and is also a common cause of conflict. It is therefore particularly likely to cause suicidal conflict. The grievances that led to Mohamad Bouazizi's self-immolation, for instance, involved his being dominated, shamed, and economically hamstrung by local law enforcement. But the stimulus that sparks the behavior is not the whole story. After all, people react to losses in many ways besides self-destruction. Even in conflicts caused by overinferiority—cases where people are angered by domination or otherwise blame someone else for their loss—they might handle their grievance using a wide variety of means. Some respond with violent aggression, directly attacking those they think have harmed them. Some negotiate for a solution to the problem or turn to such forms of avoidance as resigning in protest or firing an incompetent employee. We must still explain why the same sorts of grievances get handled in different ways, and as discussed in chapter 1, the key to doing this is to look at the social structure of the conflict. This includes its vertical structure, such as the degree of inequality between the parties and, crucially, whether the grievance is directed upward toward a social superior or downward toward a social inferior.

In any conflict, the grievance or offense has a vertical direction that helps determine how the conflict is handled. Some forms of conflict management are more likely between equals. This includes negotiation, in which both sides work toward an agreement (Black 1998:83–85). Equality also encourages a conciliatory style of social control, in which the parties are less concerned about applying explicit rules or punishing deviance than with seeking to restore harmony to the relationship (Black 1976:5, 30). Even if social control is not conciliatory, but rather punitive and violent, equality still exerts such influence as encouraging the violence to take the form of a mutual exchange, as in a duel or feud (Black 1998:75; Black 2004b). Inequality, on the other hand, encourages social control that is unilateral (Baumgartner 1984; see also Campbell and Manning 2019). In downward directions, the response to alleged deviance tends to be direct, overt, rule-oriented, and adversarial (Black 1998:144–55). Both criminal law and civil litigation are greater in downward directions, against social inferiors accused of wronging their superiors. So too is much punitive interpersonal violence, including the spanking of children, flogging of slaves, and the lynching of accused criminals. Upward grievances tend to be handled differently. True, they sometimes result in legal action or in such forms of violence as assassination, riots, and terrorism. But compared to downward moralism, upward moralism is more often muted, little more than griping and grumbling (Black 1998:144–55; see also Campbell and Manning 2019). When action does occur, it is more often covert—a disgruntled employee quietly pilfers company supplies, or a slave finds creative new ways to "accidentally" destroy farm equipment (Baumgartner 1984; Tucker 1989). It is often indirect, reliant on gaining attention and sympathy from third parties in the hopes that they will act as champions (Baumgartner 1984). And it is sometimes self-destructive. As sociologist M. P. Baumgartner observed in a discussion of social control techniques used by subordinates against their superiors, suicide is "one of the most dramatic forms of upward social control, and also perhaps the one with least appeal to people in more fortunate circumstances" (Baumgartner 1984:328).

All else being equal, suicide is more likely in stratified conflicts—conflicts in which there is status inequality between the parties. In such conflicts, it is the social inferior who is more likely to turn to suicide. This is true of suicide to escape or avoid an enemy and also of suicide to protest injustice to or punish an adversary. In a conflict, *suicide is greater in upward directions than in downward ones* (Manning 2012). Since inequality is a matter of degree, we can further specify that, all else being equal, *suicide increases with the social superiority of the adversary.* The greater the aggrieved party's degree of inferiority, the more likely he or she is to turn to suicide as a way of handling the grievance. Contrariwise, the greater the aggrieved party's degree of superiority, the more unthinkable suicide becomes. We can observe these principles at work in a number of different types of human relationship. Consider first conflict in marriages.

MARITAL INEQUALITY

Some marriages are highly egalitarian, with both spouses on equal footing: they have similar levels of wealth, education, and respectability, and neither has authority over the other. Perhaps one spouse might earn a little more income than the other, and men everywhere tend to have greater physical size and strength, but there is little inequality overall. To observe the effects of inequality on suicide it is useful to look at the opposite extreme: marriages in which one spouse monopolizes control of wealth and has a great deal of authority over the other. Such extreme inequality almost always involves a husband dominating a wife, and in highly patriarchal societies this is the typical kind of marriage.

The societies of the New Guinea Highlands, for example, tend to be highly patriarchal.[9] Women are commonly subject to severe discipline, have limited control over their sexuality, and have limited freedom to exit an unsatisfactory marriage. Though they usually have some say in their choice of spouse, girls in the Eastern Highlands may have their wishes overridden by their father and brothers and be forced to marry someone against their will. Some girls are even forcibly abducted into marriage by men of another village. In either situation, those caught trying to flee an unwanted husband face brutal discipline. A woman who flees her husband may be caught, beaten, and gang-raped by her husband's kin (Berndt 1962:136). In one case, an abducted woman who tried to escape her captors was first raped by several men and then shot in the thigh with an arrow (Berndt 1962:144–45). Similarly, among the people of New Guinea's Mount Hagen:

> Women fleeing home from their husband's clan, especially in times of warfare and if they were related to enemies, might in the past be caught and raped. A husband who was afraid that his wife would run away and estimated that he was unlikely to obtain a bridewealth return, or out of anger threw this to the winds, occasionally anticipated the event by inviting his clansmen to plural copulation before getting rid of her. Even someone anxious to retrieve a runaway wife might nevertheless punish her severely. Several stories from the past describe how a husband with supporters from his sub-clan would bodily carry the protesting woman back to his place, trussed up like a pig, and set

on her; kicking the genital area or perhaps stuffing her vagina with an irritant such as a mass of ants. (Strathern 1972:187)[10]

Throughout the Highlands, women are subject to violent social control in the form of beatings, rape, and genital mutilation (Gelber 1986:25). Husbands are within their rights to beat an adulterous wife (Ryan 1973:134). In one case among the Eastern Highlanders, an unfaithful wife was tied to two posts, stripped naked, and publicly beaten (Berndt 1962:163). Men, on the other hand, are expected to carry out extramarital affairs and have much greater sexual freedom within marriage than women do (Berndt 1962:127–28). Husbands also have control of their wives' sexuality within the marriage and might discipline wives for refusing to have sex: "Locally speaking, a man is fully justified in beating his wife for noncompliance in this respect" (Berndt 1962:188). And while women can and do initiate divorce, they face greater constraints than men in doing so, including the threat of physical retaliation and the possibility that their kin might refuse to accept their return (Strathern 1972:198).

In this highly patriarchal culture, where husbands exert a high degree of dominance over their wives, it is wives who most often turn to suicide to handle marital conflicts. Researchers report proportionally more suicide or attempted suicide by women in at least ten societies throughout the Highlands, and much of this suicide is due to conflicts between spouses (Gelber 1986:10–11). For example, among the Maring of the Bismarck Mountains suicide is almost entirely confined to female victims, many of whom kill themselves following acts of domestic violence (Healey 1979:95). Similarly, twenty-three of twenty-six recorded cases among the Huli involved female victims, and most of these were due to domestic disputes (Smith 1981–82:243). At Mount Hagen, twenty of twenty-nine recorded suicides were committed by married women, most commonly following a marital quarrel or failed attempt at divorce (Strathern 1972:256). And of twenty-six recorded cases in the Eastern Highlands, twenty-one were committed by women, again commonly in reaction to marital conflict (Berndt 1962:180).

These suicidal women do not necessarily display the sadness and lethargy consistent with Western conceptions of depression. Instead they express moralistic anger, and people in this region understand suicide as a hot-blooded act, one that will likely cause trouble for an abusive husband. In one case, "A man beat his woman at every opportunity, even during sex. She finally responded by flying into a rage, reminding him that 'Neither a pig nor a dog bore me!' She then collected all her things and threw them in the stream. That night she hanged herself from a tree near the house. Her husband cried when he found her, summoned her brothers, and killed a pig for them [as compensation]" (Berndt 1962:191).

Similar patterns are found in other parts of New Guinea. Outside of the Highlands, on the coastal island of New Britain, live the Lusi people. Though Lusi marriages appear to have less violent subjugation than those of some Highland societies, they are still quite patriarchal by contemporary Western standards. Among the Lusi a husband has rights to the products of his wife's labor and any property she inherits, it is normal for husbands to dominate their wives in household decisions, and both sexes consider it legitimate for a husband to beat a wife who defies him (Counts 1980:340). Resistance to domination is both illegitimate and impractical: "As a rule, women who publicly defy their menfolk are loudly condemned and may be physically abused by men. The inequity of physical strength between men and women makes overt defiance, or acts of physical retaliation, risky responses to male power and dominance" (Counts 1980:340). As in the Highlands, wives have limited ability to leave unhappy marriages, facing such constraints as fear of retribution, the unwillingness of their kin to accept them back, and the probability that they will have to give up custody of their children, who remain attached to the husband's patrilineal group (Counts 1990:156–59).[11] And here too wives are more likely than husbands to handle grievances with suicide: in the district of Kaliai during a twenty-year period, eight of nine suicides and two of three attempts were committed by women, and over half of these occurred after a woman had been beaten by her husband (Counts 1987).

Surely the sheer pain of abuse plays a role, but so do does the degree to which the beating is seen as deviant. While all involved accept a husband's right to discipline his wife, women object to beatings that are excessive by local standards, including those administered "for no good reason or in an unacceptable way" (Counts 1987:203). According to one female informant, "When a man just keeps beating a woman, when he won't let her explain or hear what she has to say, that's the kind of treatment that causes a woman to kill herself" (Counts 1990:151). Suicide is seen by local women as a recourse against men, one that is more feasible than retaliating in kind. In the words of one local woman, "Men are much stronger than we are. . . . Fighting back is not the way" (quoted in Counts 1980:338).[12] Suicide, however, can punish an abusive husband through shame, compensation payments, and violent retribution. It is a weapon of the weak, used when violent discipline gives rise to moral grievances.

Patriarchal domination is also the norm in much of the Islamic world, including countries in the Middle East, South Asia, and Central Asia. In Tajikistan, for example, most girls are subject to "rigid control" carried out through "physical violence, threats, and verbal humiliation" at the hands of their own kin, and after being "pressured or forced into an arranged marriage in their late teens," their husband and his family assume control (Haarr 2010:767). The domination of a young bride is often more severe in marriage than in her natal family: "Young brides find themselves in the lowest power position within the husband's family, especially in the early years of marriage when they are newcomers to the family . . . and have yet to demonstrate their ability to fulfill their new duties" (Haarr 2010:767). One survey of four hundred married Tajik women found that roughly 58 percent had been subjected to physical or sexual violence and about 19 percent had suffered both (Haarr 2010:775). The respondents who suffered violent domination were more likely to have considered or attempted suicide than those who did not, and respondents in focus groups agreed that "women who are beaten 'too much' or 'too often,' especially for 'unjustifiable' reasons, have suicidal thoughts and may eventually attempt suicide" (Haarr 2010:775–76).

In Iran, too, women are sometimes forced into marriage at a young age, may be subject to violent discipline within the marriage, and have little ability to initiate divorce. And here too suicide is concentrated among young, marriage-aged women, who commit between 60 and 80 percent of the suicides in some provinces (Aliverdinia and Pridemore 2009:309).[13] Notably, the suicide rates of women are lower in provinces of the country with higher rates of female education and labor-force participation—places where one can find more women who have a relatively high status and where women generally have more freedom from the authority of husbands and kin (Aliverdinia and Pridemore 2009). In recent decades an increasing number of suicidal women have chosen self-burning as their method of dispatch, and "many women who choose this method make it clear (via statements or suicide notes) that they burned themselves to death as a protest against their appalling family conditions" (Aliverdinia and Pridemore 2009:309). Indeed, one case-control study found that family conflict increases the risk of self-immolation by a factor of ten and that domestic violence is the chief complaint of most self-burners (Ahmadi et. al 2009; see also Zarghami and Khalilian 2002).

Self-immolation is an increasingly common method of female suicide in several Muslim countries, including Iran, Afghanistan, Pakistan, Tajikistan, and Uzbekistan. Self-burning is probably chosen because of its association

with political protest and its effectiveness as a dramatic display of one's grievances. In these countries the method is mostly confined to female victims, is
often carried out in front of witnesses, and is commonly caused by domestic
violence (Campbell and Guiao 2004:787). In Afghanistan—whose Pasthun
people have a saying that "husband is another name for God" (quoted in Black
2018:4)—there were over seven hundred burnings in 2014 alone, and most of
them were committed by women (Ministry of Public Health 2014). In eastern Sri Lanka, both Muslim and Hindu women, again, especially young and
newly married women light themselves on fire because of upward grievances
within stratified marriages: "In this male-dominated society, should a dispute
arise between partners, the woman will be advised to tolerate, forgive, and live
with it. . . . This bitter, disheartened wife may feel that she has to do something desperate to make her husband and relatives see her side of the story.
'I wanted my husband to feel sorry' said many of our patients" (Laloe and Ganesan 2002:479). Young Hindu and Muslim brides in India face similar social
conditions—a low status within the extended family of a patriarchal husband
coupled with frequent acts of violent domination—and also have high suicide
rates relative to the general population, with many suicides following episodes
of domestic conflict (Khan 2002; Hadlaczky and Wassesrman 2009:124).[14]

We see similar patterns when we look at domestic disputes in other societies with highly stratified marriages. In the agrarian villages of mid-twentieth
century Taiwan, women generally had a lower status than men, younger
people a lower status than older people, and a newly married woman had a
particularly low status within her husband's patrilineal household. Marriages
were contracted between families, with the groom's family paying a large
sum of bride-price to the bride's family. At marriage the bride left her own
family and went to live with her husband's kin, where she faced suspicion
as an outsider and extreme scrutiny as a questionable investment of family
resources. The move itself was an increase in her social inferiority, and she
would likely be subject to many specific instances of domination thereafter. Perhaps the lowest-ranking member of the family, she was expected to
obey orders from new kin. With little experience in her new role she would
likely attract constant complaints about her performance, especially from her
mother-in-law.[15] These downward grievances took the form of criticism, insults, and sometimes beatings. Such treatment might provoke grievances on
the part of the bride, though she was unlikely to respond in kind. Yet while
open rebellion was rare, sometimes brides incensed by excessive discipline
would combine escape and revenge in the act of suicide. The practice was
common enough that women of marriageable age had higher suicide rates

than any other demographic category and accounted for a large proportion of all suicides in Taiwan (Wolf 1972, 1975). Locals recognized a young wife's suicide as a rebellious act that harmed her marital family, placing them under the threat of retaliation from her vengeful ghost, shaming them in the eyes of the community, and forcing them to placate her angry natal family (Wolf 1972). Similar patterns were found in mainland China and still exist in rural parts of the country today. New brides are often subject to harsh criticism and violent discipline, and when these young women retaliate, they often do so by committing suicide (Lui 2002; Zhang et al. 2004; compare Fei 2005).[16] Family structures differ in urban areas, where modern work patterns and living arrangements preclude the kind domination found in farm families. This explains why female suicide rates are much lower in urban areas than in rural ones (Baudelot and Establet 2008:165–70; Pearson et al. 2002).

Highly patriarchal societies, particularly those in which young brides are dominated by both their husbands and their husbands' extended kin, tend to produce clear sex differences in suicide: marital conflict sparks more suicide by women than by men, most female suicides are the result of spousal abuse and other domestic conflict, and women's suicide often has an explicitly moralistic character, aimed at appeal or revenge as well as escape from suffering. This pattern is sometimes frequent enough that it produces relatively high rates of female suicide compared to other settings. And this pattern is rarely seen in societies with more egalitarian marriages. This does not mean that equality is a guarantee against suicidal conflict: wife abuse is not the only sort of marital discord that causes suicide. But even if marital conflict still causes considerable suicide in sexually egalitarian societies, the pattern of suicide is different, and such suicide is less likely to be highly concentrated among wives.

Compare the high degrees of marital inequality we have considered so far to the relative equality of the Mataco (or Wichí) of South America's Gran Chaco, a dry lowland region that stretches across Argentina, Bolivia, and Paraguay. Unlike their counterparts in rural Afghanistan, Iran, or Highland New Guinea, Mataco women are free to make their own decisions in matters of sex, marriage, and divorce (Alvarsson 1988:98; see also Fock 1963:91–92). Indeed, women take the initiative in courtship. Cooperation and mutual respect are typical of spousal relationships, and though the husband is dominant in most interactions, the wife has a "good social position" and is usually safe from abuse (Fock 1963:63; Alvarsson 1988:77, 104). Early in the marriage, the wife's position is bolstered by the custom of the married couple living with the wife's parents while the husband engages in a period of bride service, working for her parents in exchange for her hand in marriage (Fock 1963). Later in the marriage, his dominance is undercut by her ability to easily exit the relationship—a wife who initiates divorce faces no public censure and maintains custody of her children (Alvarsson 1988:138).[17] Since most serious conflicts are handled with divorce, domestic violence is rare among the Mataco. When violence does occur, women do not only participate as victims: though spouse killings are mostly perpetrated by men, jealous women will sometimes physically attack and beat an unfaithful husband, often with the help of their female kin (Fock 1963:98).

Among the Mataco, marital problems sometimes lead to suicide. In cases of infidelity or abandonment, for instance, injured parties of either sex might resort to suicide (Fock 1963; Alvarsson 1988:138). Missionaries among the Mataco estimate that suicide in general is equally distributed and cite cases arising from marital conflict with both male and female victims (Métraux 1943). Among the egalitarian Mataco, suicide is not distinctive of either sex but common to both.

Societies with egalitarian sex relations do not necessarily have a perfectly symmetrical distribution of suicide across the sexes. Inequality is not the only factor that influences suicide, and other factors might make one or the other sex more likely to turn to self-destruction in greater numbers. For instance, marriages among the Iroquois of North America were quite egalitarian by cross-cultural standards.[18] In traditional times, Iroquois peoples lived in communal longhouses shared by members of the same matrilineal clan. Each spouse took a subservient role when living among his or her spouse's clan, and since matrilocal residence was common, it tended to limit the authority husbands could exercise over their wives.[19] Though husbands still sometimes meted out violent discipline, spousal abuse does not appear to have been common, and sometimes it was the wife who was the more violent party in the relationship (Fenton 1986; Foley 1975:21; Brown 1970:156).[20] Since divorce was easy and remarriage common, marital conflict was more likely to lead to divorce than abuse. Both spouses had the right to initiate divorce, with wives usually maintaining custody of the children (Beauchamp 1900:84; Randle 1951:171; Brown 1970:175; Foley 1975:20, 77).

Both sexes sometimes killed themselves for various reasons, but accounts compiled by anthropologist and cultural historian William N. Fenton—including cases from the 1600s to the 1900s—suggest that suicide over marital problems was more common among women (Fenton 1941, 1986). Notably, though, these women did not kill themselves over abuse or domination. Instead, they mostly seemed to kill themselves out of jealousy of female rivals.

For whatever reasons, men appeared to have the upper hand in the marriage market, resulting in a "brittle monogamy" and many cases where women killed themselves when their husbands left them for someone else (Fenton 1986:451).[21] If it is true that women were more likely to kill themselves over marital problems in this culture, it may be because women were more likely than men to have the problem of an unfaithful spouse—which, as we shall see in the next chapter, is itself a common cause of suicide. Whatever the exact reason, early observers of the neighboring Delaware (or Lenape) people—who had a similar pattern of social organization—gave no indication that suicide over martial conflict was greater for one sex than the other and cited several cases of men who killed themselves over marital quarrels and infidelity (Zeisberger 1910:82; Heckewelder 1819:251).

These considerations suggest that societies with greater marital equality have a more heterogeneous pattern of suicide. Where extreme patriarchy prevails, the high degree of inequality tends to drown out the influence of other variables, leading to a more consistent pattern of suicide, with the death of abused young brides being exceptionally common. Where inequality is not so severe, the relationship between sex, marriage, and suicide is more variable.

For further comparison, consider the modern West, where marriages tend to be egalitarian by cross-cultural standards.[22] Here men are more likely to die by suicide—in the United States, the overall suicide rate for men is about three times that of women. The same pattern seems to hold when we look at particular reasons for suicide: in my sample of over two hundred suicidal conflicts from Louisville, men outnumbered women three to one. US men thus appear more likely to kill themselves over martial problems, perhaps because—like Iroquois women—they are more likely to be left by an unhappy partner (see chapter 3). On the other hand, we know that women are more than three times more likely to commit nonfatal attempts and that such attempts greatly outnumber deaths. We currently lack precise statistics on the matter, but given evidence that many suicide attempts are also a reaction to conflict, including marital conflict and domestic abuse, the overall rate of suicidal conflict may be greater for women, though the average lethality is lower.

YOUNG AND OLD

Aside from marriages, other family relationships may also be more or less stratified. Adults have more of various kinds of status than do children or adolescents, parents commonly have authority over their children, and younger relatives are often expected to defer to their elders. We would thus expect grievances against parents or other adults to result in suicide more often than grievances against children or other youth.

As with marital inequality, the effect of generational inequality is most evident in extreme cases—settings in which elders exert a great deal of authority over their juniors and in which there is a high rate of conflict between the two. One such setting is Western Samoa, where kinship groups are headed by patriarchs known as *matai* who plan and regulate much of community life, are the only ones exempt from a community-wide curfew that begins at 9:00 p.m., and who may take time to lecture their family before the evening meal, airing grievances against particular members (O'Meara 2002:55–56). Youth in this setting have a relatively high degree of subordination to their family, such that "from the time they enter childhood until they are old enough to have maturing children of their own, the lives of young Samoans are largely devoted to obeying and serving their elders" (O'Meara 2002:78). Local norms dictate that the younger generations show high levels of respect and deference to their elders, who may respond in "severe and punitive" ways to any direct challenge to their authority (Macpherson and Macpherson 1987:324). Conflict between parents and youth is increasingly common, partly because the past few decades of globalization have led to cultural differences between the generations and disrupted traditional paths to adulthood and independence. Virtually no parents kill themselves over these conflicts, but many children do: "Young Samoans usually express feelings of anger and hostility toward their parents and other authority figures only indirectly, sometimes in ways that hurt their families indirectly by first hurting themselves" (O'Meara 2002:109). The situation is extreme enough that suicide in Western Samoa is highly concentrated among youth—75 percent of all victims are between the ages of fifteen and twenty-four—and the majority of cases "are triggered by an argument, rebuff, or scolding from a parent or parent figure" (O'Meara 2002:110; see also Macpherson and Macpherson 1987).

A similar combination of generational hierarchy and high rates of conflict occurs on the Micronesian island of Chuuk (also known as Truk), where parents are strict disciplinarians and administer corporal punishment "for a wide variety of offense" (Gladwin and Sarason 1953:87). Youth, on the other hand, rarely engage in violence or overt aggression toward their elders, instead using a strategy of withdrawal culminating in suicide. Youth suicide is common on Chuuk, and "the typical triggering event" for suicides is "a quarrel or argument between the young man and his parents, or occasionally an older brother or sister, or some other older relative" (Rubinstein

2002:37). The Tikopia of Polynesia likewise use violent discipline against errant children, though children are forbidden from responding in kind: "The striking of father by son is indeed almost out of the realm of native social behavior, since a violent reaction of the son against the father would lead him to suicide direct, as not infrequently happens. This is in fact the son's remedy against injustice, and the knowledge of it acts as a check upon temperamental fathers" (Firth 1933:177).

We can see similar patterns in Western history as well. In early modern England, where children between the ages of seven and fifteen were customarily sent "from their parents' homes into service, apprenticeship, or tutelage in other households" in which they were "estranged, isolated, powerless, and without rights," young people would kill themselves when mistreated or accused of wrongdoing (Murphy 1986:268–69). Though contemporaries viewed these suicides mostly as a matter of fearing and escaping from corporal punishment, the deceased might also have counted on causing trouble for his or her elders: people in this time believed that the home would be forever haunted by the self-killer's ghost, a spirit that was "notoriously troublesome, difficult to lay to rest, and implacably vengeful" (Murphy 1986:269–70). A few centuries later, in Victorian England, child and youth suicide was more often caused by conflict with one's own parents. Historian Olive Anderson observes that "the general impression left by delving into reports of individual suicide cases in the period 1840–80 is that children and young adults who took their own lives often did so as a retort to harsh treatment, in order to make authoritarian parents repent of their conduct and to inflict punishment upon them in their turn" (Anderson 1987:180).

In the contemporary United States, youth are much more likely to commit nonfatal attempts than to die by suicide, and so cases involving the very young are rare in samples taken from the records of coroners and medical examiners. In my own study of several hundred suicides in Louisville, Kentucky, there were only seven cases with juvenile victims. Four of these were sparked by family discipline, with children or teenagers killing themselves after being scolded or punished by a parent or other older relative. For example, one eleven-year-old boy had been suspended from school for fighting: "As punishment for this the decedent was confined to his room all weekend. He repeatedly complained that this punishment was unfair. After supper he was sent back to his room. When his step-father went to check on him later he found him in the closet hanging from a belt." In another case a seventeen-year-old with a history of "behavior problems" killed himself after an argument with the aunt with whom he was staying. And one teenage girl killed herself following an argument with her mother, leaving a note complaining that "I just am not pretty, smart, outgoing, and good enough in your eyes" and urging her parents to "just love your kids for who they are and don't push them if what you want isn't what they want."

Attempted suicide is more common than completed suicide among US adolescents, and it too frequently follows a conflict with parents or parent figures (Curran 1987:64–65; Pfeffer 1986; Wagner 2009:78–90). For example: "Louisa's mother became furious over receiving a telephone call from school informing her that Louisa had been skipping classes and failing to turn in important assignments. She confronted Louisa about her dishonesty and irresponsibility that evening. . . . [Her] anger swelled into a rage. . . . She began smashing bowls and plates. . . . She screamed that Louisa was going to cause the family to fall apart. . . . Louisa raced upstairs to the bathroom, locked the door, and began ingesting any pill she could find" (Wagner 2009:78–79).

Because the United States is a large and diverse country, there is considerable variation in family structure across regions, classes, and ethnic groups.[23] The suicidal behavior of young people varies accordingly. For example, many Hispanic Americans—including immigrants from Mexico, Puerto Rico, and South America—share a culture that emphasizes the familial authority of males over females and elders over children. Relative to youth from other ethnic backgrounds, Hispanic youth are expected to show high levels of deference to their parents, and daughters in particular are subject to extensive monitoring and control. As the daughters of US immigrants adopt mainstream American culture and seek greater personal autonomy, the result is a high rate of conflict in a stratified relationship and thus an elevated rate of suicide. In 2007 about 14 percent of female Hispanic (or Latina) high school students attempted suicide, versus about 9 percent of all female high school students (Wagner 2009:33; see also Zayas 2011:36).[24] One study of twenty-seven Latina suicide attempters found that their attempts were often triggered by a fight with a parent and that these triggering conflicts were the most recent in a long history of conflicts in which "parents remained inflexible and unwavering in their demand for control. . . . Girls describe being repeatedly degraded by their parents, causing them to feel unloved or angry" (Zayas et al. 2010:7; see also Zayas 2011:113–15).

Note that the oldest people in the family are not necessarily those with the most stature. While social standing tends to increase throughout much of the life course, it often declines again in very old age. Retirement reduces income and medical bills eat up savings, while frailty of mind and body produces childlike dependence on adults still in their prime. The elderly are often socially inferior to other adults and so are more likely to turn to suicide to handle conflicts with them. Among the Jalé of New Guinea, for example, elderly persons sometimes commit suicide when neglected by their children—an act locals believe is "meant to hurt the guilty, who afterward suffer feelings of regret and self-reproach" (Koch 1974:75). The status of the very old varies across cultures according to the extent to which they are respected, exert authority, and maintain control of property. It may even vary within the same family. Among the Vaqueiro pastoralists of Spain, rules of inheritance benefit one sibling, who becomes the future head of the household, at the expense of the others, who must work for him as laborers. The household head retains respect and authority with age, but as the laborers weaken, their status declines, so that the head's old, unmarried siblings become the most structurally inferior members of the family household. Treated as servants with limited utility, and ridiculed by the rest of the family, these "old people of the house" are most likely to kill themselves in reaction to domestic conflict (Cátedra 1992:173–79).

INDIVIDUALS AND ORGANIZATIONS

When people band together for collective action, they have resources and abilities beyond those of individuals acting alone. The larger the group and the greater its division of labor, the more this is so. In Black's framework, degree of organization—or capacity for collective action—is another kind of social status (Black 1976:85–92). Organization makes groups superior to individuals, larger groups superior to smaller ones, and groups with central leadership and internal specialization superior to disorderly mobs. When individuals interact with organizations—be it a business corporation, street gang, or government—they do so on unequal terms. Grievances of individuals against organizations or of small groups against larger and more organized ones are upward grievances. Such upward grievances are more likely than downward ones to result in suicide. Thus large organizations such as states or multinational corporations virtually never employ suicide as a tactic of social control against individuals, but individuals sometimes turn to suicide to protest or oppose large organizations.[25]

Often those who commit protest suicide are acting on behalf of some organization (such as a labor union) or larger collectivity (such as a religious or ethnic group). But they are typically acting as individuals and are acting against an adversary—in most cases, a state—that is far more organized than whatever group they represent. In chapter 1, we saw that the famous suicide of Thich Quang Duc in Vietnam helped popularize self-burning as a means of political protest. Several other monks and nuns soon joined him by burning themselves to protest the government oppression of Buddhists. Others protested with lesser acts of self-destruction, such as cutting off fingers. Later, still more monks and nuns would kill themselves to protest the Vietnam War, as would some activists involved in the peace movement in the United States (Biggs 2008). In 1969, Czech student Jan Palach burned himself to protest the Soviet invasion of Czechoslovakia, while Ukrainian dissident Oleksa Hirnyk burned himself in 1978 to protest the Soviet suppression of Ukrainian language and culture (Wikipedia 2017c, 2017f). In 1981, Swedish actor Per-Axel Arosenius burned himself following a dispute with the Swedish taxation authorities, and in 1989 Taiwanese activist Cheng Nan-jung burned himself to protest the government suppression of free speech (Wikipedia 2017a, 2017g). An unusually large rash of protest suicides occurred in India in 1990 in opposition to a government proposal to set aside places in universities and government employment for lower-caste citizens: "Within 10 weeks, at least 220 people—predominantly students from privileged castes—committed self-immolation" (Biggs 2008:24). Since 1970, nearly one hundred South Koreans have killed themselves in acts of political protest. These tended to be either students protesting authoritarian government or labor activists protesting powerful businesses backed by the government (Jang 2004; Park 2004; Park and Lester 2009; Kim 2008). In one well-known case, twenty-three-year-old tailor and labor activist Jeon Tae-il set himself on fire in Seoul and "took to the street, desperately chanting, 'Observe the Labor Standards Law!'" (Kim 2008:543).

Moralistic suicide can also occur when lone individuals have a grievance against an organization. In my study of Louisville suicides, for example, there were three cases in which the self-killer expressed a personal grievance toward state agencies. One woman blamed Child Protective Services for starting the "mess" she found herself in, while another accused the Social Security Administration and Internal Revenue Service of defrauding and mistreating her, concluding her suicide note with "You are wrong you took a life. . . . Your god will talk to you." And one man publicly shot himself in the office of the Social Security Administration after having his claim denied:

> The decedent went to the social security office to meet a claims representative. He had filed for disability, but was turned down by the

Baltimore office. He came to the local office and asked the representative to reconsider his claim, stating that he was unable to work and his wife had to work and to pay his medical bills. The representative advised him that he could take the information and turn it over to another branch to handle and that this branch would give him an appointment for an interview. The decedent asked how long it would be, and the representative said 2–3 months and the decedent said that this would be too long. The representative said he did not know what else he could do and the decedent said "I do," pulled a pistol from his pants pocket, and shot his self in the head in front of the representative, 58 employees, and as many customers.

The suicide of Mohamed Bouazizi, described in the prologue, is similar. Though his death had far-reaching consequences, it was not so much the result of a larger collective conflict as his own personal losses at the hands of state officials. Like the man who shot himself at the Social Security office, he made no posthumous demands and gave no evidence that his death was meant to find justice for those left behind. Yet both deaths were nonetheless a final, desperate airing of grievances against a superior adversary.

SELF-EXECUTION

In the previous chapter, we saw that sometimes suicide is a way for a person to deal with his or her own deviance. In other words, it is what Black calls "social control of the self"—more precisely, "self-execution" (Black 1998:65). Like suicide for protest or vengeance, its likelihood varies with the vertical direction of the grievance. Like other kinds of moralistic suicide, self-execution is more likely when someone faces a superior adversary. In cases of self-execution, however, it is not the aggrieved party that commits suicide but the alleged offender. Self-execution is more likely in response to downward grievances than upward ones, and, all else being equal, its likelihood increases with the status of the aggrieved and decreases with the status of the offender.

The clearest examples of self-execution are seen in highly stratified, rank-conscious settings with strong class divisions and rigid chains of command. Premodern Japan, for example, was dominated by the samurai ruling class, themselves graded into different ranks and serving under feudal lords, who were in turn ruled by a military dictator known as a shogun. The samurai had a distinctive method of suicide called seppuku that involved stabbing or cutting open one's belly with a short sword. Samurai would commit seppuku spontaneously to escape shame or display loyalty but could also be ordered to commit it as a form of execution. Forced self-execution initially arose in the aftermath of battles as a way of eliminating enemies: "The sooner the potential troublemaker could be persuaded to cut his stomach, the sooner things could return to normal" (Rankin 2012:48). In 1439, for instance, the forces of shogun Yoshikazu surrounded the temple where his defeated rival Mochiuji was taking refuge and urged him to commit suicide. After he did so, the shogun then succeeded in ordering Mochiuji's young son to kill himself as well (Rankin 2012:47–48). The practice grew more popular, and by the mid-1500s, feudal lords throughout the land were incorporating seppuku into their official punishments for disobedient samurai. A contemporary document from the 1590s lists the punishments for samurai in Echigo Province in order of severity, with seppuku being the second-most severe after having one's entire family stripped of its weapons and expelled from the samurai class (Rankin 2012:49–50). A feudal lord in Kumamoto made extensive use of seppuku in his house's rules of conduct, prescribing self-execution for such offenses as "reckless swordplay outside of training" or even, in the case of repeat offenses, for "minor breaches of etiquette" (Rankin 2012:50). A contemporary Spanish missionary observed that men condemned to seppuku did not resist or flee but instead solemnly carried out the order (Rankin 2012:52). Such was the fate of Sen no Rikyu, who attracted the wrath of the powerful lord Hideyoshi. When Riyku failed to apologize for an unintentional slight against his ruler, Hideyoshi sent representatives to inform him that he must commit seppuku. Rikyu responded by bowing and calmly offering the representatives tea. After drinking tea with them, Rikyu followed custom by composing two death poems and slitting his stomach with a single cut (Rankin 2012:68).

By the eighteenth century, forced seppuku had evolved from an agonizing form of suicide into something that was more often a form of voluntary execution, with many condemned nobles only going through the motions of stabbing themselves before being beheaded by an executioner. But those who voluntarily committed seppuku continued to cut their bellies as before.[26] In 1755, an ill-fated public works project aimed at building a series of dams led to the suicides of over fifty of the samurai sent there to oversee the effort. Some killed themselves to protest the poor management and bad working conditions, others because of their own errors and failures. For example, one man was found still breathing the morning after having cut open his belly in his room at the local inn; before he died, he explained that he was dying from shame because he was responsible for a construction delay (Rankin 2012:144).[27]

Forced seppuku died out in the late nineteenth century. Voluntary seppuku, especially as a means of self-punishment, also became rare, though it enjoyed a brief resurgence during World War II, particularly among military men. In one case, for instance, a Japanese naval officer disemboweled himself to atone to his superiors because "he could not complete his assigned task within the given period of time" (Seward 1968:39). And War Minister Korechika Anami committed seppuku the morning after signing Japan's surrender, leaving a note apologizing to the Japanese emperor (Kameda 2015.[28]

Self-execution might play an unusually prominent role in Japanese culture, but it is by no means unique to it. Suicide as capital punishment is found in other times and places where rulers have dictatorial power over their subordinates. Chinese kings and emperors could also order their officials to kill themselves, and the officials would comply, perhaps viewing the sentence as a mercy compared with the torturous methods of execution common in premodern states. Such forced executions have a long history. In 273 BCE, for instance, the king of the Qin state forced the renowned general Bai Qi to commit suicide (Hawkes 2011). In 904 CE, during the Tang dynasty, a purge of the administration led to thirty high-ranking officials being ordered to commit suicide (Wikipedia 2017a). And in 1858, during the Qing dynasty, the emperor ordered a Manchu statesman named Keying to kill himself for abandoning his post after he walked away from negotiations with the British (Fang 1943). Nor is forced self-execution solely an Asian phenomenon. As we saw in the last chapter, condemned criminals in ancient Greece and imperial Rome would also act as their own executioners. Among others, the philosophers Socrates and Seneca the Younger were sentenced to die by their own hands. Likewise, when the Roman emperor Nero became suspicious of his general Corbulo, he sent messengers who summoned Corbulo and ordered him to commit suicide. Corbulo promptly obeyed and fell on his sword (Rankin 2012).

Even inequality less extreme than that found in ancient states and empires might be sufficient to produce this form of capital punishment. Some tribal chiefs, for instance, can also demand such behavior. While Tikopian chiefs can strike commoners "with impunity," a commoner who strikes a member of a chiefly family "will probably have to expiate this offense by going off to sea" on a suicide voyage, taking his canoe out into the open ocean, where he will eventually die of drowning, sharks, or exposure (Firth 1933:358). Usually such suicide voyages are ordered by the chief himself—who will have an official announce the sentence and drag the offender's canoe to the edge of the water—though in some case the offender "anticipates the sentence by setting off in a canoe on his own initiative" (Firth 1949:180).

Inequality is a universal feature of social life. Even in societies with little stored wealth, people will differ in their health and strength, their knowledge and skill, and their reputation for being good or bad. But inequality is also variable. Some societies and relationships are relatively egalitarian; others are rigidly stratified. And inequality constantly changes, fluctuating with every gain and loss, every compliment and criticism, every act of discipline and rebellion. Suicide and conflict both vary accordingly, and thus moralistic suicide does as well. It arises from downward mobility and varies with the degree of loss. It waxes when stratification increases and wanes when it declines. As protest or punishment of another, it is relatively common against superiors but rare against inferiors. It is a weapon of the weak, often used against those whose strength and stature repel more direct aggression. And as self-punishment, it responds to upward offenses and downward complaints. Suicide is not randomly distributed across vertical space or vertical time. The same goes for the other dimensions of the social universe. This includes the subject of the next chapter: the distribution of relationships.

3

Suicide and Relationships

The 28-year-old factory worker had been drinking all day and began arguing with his live-in girlfriend. He accused her of cheating on him. She next heard him in the bedroom at midnight and went to see what he was doing. He was sitting on the floor with a .45 against the side of his head. She reached for the gun and he pulled the trigger. (Case from my Louisville study)

There is an old saying that compares friends to wealth: "Make new friends, keep the old, the former are silver, the latter are gold." The adage reflects the fact that if there is one aspect of social life that preoccupies people at least as much as social status, it is their social ties to others. Friends, family, spouses, lovers, coworkers, allies, business partners, and even casual acquaintances—such relationships attract a great deal of time and attention, and their patterning exerts powerful effects on social life.

If inequality is the vertical dimension of social space, then the distribution of social ties is the horizontal dimension (Black 1976:37). Like inequality, it has several variable features. Relationships can be more or less close, and this closeness can come from varying degrees of intimacy and interdependence (Black 1976:39–41). Entire social networks might be more or less close depending on the strength of all the ties within them. Just as people can inhabit higher or lower elevations in the distribution of wealth, they might inhabit more central or more marginal positions in a network of relationships (Black 1976:48). Just as levels of social elevation and status inequality are subject to change, so too are network position, intimacy, and interdependence. And just as suicide varies with inequality, so too it varies with relationships.

Suicide and Social Integration

Emile Durkheim long ago observed, based on his study of government statistics in France and elsewhere, that the married had lower suicide rates than the unmarried and people with children had lower suicide rates than the childless. To explain this pattern, he posited a simple relationship: *suicide varies inversely with social integration* (Durkheim [1857] 1951:171–216). He originally used the term *integration* to refer to shared beliefs and sentiments—"collective states of mind"—that arise from involvement in close social ties and cohesive social institutions (Durkheim [1857]1951:170).[1] Since then, sociologists have come to use *integration* to refer to social ties and involvements as such, meaning that people are more integrated to the extent that they are enmeshed in networks of stable relationships and participate in social institutions and activities (e.g., Black 1976:48; Hassan 1995:5; Wray, Colen, and Pescosolido 2011:514). And they have continued to find that people with fewer ties, weaker ties, and less social involvement are generally at greater risk of suicide. For instance, many studies—including analysis of public health statistics from the United States, Europe, Australia, South Korea, and elsewhere—support Durkheim's claim that married people have lower suicide rates than the unmarried (e.g., Danigelis and Pope 1979; Dublin 1963:27; Lorant et al. 2005b; Park, Lee, and Kim 2018; Smith, Mercy, and Conn 1988; for meta-analysis see Woo et al. 2018).[2] For reasons we will discuss below, the effect of being divorced is especially strong (Kposowa 2000; Stack 2000b). Studies of official statistics and large longitudinal surveys also find evidence for the protective effect of having children, of being involved in religious congregations, and of living in areas with greater residential stability (Baller and Richardson 2002; Breault 1986; Danigelis and Pope 1979; Duberstein et al. 2004; Pescosolido and Georgianna 1989; Tsai et al. 2014; on religion, compare Van Tubergen, Grotenhuis, and Ultee 2005).

Other indicators also point to suicide victims being more isolated and less integrated. For example, surveys tracking a cohort of nearly thirty-five thousand US men for twenty-four years show that suicide risk is greater for those with smaller social networks and that scoring high on a seven-item index of social integration led to a twofold reduction in suicide risk (Tsai et al. 2014). Studies in Australia and Sweden find that those who live alone are more prone to suicide than those who live with a family (Hassan 1995:28). Coroners' records from a nineteenth-century English town show not only that suicide victims were disproportionately single or widowed but also that suicide victims had few relatives of any kind who could testify regarding the circumstances leading to their death, such that "it was not uncommon for those testifying at inquests (notably landlords) to have had only a contractual relationship with the deceased" (Bailey 1998:259). Sociologist Ronald Maris found the same pattern in Chicago during the 1960s, where a landlord was often the only person available to answer the coroner's queries, as "it was not uncommon for there to be no relatives present at the inquest or for the relatives who were present to have had no contact with the decedent for quite some time" (Maris 1969:99). Chicago coroners' records also show it was common for victims to live alone, have no dependents, and to be described as lacking any close friends (Maris 1969:99; Maris 1981:60). Maris's follow-up study of Chicago suicides had the benefit of utilizing a comparison group of people who died by other causes and of conducting interviews with both groups' surviving relatives. He found that suicide victims had, on average, a smaller number of friends, fewer organizational involvements, and fewer close ties of any kind (Maris 1981:107, 114). A more recent case-control study in Syracuse and Rochester, New York, compared eighty-six suicide victims to eighty-six living people and found that in addition to being more often unmarried, childless, and not living with family, the suicide victims were also less likely to participate in community activities and generally had lower levels of social interaction (Duberstein et al. 2004). And because isolated or marginal people are more likely to kill themselves, places that attract them often have higher suicide rates. Thus studies of suicide in early twentieth-century cities found that suicide rates were greatest in areas with a high concentration of boarding houses that catered to detached, transient people (Schmid 1928; Cavan 1928:81–105; Sainsbury 1955:18).

There is thus a good deal of evidence that suicide concentrates at the margins of social networks. We might immediately think of psychological mechanisms behind this, such as suicidal motivation arising from loneliness or, as Durkheim posited, from a need for individuals to be attached to something greater than themselves to justify life: "The individual alone is not a sufficient end for his activity" (Durkheim [1857] 1951:210). There are also sociological mechanisms that contribute to the association. In chapter 4, we will consider the effect of social isolation on moral support, suicide prevention, and rescue. Another consideration is that, in addition to the effect of being more isolated, the association is partly due to the effects of *becoming* more isolated—that is, to the loss of social ties.

Suicide and Underintimacy

Social ties vary in their degree of intimacy, or *relational closeness*. Relational closeness is the degree to which individuals or groups participate in one another's lives. It increases with the length of the relationship, the frequency of contact, the amount of time spent together, and the range of shared activities (Black 1976:40–41; Black 2011:21). Activities can themselves be more or less intimate—compare having sex with someone to sitting next to them at a bus stop—and relational closeness varies accordingly. Relational closeness also increases with exposure to information about someone else. The more we observe and learn about someone, the closer we get—something that allows a one-sided closeness to people who may know nothing about us, as when fans spend much time watching and reading about their favorite celebrities (Black 2000:349; Black 2011:21). And even mutual strangers might be more or less distant from one another, depending on their position in a larger social network (Black 1976:41). Not all strangers are equally strange, and those who share network ties ("You know Bob? I know Bob too!") are relationally closer than those who do not.

Like any other aspect of the social world, relational closeness is subject to change. People form new relationships and end old ones, increase their contact with one another or decrease it. In Black's language, any decrease in relational closeness is *underintimacy*, while any increase in closeness is *overintimacy*. In the previous chapter we considered how fluctuations in the level of inequality can cause both conflict and suicide, and the same goes for fluctuations in intimacy. Overintimacy conflicts erupt over increases in closeness, such as when someone complains about another invading his or her privacy, overstaying his or her welcome, or acting too familiar (Black 2011:21–42). Underintimacy conflicts erupt when people complain about someone failing to keep in touch, giving the cold shoulder, or being too secretive (Black 2011:43–55). But just as not every fluctuation of inequality is equally likely to cause suicide, neither is every fluctuation of intimacy. Around the world and throughout history, underintimacy causes much more suicide than its opposite. And as with all types of social time, its effects are greater when the change is greater: a slight reduction in contact is less dangerous than the complete termination of a relationship, and the termination of a close relationship is more dangerous than the termination of a distant one. In other words, *suicide varies directly with underintimacy* (Manning 2015d). Thus one of the most common causes of suicide is the end of a marriage.

DIVORCE AND SEPARATION

Many studies, going back at least as far as Durkheim's pioneering work, find a connection between divorce and suicide risk. These include correlations at the aggregate level, such as the finding that states and counties with higher divorce rates also have higher suicide rates (e.g., Faria et al. 2006; Stack 1980; Breault 1986). Longitudinal studies show that suicide rates rise and fall in tandem with divorce rates—as they did, for example, in Denmark between 1951 and 1980 (Stack 1990a). One analysis of US data shows the causal priority of divorce, finding that shifts in the suicide rate occur after shifts in the divorce rate, with a spike in suicide occurring during the first few months after each spike in divorce (Wasserman 1984). Data on individuals confirm the relationship between divorce and suicide (Stack 1990b). We have already seen that much research finds a link between being unmarried and committing suicide. But the effects of being divorced are stronger and more consistent than those of being single, indicating that losing a marriage is more dangerous than merely lacking one. In a longitudinal study of over 400,000 Americans, divorced persons were over twice as likely to kill themselves within the follow-up period (Kposowa 2000). An analysis of World Health Organization data from ten European countries and the United States, Australia, and New Zealand found that suicide rates were higher for divorced individuals (Danigelis and Pope 1979). So too did a study of suicide in Hong Kong, Taiwan, Japan, and South Korea (Yip et al. 2012).

While it is hard to sort out exactly how much of the association between divorce and suicide is due to *being* divorced versus *becoming* divorced, the latter clearly has an impact. To the extent that underintimacy as such is the cause of suicide, we would expect the greatest danger to be during the period immediately following the end of the marriage, and this appears to be the case. For instance, a study of a cohort of over 200,000 Finnish men found that the increase in suicide risk was greatest immediately after divorce and declined over time afterward (Metsä-Simola and Martikainen 2013). Likewise, a study of twelve thousand US individuals found that recent divorce has a greater impact on suicide risk than does divorce further in the past (Stack and Scourfield 2015).[3] But even these studies probably underestimate the impact of marital breakdown on suicide. Marriage in modern societies is a legal institution, and in many jurisdictions obtaining a divorce is a legal process that can take several months to complete. By that time the formal divorce may simply be a legal ratification of a split that is in every other way already complete, as the estranged spouses have already moved apart, ceased regular communication, and otherwise disentangled their lives. While the legal divorce may be the proverbial last straw for some abandoned spouses, for many others the initial separation is the more severe blow. Thus a study of over six thousand suicide cases in Queensland, Australia, found that people who were "separated" had a risk of suicide four times that of any other marital status, including those who were officially divorced (Wyder, Ward, and De Leo 2009).

Looking in more detail at individual cases, as described in the investigations of coroners, police detectives, and others, confirms the importance of underintimacy in causing suicide. In one sample of thirty-one suicide cases taken from a coroner's records, seven victims had been separated from a spouse within the past six weeks, with another three being separated or divorced in the past year. A follow-up study of fifty suicide cases found that nine had separated within the past six months, with an additional eighteen separated or divorced in the past year (Murphy et al. 1979). There were also several more cases where the deceased was facing an impending separation, as when one twenty-six-year-old shot himself after his wife ordered him to leave their home. In another case, a thirty-four-year-old man's wife had announced her intention to divorce him the month prior, but while they had already scheduled a divorce hearing, they were still living together (Murphy et al. 1979). In my study of suicide in Louisville, breakups, separation, and divorces were mentioned by either investigators or by the victims themselves in 9 percent of a sample of 260 suicide cases. Examples include a twenty-nine-year-old man, recently divorced, who left a note addressed to his ex-wife in which he reminisces about significant events in their relationship, such as their first meeting and their first kiss. Another man, described by investigators as "depressed because of his pending divorce," had "driven to his estranged wife's home and threatened to kill both her and her child with a knife" before hanging himself the next day. Separation is also a drastic degree of underintimacy for those who were never formally married in the first place. Several cases involved unmarried partners, most of whom had been living together in long-term relationships. For instance, one African American woman who had broken up with her cohabiting boyfriend shot herself as he was loading the last of his possessions into a van parked outside. The role of underintimacy was even greater in a study of suicides in England and Wales. When Ben

Fincham and colleagues conducted a "sociological autopsy" of one hundred cases by analyzing police interviews, suicide notes, and other records, they found that "slightly more than half the cases mentioned relationship problems or breakdown and a third indicated that these difficulties were the main trigger for suicide" (Fincham et al. 2011:150). For example, one self-killer's mother recalled that before his death "he came to my door covered in blood. He said 'she's ripped my heart out, she's thrown it on the floor and she's bouncing on it'" (quoted in Fincham et al. 2011:162). As the authors of the study note, the importance of separation in causing suicide helps explain why in Britain the peak age for male suicide corresponds to the peak age for divorce (Fincham et al. 2011:148).

Sometimes the end of a romantic relationship results in the abandoned party killing his or her estranged partner and then committing suicide. In the United States, for instance, such cases of homicide-suicide account for about 8 percent of all homicides and 4 percent of all suicides (Riedel 2010:430; see also Bridges and Lester 2011). The perpetrators in these cases are usually men, and men killing themselves along with their estranged wives and girlfriends is by far the most common scenario of homicide-suicide (Marzuk, Tardiff, and Hirsch 1992:3180; Milroy 1998; Websdale 1999; Koziol-McLain et al. 2006; Liem and Nieuwbeerta 2010). Consider for example, a case from a study of several hundred Canadian homicides: "Witnesses claimed that the victim and the offender fought like cats and dogs. They were in the process of getting a divorce. . . . The offender had made several comments in the weeks prior regarding 'it being all over.' He also saw a lawyer and made a new will. The offender told his friend that there would be no court case (with respect to divorce and/or property settlement), but only two pine boxes. The offender strangled the victim with a vacuum cleaner cord and then stabbed himself" (Dawson 2005:82). In my own (Manning 2015b) study of West Virginia homicide-suicides, fourteen of the twenty cases occurring over a three-year period were sparked by some kind of underintimacy, usually a breakup or marital separation. One middle-aged man continued to stalk and harass his estranged wife for months after their separation, until he finally cornered her at her new home, shot her, and then turned the gun on himself (Manning 2015b:9). In another case a man who killed his estranged wife and then himself left a series of suicide notes that demonstrate how his initial plan to commit suicide evolved into a plan to take his wife with him. His last entry, written as he hid waiting to ambush his victim, read: "I'm going to have a heart to heart with [my wife] and we are both going to die" (quoted in Manning 2015b:11).

Divorce and separation might involve an additional source of underintimacy: reduced contact with one's children. For instance, one recently separated British self-killer left a suicide note reading: "I've lost everything and ain't got no contact with my son or family phone number. . . . I love and miss Nicholas David I love and miss and can't go on with heartache" (quoted in Fincham et al. 2011:162–63). Another suicide victim's mother told police, "He hasn't seen his two children for a few months now, Rachel 6 and Jack 5. Not seeing his children has broken his heart. . . . Joe has told me that he wanted to kill himself because of his children" (quoted in Fincham et al. 2011:163). The sociologists reporting these cases note that "given prevailing legal and social norms, separation and divorce routinely distances men from their children in a way that it rarely does for women"—a fact that can help explain why, in this setting, marital breakdown seems to play a larger role in suicide by men (Fincham et al. 2011:156). On the other hand, mothers are usually closer to children than are fathers, and so we would expect them to be more likely to commit suicide if they are separated from their young. Thus the authors report, "Female suicides were further distinguished by the extent to which they were more widely associated with problems related to children. . . . Such problems included separation from children due to divorce, estrangement (especially from older children), and children being taken into care" (Fincham et al. 2011:156). A crumbling marriage can sever other relationships as well, breaking off ties to in-laws or common acquaintances. For example, after parting ways with her prominent husband, Ted Hughes, poet Sylvia Plath "was lonely, almost friendless as well as husbandless" for "the flattering courtiers had departed with the king" (Becker 2003:2).

The suicidal effect of underintimacy is not limited to modern industrial societies. As noted in the previous chapter, failed marriages have been a major cause of Iroquois suicide since at least the 1600s. In 1672, a Jesuit missionary described a case among the Onondaga Iroquois: "[A woman] took some hemlock juice, because she could not bear to see herself abandoned by her husband, who married her rival. I am summoned in the capacity of a physician who has already succeeded in counteracting the effects of the poison. . . . I give an emetic. . . . The poison has already penetrated the intestines. . . . She utters loud cries and is seized with dreadful convulsions. . . . 'I have not sinned,' she says, 'he who has abandoned me is the one who is guilty'" (quoted in Fenton 1941:128). In a case from the late nineteenth century, a Seneca Iroquois couple "had a falling out, and he went home in the night telling her that he was leaving her for good, that he would not return. The following morning she went out and dug up the [poisonous root] and ate it and died" (Fenton 1941:93). Though we have seen that such suicide was more common among Iroquois women, men did it as well. An eighteenth-century observer reports the case of another Seneca couple who had a quarrel: "She told him to leave her, and forbad his inhabiting with her any longer. He went away and poisoned himself" (quoted in Fenton 1986:450). Men among the neighboring Delaware people sometimes killed themselves for the same reason—in one case, a Delaware man was especially upset at the idea of separating from his wife because, as was customary, she would take the children with her (Fenton 1941:105). Far away in India, the Bison-Horn Maria (or Muria) people also kill themselves over abandonment: "Kawasi Hurra's wife Lakhmi did not care for him and was always slipping away to her parents' house. He brought her back five or six times, but she would run away again after staying with him for a few days. Hurra seems to have been very fond of the girl, and her constant absence made him so miserable that he ended his life" (Elwin 1943:123). The Palawan people of the southern Philippines also experience suicide caused by desertion (Macdonald 2007:171–203). For instance, one relatively wealthy, middle-aged planter was married to a younger woman, who left him and went back to live with her father. He asked her to return but she refused; shortly after hearing this he hanged himself from a rafter (Macdonald 2007:171).

INFIDELITY

Breakups and divorces are obviously a substantial increase in relational distance and thus entail a high degree of underintimacy that is prone to cause both serious conflict and suicide. Infidelity is another relational breach that is likely to cause serious conflict. Societies vary in the extent to which they condemn extramarital affairs, and in some they are tolerated more for one sex (usually males) than for the other. But all expect marriage to involve at least some degree of exclusivity, and sexual jealousy causes conflict everywhere, including much violent conflict. There are of course evolutionary reasons for people—or any other animals—to be sensitive to mate fidelity, which can have a massive impact on reproductive success. Humans, after all, are far from the only species to guard mates and attack rivals. But we can also make sense of conflict over infidelity from a purely sociological perspective. One of Black's innovations is to conceptualize intimacy as zero sum: becoming relationally closer to one person necessarily means becoming more distant from everyone else (Black 2011:21–22).[4] Sexual and romantic interactions are particularly close, and so an affair creates a new close relationship and a corresponding increase in distance within the marriage (Black 2011:44–45). Infidelity is thus another kind of underintimacy.[5] The same principles that allow us to understand why people get upset or angry over sexual rivals also help us understand why they sometimes get jealous of nonsexual rivals as well—why people sometimes express resentment of their partner's children or pets or express annoyance when a close friend invites a newcomer along on what was previously an activity the friends shared alone. But the degree of underintimacy in romantic infidelity is usually greater and the conflicts more severe. And infidelity is also more likely to cause suicide.

We can see this in the ethnographic record. One observer of North America's Delaware Indians writes, "Many a [husband] takes [his wife's] unfaithfulness so to heart that in the height of his despair he swallows a poisonous root. . . . Women, also, have been known to destroy themselves on account of a husband's unfaithfulness" (Zeisberger 1910, quoted in Fenton 1941:21). Adultery is also a major cause of suicide among the Palawan of the southern Philippines (Macdonald 2007:145–203). In one case among the Palawan, a young man named Nalde killed himself by drinking poison out of jealousy over his wife, Rusida, who was "somewhat promiscuous" (Macdonald 2007:170). Another young man also drank poison because his wife had an affair—he drank it by the river after a quarrel and then returned home to her to die (Macdonald 2007:171–72). And a young woman named Sumling killed herself, partly out of anger and jealousy at her husband Durmin's continued affair with another woman, partly because her brothers were going to handle the infidelity by forcing the two to divorce (Macdonald 2007:145–46). Describing patterns of violence among Africa's !Kung hunter-gatherers, anthropologist Nancy Howell notes that "in cases of sexual jealousy . . . the angry party might attack the spouse or the other person, presumably depending upon whether he or she wanted the marriage to continue. The third possibility is that one may attack oneself, in the form of suicide. . . . Several women have been known to take poison arrows to injure themselves, as have several men" (Howell 1979:83).

Again, different societies have different norms about marriage and monogamy, but sexual jealousy appears to be universal, and underintimacy can cause conflict and suicide even when it is widely considered legitimate. In societies where polygyny is an accepted form of marriage, it is not a breach of vows or violation of trust when a man takes a second wife. But while it is not technically adultery, it is still underintimacy and is likely to cause grievances against both the husband and the new wife. Indeed, in polygynous societies hostility between cowives is often proverbial, and local wisdom might hold that only a strong-willed or interpersonally skilled husband can manage the inevitable conflicts that result. Here too jealousy can lead to suicide, and sometimes a jealous wife might turn to suicide when her husband takes a second bride or if he begins to favor one of her cowives with more time and attention (see, e.g., Elwin 1943:114).

Infidelity causes suicide in the modern United States as well: "As soon as American poet Robinson Jeffers' wife learned he was having an affair with another woman . . . she lay down in a bathtub and shot herself in the heart" (Black 2011:46, citing Karman 2001). Likewise, one Kentucky woman killed herself after discovering her girlfriend's infidelity, leaving the words "I loved you" scrawled in lipstick on a mirror (Holmes and Holmes 2005:16). My own sample of Louisville cases contained several examples, including the one quoted at the beginning of the chapter, where a young man shot himself after accusing his cohabiting girlfriend of infidelity. Another male self-killer left the following note before shooting himself: "This is my divorce from Debbie. Cheating bitch." In still another case, a woman had "caught" her husband with his ex-wife and was arguing with him about the issue when she threatened to kill herself. Having heard several such threats before, he handed her a loaded gun and dared her to follow through—which she did.

Infidelity often occurs as a prelude to ending a marriage, with the growth of the new relationship strangling the old one, and people are often inclined to end a relationship only when they see a better option available. This may be especially so in small-scale societies where people are highly intimate, there is a strong sex division of labor, and there is little conception of what modern people would call "the single life." Whatever order they occur in, the succession of ending one relationship and beginning another is likely to cause a severe reaction. In some cases, the jilted lover survives the initial breakup for some time but reacts explosively when his or her estranged partner forms a relationship with someone else. One case in my study of the Louisville coroners' files involved a man who, distraught over his ex-girlfriend's plans to marry another man, confronted her and shot himself at her wedding rehearsal. As he lay mortally wounded before her, he said, "I am dying and it's your fault because you don't love me anymore." In another case, a man who learned that his ex-wife had started a new relationship called her up and shot himself while on the phone with her (Manning 2015a). A new competing relationship might likewise trigger a homicide-suicide, and some homicide-suicide perpetrators kill their rival along with their former partner before dispatching themselves (e.g., Manning 2015b:10). One Florida man, for instance, shot and killed both his ex-girlfriend and her new boyfriend as they walked down the street; after fatally wounding them, he lay down next to his ex-girlfriend and shot himself (Websdale 1999:41).

BEREAVEMENT

Relationships sometimes end because one party intentionally leaves, as is usually the case in divorce. In other cases, however, relationships end because of forces beyond either party's control, such as death due to accident or illness. Suicide might follow the death of a close relative, especially a spouse or a child, among such diverse peoples as the ancient Romans, the Iroquoian and Algonquian peoples of North America, New Guinea Highlanders, and the Tikopia of Polynesia (Berndt 1962:183; Fenton 1943:125–26; Firth 1967; Van Hooff 1990:103–4). The time immediately following an intimate's demise is particularly dangerous. When illness claimed his wife, to whom he was unusually devoted, Roman military leader Marcus Plautius did not survive her funeral: "During the obsequies he drew his sword and threw himself on it" (Van Hooff 1990:103). In a similar case among the Tikopia, a man "wailed and wailed" before hanging himself on the very day of his wife's death (Firth 1967:126). Another Tikopian likewise killed himself on the day of his wife's death; another still tried to kill himself during his son's funeral (Firth 1967:126). When a death occurs among the Aguaruna Jívaro of Peru, "people keep close watch on distraught relatives to make sure that no poisons are within their reach and that they are not left alone long enough to hang themselves" (Brown 1986:315). But such precautions are not foolproof: during the funeral of one Aguaruna woman, "her daughter . . . escaped notice long enough to drink a mixture of water and laundry detergent. At about the same time in another part of the community, the deceased woman's brother, a man in his early twenties, was also overcome with grief and drank a bottle of insecticide. The next day, both died" (Brown 1986:315). The death of a spouse or close kinsman is also a frequent cause of suicide among the Palawan of the Philippines, where it accounted for 15 of 107 cases recorded by an ethnographer (Macdonald 2007:210). Bereavement leads to suicide among the Netsilik Eskimo as well: when one woman heard that her son had been killed during a hunt, she "immediately took a thong . . . and a few moments later hanged herself from a high rock" (Balikci 1970:165).

Some who kill themselves after another's death speak only of escaping their grief, much like those who kill themselves to escape the pain of illness, depression, or torture at the hands of an enemy. While escape is likely a component of most such suicides, they can have other aspects as well. Some speak of joining the deceased in the afterlife, as when one South African woman wrote—shortly before asphyxiating herself and her children—that her late husband was "coming to fetch us in a few days' time, you see, he loved us very much and could also not live without us in heaven" (quoted in Graser 1992:58–59). The notion that suicide is a way of following another person into the afterlife is found in many times and places, and in some societies this sort of suicide might even be an institutionalized way of showing loyalty and reverence for the dead. For example, widows in traditional India might pledge to die atop their husband's funeral pyres, an act that was praised and encouraged (Fisch 2006). Knowledge of an impending death can cause suicide as well. Sometimes when one spouse is about to die from a terminal illness, both partners might choose to die together in a suicide pact. Indeed, a study of such suicide pacts in England and Wales found that diagnosis of a terminal illness was the most common reason for suicide pacts between spouses (Brown and Barraclough 1999). In the words of one researcher, "The relationship between victims of suicide pacts is typically exclusive, isolated from others, and the immediate trigger is usually a threat to the continuation of the relationship, for example, impending death of one member from an untreatable illness" (Rajagopal 2004:1298). In this respect, modern Britain is not much different from ancient Greece (Van Hooff 1990:75–76).

Suicide and Overintimacy

The opposite of underintimacy is overintimacy—an increase of relational closeness (Black 2011:21–42). Judging from the evidence discussed above, underintimacy is the more frequent cause of suicide, and breaking a relationship is generally more dangerous than forming one. But there are two major circumstances in which people kill themselves due to overintimacy: forced marriage and rape.

People in the modern West, among other places, might take it for granted that people choose their own spouses, but in many social settings around the world and throughout history this is not the case. Instead, marriages are arranged by parents or other family elders and may be contracted with little regard for the wishes of the betrothed. Where people can be forced into such a close and permanent relationship against their will, they may turn to suicide to avoid it. This is especially the case for young women, who, in settings where arranged marriage is common, are likely to have the least say in choosing a spouse. An anthropologist studying the Bedouins of Libya remarks, "I heard of a number of both young men and women who

committed suicide in desperate resistance to their fathers' decisions, especially regarding marriage" (Abu-Lughod 1986:101). Sometimes threatened
or attempted suicide is enough to make their parents reconsider and thus
give the young women some influence over the decision. In rural Turkey,
"both boys and girls usually have personal preferences, and a girl faced with
the prospect of unyielding parents and an undesirable match may threaten
to commit suicide in order to force her parents to relent" (Starr 1978:71).
Such threats are credible in settings where female suicide is common: "In
the early 1970s, a young bride in a village in southwest Iran, apparently
traumatized by her husband's sexual demands, killed herself shortly after
her wedding. Several years later, her younger sister successfully resisted her
parents' plan for her marriage by threatening to kill herself like her elder
sister. Thus, she turned her sister's death into a source of efficacy for her
own resistance" (Friedl 1994:153). Note that arranged marriage can also involve a kind of underintimacy, in that it might force a young person to sever
an existing relationship with a lover in order to marry the spouse of his or
her parents' choosing.[6] Thus suicide might still result in part from a broken
relationship, and the threat of suicide might be used to convince parents to
condone the preferred relationship as well as to avoid the unwanted one. In
Highland New Guinea, for instance, "girls sometimes threaten to commit
suicide in order to persuade their parents and brothers to allow them to
marry a man of their choice, or to avoid marrying a man chosen for them"
(Healey 1979).

Though it is not considered a crime in societies where it is common,
being forced to consummate a marriage against one's will is nonetheless a
type of rape. Whether it occurs in the context of marriage or not, rape is also
a kind of overintimacy that can cause suicide. One of history's most famous
examples of female suicide is that of the ancient Roman woman Lucretia,
who, after being raped by the Etruscan king's son, called on her fellow Romans to take vengeance prior to publicly stabbing herself to death. Others
kill themselves preemptively to avoid being raped. For instance, one of the
few recorded suicides by an ancient Greek female is that of a fourteen-year-
old bride who "killed herself in AD262/3, to escape being raped by Gothic
invaders" (Van Hooff 1990:24). Military conquest in the ancient world was
often accompanied by the mass rape or sexual enslavement of women on
the defeated side and so might lead to the mass suicide of women seeking
to avoid this fate. In medieval India, military defeats sometimes resulted in
thousands of women and girls killing themselves by sword or by fire, often
led by a queen or a number of princesses (Thakur 1963:166–68).

It might seem strange to call rape overintimacy if we think of intimacy in emotional terms, as a feeling of closeness. But if we think of it in sociological terms, sexual intercourse is still a form of close interaction even if unwanted and despised. Sociologically speaking, unwanted sex belongs to the same family as unwanted looking, unwelcome conversation, or inappropriate staring—all actions that increase someone's participation in our lives and thus increases relational closeness (Black 2011:22–34). Only rape is a more drastic action, invading not just the victim's privacy or personal space but her body. According to Black's (2011:23) theory of conflict, this is exactly why rape is such serious deviance, generally causing more conflict and condemnation than do lesser intrusions. For the same reason it is more likely to cause suicide. Furthermore, rape is carried out by force and is therefore a form of violent domination. Thus it is not only overintimacy but also overstratification, something that subjugates the victim. The downward mobility involved in rape is amplified in many settings by the shame and stigma that attach to rape victims or by the fact that it destroys their value on the marriage market. Here, then, is the main context where overintimacy causes suicide: when it is both drastic and coupled with overinferiority. Indeed, the mass rapes accompanying military conquests, especially at the end of ancient sieges, would have often been a prelude to slaughter, the beginning of sexual slavery, or otherwise the end of a conventional and respectable life—all the more so for the upper classes of the conquered cities, who seem generally more prone to choosing death over submission.

Forced marriage is rare in the modern West, and rape victims are not stigmatized to nearly the same extent as in many traditional settings, where victims might be punished alongside perpetrators or barred from marriage or any respectable role in society. Indeed, the modern increase of equality between the sexes has coincided with campaigns to win more sympathy and respect for rape victims along with greater efforts to punish and stigmatize those who commit sexual assault. Perhaps this is why studies of coroners' records (e.g., Cavan 1928; Fincham et al. 2011) rarely mention rape as a reason for individual cases of suicide, though this could be a consequence of the same factors that lead to rape being underreported in other official records. It may also partially reflect that women's self-violence tends to be less lethal. Studies that focus on attempted (rather than fatal) suicide in the United States do find that victims of rape and sexual assault have elevated rates, though there is little information on whether such victimization was the proximate cause of the attempted suicide (see, e.g., Resick 1993; Rosellini et al. 2017). Rape is a traumatic form of violence, and it is plausible that the combination of violent subjugation and overintimacy still contributes to self-destruction in the modern world, especially if it occurs in the context of an ongoing abusive relationship—something more analogous to the long-term subordination of a forced marriage.

Suicide and Integration Reconsidered

As we have seen, there is substantial evidence that both losing connections and lacking connections make suicide more likely. But Durkheim also argued that sometimes *having* social connections could also make suicide more likely. When integration is too high, he argued, people become so fully immersed in the social group that they devalue their own individual existence and are therefore more prone to suicide (Durkheim [1897] 1951:217–40). Thus he claimed that too much social integration was as dangerous as too little, making the relationship between integration and suicide a U-shaped curve, with the greatest rates of suicide among the most and the least integrated.

As a prediction about the overall frequency of suicide in different social settings, we have little evidence that Durkheim's idea about excessive integration is correct. Granted, this is partly because most studies focus on the effects of low integration, something that Durkheim suggested will be the more common in modern society. It is in tribal and traditional settings, Durkheim argued, where we are more likely to see the effects of too much integration, since these societies have much higher levels of integration overall (Durkheim [1897] 1951:217–28). He was certainly correct that life in band and village society is highly intimate, with degrees of integration and solidarity modern Westerners might find difficult to imagine.[7] And some tribal societies certainly have rates of suicide that are much higher than those of modern nations.[8] But there is little reason to think tribal societies have higher suicide rates in general.[9] More importantly, there is little evidence that individual cases of suicide in tribal societies concentrate among the most integrated people. When they describe patterns of suicide, anthropologists almost never mention low involvement or social isolation as a protective factor in such settings. Indeed, it appears the opposite is often true: just as in wealthy industrial societies, suicide in traditional societies often concentrates at the margins of the social network (La Fontaine 1975). In New Guinea, for instance, suicide is more likely among orphans, as well as among men who are childless, friendless, and do not participate in cooperative hunting and gardening (Panoff 1977; Poole 1985). And among the Munda, a farming people of India, suicidal people are often as isolated as one can be in an intimate village setting. Consider the relative marginality of one self-killer: "Though the Munda regale themselves by dancing, drinking and singing in the evening after a hard working day, Koka never took part in music or dance. . . . He had neither the inclination nor the knack to attract girls. . . . While the other persons of his village went to graze their cattle in the company of others, Koka went with his cattle all alone in a different direction" (Saran 1974:175–76). Sociologist Wilfred Masumura goes so far as to argue that the impact of marginality is even greater in tribal societies than in modern ones. If many tribal societies have high suicide rates, he suggests, it is because "socially alienated individuals . . . are more likely to commit suicide in highly integrated societies" (Masumura 1977:265). Black similarly proposes that because of high overall closeness, tribal morality views any reduction or lack of closeness as seriously deviant (Black 2011:138–43). Those who seek solitude are viewed with intense suspicion and perhaps accused of witchcraft, widows and orphans might be treated with open contempt, and exclusion or ostracism are extremely severe sanctions. In any case, social isolation and marginality do not seem to generally lower the likelihood of suicide in either modern or tribal settings.

But even if it is incorrect about the overall volume or risk of suicide, Durkheim's theory might contain lessons about variation in the type and form of suicide. Not only did Durkheim suggest that very high integration leads to more suicide, but he also argued that it leads to distinctive patterns of self-killing. He noted that many tribal and traditional societies had scenarios in which suicide was socially accepted and approved, including such practices as the suicide of widows at the death of their husbands, the suicide of the elderly, and holy men who fasted to death so as to reach a higher plane of existence. His catchall term for such behavior was "altruistic suicide," because he believed such suicides were oriented toward external norms. In his own words, "Having given the name of egoism to the state of the ego living its own life and obeying itself alone, that of altruism adequately expresses the opposite state, where the ego is not its own property, where it is blended with something not itself, where the goal of conduct is exterior to itself, that is, in one of the groups in which it participates" (Durkheim [1897] 1951:221). Today the term "altruistic" is somewhat misleading, in that most of us think of altruism as helping behavior, such as giving other people material assistance. This would match many cases in which elderly or ill people kill themselves to spare others the burden of their care but would not necessarily fit other patterns of suicide we see in tribal and traditional societies, such as suicide meant to harm someone else. For the purposes of asking why different social behaviors occur, and why they sometimes take on self-destructive forms, we would probably prefer to distinguish helping behavior from moralistic aggression or from any other sort of suicide that are externally directed.

As several critics (e.g., Masumura 1977) have pointed out, there is little reason to think the typical suicide in settings of high social integration is altruistic in the common sense of the term. Still, Durkheim's ideas point us toward the question of how social conditions shape the character of suicide. Settings with high social solidarity will tend to produce different patterns of self-destruction than socially atomized settings. They may indeed produce proportionally more suicide that is altruistic in the sense of being a helping behavior, a sacrifice on behalf of another. Institutionalized old-age suicide is one example, as is the practice—found in some Inuit groups—of sacrificing oneself to appease the spirits believed to be causing someone else's illness (Leighton and Hughes 1955). If it is true that suicidal altruism is relatively more common in settings of high solidarity, it might be because close relationships generate more intense helping behavior of all kinds. Yet when we look at the cases of suicide recorded in the ethnographic literature, suicidal altruism is much less prominent than suicidal moralism. This is because close relationships also have a dark side. They can be a site of conflict, and close conflicts can be devastating.

Suicide and Relational Closeness

Some ways of handling conflict are more likely when the disputants are relationally close. For instance, Black predicts that grievances against an intimate are more likely to be expressed in a therapeutic style, with the objectionable conduct being treated as a symptom of illness or disorder rather than as a crime or sin (Black 1976:47; Black 1995:835n7; Horwitz 1990:81–83; see also, e.g., Tucker 1999). Closer grievances are also more likely to be tolerated, with the aggrieved doing little or nothing at all (Black 1998:88–89, 143–44; see also, e.g., Cooney and Phillips 2017). As relational distance increases, other ways of handling conflict become more likely. Black proposes that greater distance generally increases the severity of moralism, making it more uncompromising, coercive, and punitive (Black 1998:144–56). With this comes an increase in the likelihood and severity of interpersonal violence, including such forms of collective violence as lynching and rioting (Senechal de la Roche 1996).[10] Of course violence occurs in close relationships as well. Even if intimacy makes any given conflict less likely to result in violent punishment, frequent interaction means that there are many more occasions for conflict to occur. If only a small proportion of these conflicts produce severe reactions, domestic violence can still make up a substantial proportion of all violence in a society. This is especially so in modern societies where legal systems are more effective at suppressing public violence between strangers than private violence between intimates (Cooney 2003). Still, the most extreme instances of moralistic violence, such as the mass killings of genocide and terrorism, typically cross the gulf of distance between unrelated people from different nations or socially segregated ethnic groups (Black 2004a; Campbell 2015b). And even domestic violence appears to increase with distance, with closer couples having less and more distant couples having more (Black 2018). But suicide is different from other kinds of violence in that it targets the self instead of another. And as its direction is opposite, so is its distribution: in a conflict, *suicide varies directly with relational closeness* (Manning 2012, 2015b). All else being equal, closer grievances are more likely to result in suicide.

INTIMATE-PARTNER CONFLICT

Conflicts between spouses and other intimate partners are probably the most common type of dispute leading to suicide and are a major cause of suicide in a variety of cultures. For example, when anthropologist Bronislaw Malinowski described suicide among the Trobriand islanders of the South Pacific, nine of the ten cases he described were due to spousal conflict. In one of these cases, "a Trobriand man was having an affair. In retaliation, his wife ceased to cook or bring water for him, and he had to depend on his married sister for these services. One night his wife made a public scene, insulting him severely. He then flew into a rage and beat her senseless. The next day she took a fatal dose of poison" (Malinowski [1929] 1962:120). He also notes that he learned of a number of attempted suicides during his stay and that these were limited to "lovers' quarrels, matrimonial differences, and similar cases" (Malinowski [1926] 1976:94). An anthropologist studying a Thai village similarly reports that all three suicide attempts that occurred during his stay arose from marital conflict and appeared aimed at making the offending spouse feel bad (Phillips 1965:186). According to anthropologist Raymond Firth, marital arguments are also a major cause of suicide on the Polynesian island of Tikopia. One Tikopian man took a second wife and "fought with her so strenuously that both of them rushed off in opposite directions and committed suicide, separately, by hanging" (Firth 1967:128). Another man was offended that his wife's strict observance of mourning taboos for a deceased chief was keeping her from eating with him: "He objected, saying, 'Are we not married? And don't we eat together? Stay in your taboos. But I'm going, and you can stay and keep your taboos for me.' By this he meant that she could now start mourning for him instead. He did not steal away secretly, but ostensibly joined a searching fleet looking for three young women who had swum off to sea [in an unrelated collective suicide attempt]. Then he slipped away to pursue his own suicide attempt, and it was only discovered later that he had had a row with his wife" (Firth 1967:128).

Among the Luo of East Africa, "the most common cause" of female suicide is "domestic quarrels" (Wilson 1960:204).[11] In one case, a man who believed his daughter's misbehavior was responsible for the disease that was killing his cattle told his wife: "I wish the disease which killed my heifers would kill you, my wife, for your daughter is a whore who has brought the disease of her womb to my cattle." Outraged by this, the wife made her other daughters swear they would never marry a man who would give cattle (the customary bride-price) to her husband, placed a curse on his village to prevent him from obtaining a new wife, and then hanged herself (Wilson 1960:208). Another woman killed herself because her husband would refuse to eat her food (a form of curse in their society) and compounded the injury with the insult of feeding the food to one of her cowives (Wilson 1960:205). Yet another killed herself to prove her innocence when her husband charged her with adultery; had she been guilty, local reasoning goes, she would have instead chosen to be ritually cleansed of the offense (Wilson 1960:205).

Far away in eastern North America, Seneca Iroquois informants cited intimate-partner conflict as the main cause in nine out of seventeen reported cases (Fenton 1941:92). In South America, according to one ethnographer, moralistic suicide among the Aluku Maroons typically occurs "in the context of lovers' quarrels" (Bilby 1990:46). Likewise, among the Saramaka Maroons, where people kill themselves to mobilize vengeful spirits against their enemies, most of these spirits arise from "a person dying during the course of a stormy marriage" (Price 1973:88). Among the Mataco of the Gran Chaco region, "a person who feels himself rejected or a victim of unhappy love sometimes commits suicide, which with the Mataco appears to occur particularly in this connexion" (Fock 1963:100; see also Alvarsson 1988:138).

According to historian Jeffrey Watt (2001:232), marital conflict lay behind many suicide cases in eighteenth-century Geneva, Switzerland. After one young Genevan couple committed suicide within hours of one another, witnesses testified to the love they had for one another, a love, however, that "'was so violent that at times they quarreled over very insignificant things, always convinced that their passion was at stake in even the slightest things'"

(Watt 2001:225). Conflicts with spouses or lovers were also a prime cause of suicides in eighteenth-century England, where "typical newspaper stories reported in 1729 that during an argument with his wife a schoolmaster at Westminster School leaped out of a window and ran into the Thames up to his neck and in 1766 that a Mr. Pernell of Holborn committed suicide on his wedding day after a row with his young bride" (MacDonald and Murphy 1990:263, 290–91; see also Bailey 1998:191, 202).

We see the same patterns in the contemporary United States. According to a seven-state study by the US Centers for Disease Control, nearly a third of suicide cases were triggered by a conflict with an intimate partner (Centers for Disease Control 2006; Zwillich 2006). A study of adolescent suicides in Western Pennsylvania compared a sample of sixty-seven suicide victims to sixty-seven matched controls from the same region and found that suicide victims were more likely to have experienced conflicts with a boyfriend or girlfriend (Brent et al. 1993). In my study of all 260 suicides from five years of coroners' files in Louisville, about 20 percent of all suicides in the area involved some form of intimate-partner conflict. In a second overlapping sample of 202 cases precipitated by interpersonal problems, 88 percent involved conflicts with a spouse or other intimate partner—usually, in the case of unmarried partners, a long-term cohabiting union, often with shared children.

At least some of the association between intimate conflict and suicide is due to the sort of things intimate partners tend to fight about: as Black's theory of conflict predicts, infidelity, abandonment, and other kinds of underintimacy are distinctive and severe sources of conflict in such relationships (Black 2011:139).[12] And as we have seen, such drastic losses of intimacy are a major reason for suicide. But intimate conflict appears more prone to cause suicide even when it is over other matters. Several cases of Trobriand suicide described by Malinowski involve spouses outraged by insults or accusations of wrongdoing. In one, a polygynous man quarreled with a wife to whom he was "very attached." During one quarrel "he insulted her by one of the worst formulae . . . which, especially from husband to wife, is regarded as unbearable," and she committed suicide on the spot by climbing and jumping from a palm tree (Malinowski [1926] 1976:96). In another case, a man whose wife pestered him with accusations of adultery eventually committed suicide by poisoning himself (Malinowski [1926] 1976:96). Or consider an example from New Guinea's Eastern Highlands. In this case, a fight over sex led an aggrieved husband to burn his wife's genitalia with a piece of flaming bark: "She responded with abuse and ended her tirade by saying, 'I am no malignant spirit: a human being bore me. . . . You burnt me, and my belly is hot [i.e., she was angry].' That night she decorated herself in the usual way and, taking a length of rope, went to her husband's garden . . . where she hanged herself from a tree" (Berndt 1962:189). In the previous chapter, I noted that spousal abuse is a common reason for female suicide, particularly in extremely patriarchal settings. Highly patriarchal marriages may be less intimate than more egalitarian marriages, but they are still fairly close, and the combination of closeness and inequality contributes to the prevalence of wife suicide. Relational closeness also explains why, even though their superiority makes it much less frequent, men in patriarchal marriages also sometimes kill themselves over marital conflict. For example, when one woman in the Eastern Highlands of New Guinea insulted her husband by calling him lazy, and he "was so deeply offended that he strode out into the bush" to hang himself (Berndt 1962:191–92). Whether the issue is jealousy or insult, abandonment or violent abuse, a grievance is more likely to lead to suicide when it occurs between spouses or other intimate partners.

In my sample of suicidal conflicts from Louisville, discounting any cases that mention breakups, separations, or accusations of infidelity still leaves the majority of cases involving some grievance against an intimate partner. Consider some examples of suicidal conflict within an intact relationship:

> On the evening in question the victim and his wife had been down to the waterfront. Apparently, he had not wanted to spend the evening there, preferring instead to go to a college alumni gathering. His wife claims she did not realize this at the time. On their way home they argued in the car, and eventually she got out of the vehicle and called a colleague to come pick her up. A few minutes later the victim called her and asked for her location. He came back and picked her up. According to his wife they began to argue again over his claim that she didn't listen to him. She says that they were both "pissed." She was looking out the window when the car stopped and her husband shot himself in the head. She jumped out of the car, thinking at first he had fired a shot into the air, and looked back to see him slumped over the wheel.

> Per the decedent's girlfriend, they had been fighting all day. The decedent began drinking beer at 3:30. The girlfriend was on the front porch and heard a gunshot. She went to the side yard and found the decedent sitting on the ground with a 20 gauge shotgun. He had fired a shot into the air. They exchanged words and she returned to the porch.

She heard a second shot, and returned to find the decedent had shot himself in the head.

A 62 year-old housewife lived with her husband of 40 years. According to the husband, during the last 5 they had been fighting almost every day about him not working. On the night before her death his wife had knocked him down the basement steps, cut him with a butcher knife, and also struck him with a piece of iron pipe. The morning of her death, she resumed fighting with him and at 7:00am ran him out of the house, telling him to leave and never come back. She was last seen by a neighbor at 10:00am in front of her house. She told the neighbor that she was going to kill herself because she couldn't take the domestic trouble anymore. Her husband returned at noon and found her on the couch with a gunshot wound to the head.

In yet another case, a man hid his worsening financial situation from his wife, who was enraged upon finding their bank account overdrawn. Her suicide note expressed a great deal of anger over her husband's secrecy, stating that "I don't deserve that because I have been good to you for a great many years" and closing with the remark "Try to keep your delusions under control."[13]

FAMILY CONFLICTS

In modern societies nuclear families tend to be close, and in tribal societies extended family units might be even closer. In some settings conflict between close kin is the most common situation for moralistic suicide, while in most others it is second only to conflict between spouses and other intimate partners.

In the previous chapter I discussed conflicts between parents and children as a cause of children's suicide. As with marriage in patriarchal societies, the relationship is not only unequal but also close. Inequality explains why it is more often children than parents who threaten or commit suicide when conflict erupts between the two, but closeness helps account for the frequency of such suicide and the fact parents occasionally resort to it as well. Among the Chukchee (or Chukchi), a reindeer-herding people of the Russian arctic, such behavior takes an unusual form. A Chukchee father has the right to demand that another family member kill him, something usually reserved for dealing with the effects of advanced old age and severe infirmity. But it could also be invoked as an act of punishment: "Among our people, when a father is very angry with his lazy and bad son, he says, 'I do not want to see him anymore. Let me go away.' Then he asks to be killed, and charges the very son who offended him with the execution of his request. 'Let him give me the mortal blow, let him suffer from the memory of it'" (Bogoras 1909:561). Closeness also explains why children and youth are more inclined to kill themselves over conflicts with parents than over conflict with other social superiors, even if the issues involved are similar. For instance, in his discussion of suicide among the Chuukese of Micronesia, anthropologist Donald Rubenstein observes: "It is virtually unknown for a Micronesian adolescent to commit suicide after being scolded by a teacher, a neighbor, a priest, a policeman, a friend, or a collateral relative. If a young man seeks to marry a young woman of his choosing, but is thwarted by his sweetheart's parents, suicide is quite improbable. However, if his own parents reject his plea for approval of the match, his suicide would be an accustomed response" (Rubinstein 1995:33; see also Rubinstein 1983, 1992, 2002). A second ethnographer concurs, adding that even "other distant members of the family normally could not precipitate a suicide by scolding or rebuking [the potential victim]" (Hezel 1984:200).

While strict hierarchy and harsh parental discipline increase the likelihood of children's suicide, familial closeness means that milder degrees of discipline can provoke it as well. Iroquois parents are not particularly authoritarian by cross-cultural standards, but Iroquois children nonetheless turn to suicide "to escape restrictions or in revenge of punishment" (Fenton 1941). Suicide of this kind is mentioned by several early observers during the colonial era, one of whom refers to the Iroquois as "thin skinned" and reports that "it was not extraordinary to see [children] poison themselves . . . over a moderately severe scolding" (quoted in Fenton 1941:107). The pattern appears to have persisted into modern times, as in the twentieth-century case of a fifteen-year-old Seneca girl who, "discontent with parental discipline," killed herself after being made to stay home and watch younger children while her parents attended a lacrosse game (Fenton 1941:97).[14]

Closeness is not limited to parent-child relationships. Attempted suicides in traditional Chuukese society sometimes arose due to conflicts with siblings, as when one young man, insultingly excluded by his brothers from practicing fighting techniques, "climbed a coconut tree, and jumped off, landing on a rock and breaking an arm and a leg" (Gladwin and Sarason 1953:145). Among the Cheyenne of the North American Great Plains, where suicides to "appeal to the public for a redress of a wrong" almost always involve "a grievance within the closest family," brother-sister conflict was as much of a fault line as mother-daughter conflict (Llewellyn and Hoebel

1941:159). In my sample of Louisville cases involving conflict, most of those that did not involve intimate partners involved close kin, usually members of the same nuclear family.[15] These were mostly parent-child conflicts, but some involved sibling and other kinds of relationship as well. One sixty-six-year-old retiree appeared to have grievances against most of her immediate family: "After her husband died, the decedent came to live with her daughter, son-in-law, and grandson at their home. She had been living there for four years. She had a history of conflict with her family: she had a habit of locking herself in her room when angry and had threatened suicide several times in the past. In her suicide note, she complained bitterly of her treatment within the house and accused her brother (who lives in another city) of turning her grandson against her."

SUICIDE AND HOMICIDE

The best scientific evidence for the existence of a relationship between one thing and another comes through comparison. An ideal test of the effect of relational closeness on suicide would be to generate a random sample of conflicts that involved varying degrees of closeness and then compare their different outcomes. Sampling conflicts in this way would be challenging, especially if we sought a large enough sample to capture relatively rare outcomes like suicide and to include conflicts with such minor outcomes that the participants themselves are not likely to remember them. A large sample adequately representing the entire universe of human conflict would be a Herculean task. But even lacking such a sample, we can still make more focused comparisons between conflicts that get handled in different ways. For instance, consider homicide versus suicide.

Homicide too is lethal violence, and it too is often a reaction to conflict. Killings arise out of arguments and fights, unpaid debts and acts of disrespect, sexual jealousy and broken relationships. Most homicide is moralistic, an expression of grievances against someone. Like suicide it is an extreme and violent reaction, and rare compared to the milder ways of handling conflict. Because of this, factors that encourage more severe conflict—such large movements of social time—might encourage both homicide and suicide relative to other, less severe behaviors. But since they are different reactions—inward violence versus outward violence—there must be factors that encourage one relative to the other. One of these is relational distance. Whereas suicidal conflicts are overwhelmingly issues between family members and intimate partners, only about 25 percent of homicide cases occur in these relationships (see data cited in Cooney and Phillips 2002:82–86). The difference is somewhat inflated by the fact that some homicides (an estimated 20 to 40 percent) are not due to conflict at all but occur in the course of armed robbery and other acts of predation—crimes that are more likely to target strangers. Even discounting such predatory homicides, though, no more than half of homicides occur between intimates. Conversely, distant adversaries are much more common in homicide cases than they are in suicide cases. One criminological study of homicide in Miami in the early 1980s found that out of 569 homicide victims 11 percent were killed in domestic arguments, while 29 percent were killed in arguments of other kinds (Wilbanks 1984:32). Of homicides occurring in Philadelphia between 1948 and 1952, 28 percent involved "close friends," and another 14 percent involved "acquaintances"—categories barely represented among moralistic suicides (Wolfgang 1958:207). And of 508 homicide cases in Detroit in 1972, 48 percent involved "unrelated acquaintances" (Daly and Wilson 1988:19). Such patterns provide more evidence that distant grievances are relatively more likely to result in interpersonal violence, while close grievances are relatively more likely to result in self-inflicted violence (compare Henry and Short 1954:17, 108–16). That is, closeness makes suicide more likely than homicide, while distance makes homicide more likely than suicide.

We can narrow the comparison even further. We have seen that intimate-partner conflict is one of the most common occasions for suicide. But such conflicts can also lead to homicide (as when someone kills his spouse) or to the combination of both homicide and suicide (as when someone kills his spouse and then himself). There are usually similar sorts of grievances in all three cases—most lethal domestic conflicts arise from separation, divorce, and sexual jealousy (Block and Christakos 1995; Kelly and Johnson 2008; Miethe and Regoeczi 2004:155–56; Websdale 1999; Wilson and Daly 1993).[16] But not all intimate partners are equally intimate: some have been together longer than others or spent more of their time together than others or share more activities than others (Black 2018). We would expect the relative likelihood of homicide and suicide to vary accordingly and that cases ending in suicide would tend to involve more closeness than cases ending in homicide, with cases of homicide-suicide falling somewhere in between. There is presently little research aimed at making these comparisons, but some findings suggest the predicted relationship exists. For instance, in a sample of thirty-two intimate-partner homicides from West Virginia, I found that victim and offender tended to have much older relationships in cases of homicide-suicide, being together on average for twelve years, than in cases of homicide alone, with an average relationship length of five years (Manning 2015b).

The closer the partners, the more likely the killer was to join his victim in death—or to choose death and force her to join him. Likewise, a study of 112 intimate-partner homicides in Hong Kong also found that relationship length predicted likelihood the offender would commit suicide (Chan, Beh, and Broadhurst 2010).[17]

Suicide and Interdependence

In Black's terminology, *functional interdependence* refers to the extent that two parties rely on one another for survival and well-being (Black 1998:77). We might understand this as a source of relational closeness, with those who co-operate and exchange goods and services being closer than those who do not. But Black and his students often treat it as a separate variable, a kind of social closeness in its own right. One reason for doing so is that functional interdependence appears to have a major impact even when relationships are in other ways quite distant. For instance, in his work on genocide, Bradley Campbell (2009; 2015b:17) argues that when foreign colonists rely on the labor of con-quered strangers, they are less likely to exterminate them. People are less likely to kill those they cannot easily do without (Black 1998:77). They are also less likely to cut off ties with them in other ways, making conflicts less prone to such forms of avoidance as divorcing an abusive spouse or resigning from a corrupt organization (Baumgartner 1988:61–62; Black 1998:80).[18] The effects of interdependence can arise whether it is mutual, with both parties relying on the relationship, or one-sided, with one party needing the other but not vice versa. Where it is uneven, it sometimes produces a kind of inequality, with the more dependent party having a subordinate position in the relation-ship. It can exaggerate inferiority by robbing the inferior of the option to flee the relationship and can discourage avoidance as well as open rebellion (Black 1998:80–81, 153–54). Contrariwise, one-sided dependence on a social inferior might effectively reduce the inequality in the relationship, giving the infe-rior the ability to negotiate greater privilege and autonomy. But dependent superiors might also use force to compel cooperation, and dependence can thus still discourage avoidance and other disruptions to the relationship: most slaves could do without their masters more easily than the master could do without slaves, yet the masters take great pains to keep the slaves from fleeing. Partly because it discourages such alternatives as avoidance, extermination, and rebellion, functional interdependence encourages suicide. In a conflict, *suicide varies directly with functional interdependence.*

Just as they can be more or less intimate in other ways, family relation-ships can be more or less interdependent. Children depend on their parents to provide food, shelter, and almost everything else, and this can contribute to the suicide of children over conflicts with parents. In some cultures, material dependence persists well past the age of physical maturity. Adolescence is sometimes associated with increasing frequency and severity of conflict as the child's stature rises and he or she challenges authority and seeks greater autonomy or, conversely, parents demand that the child display more autonomy and take more responsibility. In either case, a high level of dependence can be both a source of conflict and something that encourages an aggrieved youth to handle conflict with suicide.

Nowhere is this illustrated more dramatically than on the islands of Chuuk and Western Samoa, where youth suicide has risen dramatically during the latter half of the twentieth century (Rubinstein 1983; Macpherson and Macpherson 1987). Between 1960 and 1981, the rates of suicide for Micronesia (including Chuuk) skyrocketed from 6.4 to 49.5 per 100,000, an increase mostly due to the increase in the suicide of young men in their teens and twenties (Rubinstein 1983). The triggers of suicide in these societies remain similar to that found in earlier times, with most cases being due to conflicts between young men and their close senior kin (Gladwin and Sarason 1953:146; Freeman 1983; Hezel 1984; Rubinstein 1995). For example, one father "had provoked growing resentment in his son through his insults and beatings," leading his son to commit suicide when ordered to do something that he did not want to do (Hezel 1984:198). But why did suicide become more frequent?

One explanation is that youth have become more dependent on their parents and for longer periods of their lives. In earlier times, family hierarchy was tempered by an early age of independence. Once Chuukese youth reached puberty they began to take an important role in subsistence activities and to rely on a wider network of kin and age-mates, reducing their exclusive dependence on their parents or, indeed, on any one person (Gladwin and Sarason 1953:97). Furthermore, young males would usually move out of their parents' homes to live with relatives or in a communal men's house, and by their late teens and early twenties men were largely self-sufficient (Gladwin and Sarason 1953:98–99). The situation changed when the economic modernization of Chuuk began in earnest in the 1960s (Marshall and Marshall 1990:10–29). Since that time, the subsistence economy has been supplanted by a reliance on wage labor and manufactured goods. But there are few jobs, and most of these are government positions monopolized by the older generation. Thus unemployment among the young is very common, and youth no longer become materially independent at an early age

(Marshall and Marshall 1990:19). Dependence on nuclear family was further increased by the decline of the extended matrilineal clan and the extinction of the communal men's houses. Now young men depend upon their parents for subsistence and shelter to a much greater extent than in earlier times, and this dependence lasts well into their twenties (Rubinstein 1995). The same is true of youth in Western Samoa, who also lack employment opportunities and remain at home and dependent upon their parents well past an age where they would have, in older times, established their own household (O'Meara 2002:111).

Dependence keeps youth under the authority of their elders and robs them of other options for managing family conflict. Their dependence is even visible in the issues at stake in family disputes. Many young Chuukese become upset and kill themselves when older relatives refuse to grant them some material request. For example, "One 16-year old boy hanged himself when his parents refused to buy him a new shirt for Christmas; another young man of 23 killed himself after his older sister would not give him the yeast he demanded for a drinking party" (Hezel 1984:196). Other conflicts occur when parents become angry at the dependence of their sons, a phenomenon which runs against traditional patterns of child-rearing and norms of masculine behavior (Rubinstein 1992).[19] According to one observer, "Young men are now held in a position of greater dependency vis-a-vis their parents. The parents' response, especially that of the father toward his older sons, is one of growing impatience and severity—yielding the many small incidents of the rejection that commonly occasion a son's suicide" (Rubinstein 1995:39). Rising dependence on the part of Chuukese and Samoan youth has resulted in both a greater frequency of conflict and a greater likelihood that conflict will be handled with suicide, resulting in a sharp spike in suicide rates.[20]

Spouses can also rely on one another, and such reliance is generally greater in settings with a pronounced division of labor between the sexes or where legal and financial barriers prevent women from making a living on their own. Because economic dependence reduces avoidance, it makes wives less likely to handle marital dissatisfaction by seeking divorce (Hannan, Tuma, and Groeneveld 1977, 1978; Schoen et al. 2002). Contrariwise, it makes them more likely to turn to suicide. Until recently, for example, divorce was rare in Japan and difficult for women to initiate. Thus an observer of suicide in Japan in the 1980s remarked that "[a Japanese woman] does not usually seek divorce, because legal protection and job opportunities are lacking. . . . The more likely alternative for ordinary Japanese women who believe they have failed in building a happy family is to resign themselves to the situation. . . . When she is not tolerant, she may be pushed to suicide" (Iga 1986:58). At least one study of Japan during this period found that prefectures with higher divorce rates had lower rates of female suicide, suggesting that divorce was indeed an alternative to self-destruction (Chandler and Tsai 1993:250). And it is an alternative that is more likely in settings where women have access to employment or other sources of material support, better enabling them to leave abusive or unsatisfactory relationships.

A Note on Cultural Closeness

Cultural distance refers to differences in culture between individuals or groups, such as differences in dress, language, and religion (Black 1976:73–74). People who share such cultural traits are culturally closer than those who do not, and the more traits they share, the closer they are. In most Blackian theories, cultural distance and relational distance have similar effects on behavior. For instance, violent aggression tends to increase with both—genocide, terrorism, rioting, and the like are more likely and more severe against people with different religions, languages, and ethnicities (Black 2004a; Campbell 2015b; Senechal de la Roche 1996). We might thus expect that both kinds of social closeness have similar effects on suicide, such that cultural closeness also encourages people to handle grievances with self-destruction. The effect is difficult to observe, though, since moralistic suicide is highly concentrated in intimate conflicts and intimates tend to be culturally close as well. Thus samples of suicidal conflicts tend to lack gross variation in cultural distance, and most sources of information do not address fine variation. We might still hypothesize that conflict in interethnic and interreligious relationships is more likely to result in homicide or homicide-suicide rather than suicide alone.[21] And as cultural distance makes political grievances more likely to result in terrorism and guerilla war, we should expect cultural closeness to make them more likely to result in protest suicide. Cultural closeness thus contributes to protest suicide being relatively more frequent in domestic conflicts than international ones.

Social Closeness and Self-Execution

Social control of the self also varies with the social closeness of the adversaries, including their degree of relational closeness and functional interdependence (Black 1998:65). For example, people are more likely to apologize for offending someone who is closer to them (Exline, Deshea, and Holeman 2007). Close offenders are also more likely to kill themselves than those who offend distant parties. Sometimes this is because close adversaries allow an offender the opportunity to commit suicide rather than directly taking vengeance themselves. As discussed in the preceding chapter, in some highly stratified societies, rulers might order inferiors to kill themselves as a kind of punishment. Where this is so, the practice is usually restricted to members of the governing class or military officials—individuals who, relative to peasants and commoners, share more social ties, culture, and interdependence with the central authority (Otterbein 1986:118 n1). In premodern Japan, for instance, forced self-execution was limited to members of the samurai class—the lord's military retainers and administrators—while those of lower rank were simply beheaded (Pinguet 1993:129–35; Seward 1968). Similarly, in imperial Rome, the emperor might demand suicide from members of the elite senatorial class, while others received standard executions (Van Hooff 199095–96; Griffin 1986b:112). Allowing an offender to commit suicide was in these societies a form of leniency—such deaths were less dishonorable than dying at the hands of another person, and so they were a privilege that rulers extended to their fellow elites. In the twentieth century, Germany's Nazi regime took a similar approach. Those socially close to the Nazi leadership, including eminent military leaders and Hitler's longtime associates, would be offered a chance to kill themselves rather than be executed. Thus Field Marshall Erwin Rommel, when accused of participation in a plot to assassinate Hitler, was allowed to take poison rather than face court-martial (Goeschel 2009:140).

Suicides expressing guilt, remorse, or expiation also are more likely when the victim is an intimate, such as a family member. Chuukese youth sometimes kill themselves due to shame at their own offenses but only when the offense injures their family: "The young [Chuukese] can live with the fact that he is the subject of public opprobrium in the community, but he cannot at all live easily with the feeling that he is the cause of disgrace for his family" (Hezel 1984:203). Among the Bison-Horn Maria of India, individuals may kill themselves out of "regret for harsh behavior toward someone loved" (Elwin 1943:48). Self-destruction is more likely when the offender is dependent upon the aggrieved as well. Again, dependence itself may even be the source of the conflict. In one case described in the psychiatric literature a husband who cared for a bedridden wife "began to express distaste for his own care-giving role, to blame his wife more and more for the constriction imposed on his own activities, and to voice barely disguised antipathy toward her for continuing to live. . . . He began to talk of burglaries and purchased a gun which he discharged in a 'how to work it' session, he then left the loaded gun within arm's reach of his bedridden wife. After the demonstration and a particularly bitter soliloquy, the husband went to work. The wife killed herself shortly afterwards" (Perlin and Schmidt 1975:157).

Social closeness thus encourages two varieties of moralistic suicide: those that act against another person and those that act against the self. Given this, we should not be surprised to find that the same case of conflict can generate both. For example, one Trobriand man insulted his wife during the course of a quarrel, causing her to commit suicide on the spot. The next day he followed suit, killing himself out of grief and remorse. So did another man whose wife fatally jumped from a palm tree following an accusation of infidelity (Malinowski [1926] 1976:96). Indeed, Black (1998:145–54) proposes that social closeness reduces the one-sidedness of moralism: the closer the adversaries, the more likely there is to be some compromise and mutual acceptance of blame. Close adversaries are not simply enemies to be attacked or avoided, and hostility is often mixed with affection and concern. Right and wrong lose their clarity, as does the distinction between victim and offender. Often this can lead to remedial forms of social control, aimed at compromise and social repair (Black 1976:47). But even when social control is more accusatory, it can still display a kind moral ambiguity. We should not be surprised, then, to find suicide notes that display such ambiguity, perhaps simultaneously identifying someone else as the reason for the suicide and absolving them of blame or mixing criticism and blame of another person with criticism and blame of the self (Manning 2015a). Survivors of serious suicide attempts, describing the issues that drove them to their desperate act, may likewise vacillate between describing mistreatment by others and complaining of their own inadequacy (see generally Heckler 1994). Thus one survivor, describing her family conflicts, recalls thinking, "It was my fault. I shouldn't have told my mother I was being molested. I'm responsible for the family falling apart" (quoted in Heckler 1994:108). In these cases it may be difficult to draw a line between social control of the self and social control of others, but such is the nature of intimate conflict. Extreme closeness muddies the waters of conflict and sometimes leads a conflict with others to become a conflict with the self.

Self-Conflict

People not only interact with others, they also interact with themselves. This includes complaining about oneself and defining one's own behavior as deviant. For instance, one victim from my study of Louisville coroners' records left an extremely lengthy note detailing her self-described "fake life and misuse of money," judgmentally recalling bad decisions she had made over the course of a lifetime and detailing what she saw as her own flaws. People might harshly judge themselves in this way even in the absence of external complaints and might do so for things that are invisible to other people, such as their own closely guarded thoughts and feelings. Consider the case of a young suicide attempter who reported a long-standing conflict with himself over his secret homosexuality and artistic aspirations, both of which ran counter to his public image as a heterosexual football player: "I hated myself in many ways because I didn't like this—this double life I was trying to lead. I liked to write poetry. I liked to write things like that and be sensitive, and whenever a damn teardrop hit me, I'd say, 'You fucking chump! What are you feeling that way for?'" (quoted in Heckler 1994:60). His self-conflict seemed to escalate soon after he had his first sexual encounter with another man: "I would wake up in the middle of the night and look in the mirror and my eyes would just start getting real wild. I'd scream at myself, 'You're a disgrace to your family!'" (quoted in Heckler 1994:60). Not long after, he attempted suicide by jumping from a dam, an act that left him alive but paralyzed from the waist down.

The notion that suicide is a way of handling self-conflict is similar to psychologist Roy Baumeister's argument that the typical suicide is an "escape from aversive self-awareness" (Baumeister 1990:90). He argues that not only is escape the most common motive for suicide, but what most suicidal people are escaping from is themselves—or more specifically, from their own harsh judgements about themselves. For various reasons, including external setbacks, people see themselves as having fallen short of their own standards, and so they become "acutely aware of self as inadequate, incompetent, unattractive, or guilty" (Baumeister 1990:91). There are various ways of trying to escape this negative self-awareness, from becoming engrossed in activities to becoming intoxicated to sleeping excessively—all limited forms of self-avoidance. But should negative self-awareness be severe enough or persist long enough, some will turn to permanent oblivion in the form of suicide. People can therefore turn to suicide to escape or avoid themselves, just as they would escape or avoid an external adversary.

We can also understand this in sociological terms. As Black observed in his work on the self-application of social control, "Self-interaction is a form of social interaction" (Black 1998:72). Thus, he argued, the same principles that predict and explain how people behave toward one another can predict and explain how they behave toward themselves. So if social closeness makes grievances more likely to result in suicide, this should be true of self-conflict as well. People can indeed be more or less close to themselves, as measured by such things as the time they spend alone and the absence of competing relationships with other people (Black 1995:835n37). Self-closeness might therefore contribute to the relationship between social isolation and suicide. Discussing changing patterns of intimacy in the modern world, Black argues that "whereas tribal people devote most of their attention to one another, modern people devote ever more attention to themselves" (Black 2011:148). The result of greater self-interaction, he proposes, is a greater rate of self-conflict: "Some complain about losses of closeness with themselves: 'I've lost touch with myself'; 'I don't know who I am'; 'I don't know what I want.' Others complain about their own thoughts and feelings, their behavior toward themselves or others, or their level of performance in their work or other activities. They expect to be happy, and complain when they are not: 'I don't like myself'; 'I worry too much'; 'I'm depressed'" (Black 2011:148). And greater self-closeness—more often making oneself a focus of time and attention—could also encourage people to handle self-conflicts with suicide. Perhaps this is why psychological studies have found that people who are depressed—and thus at greater risk of suicide—tend to report higher levels of self-focus (Greenberg and Pyszczynski 1986; Mor and Winquist 2002).

Very close conflicts tend to attract a therapeutic style of social control, in which both the principals and third parties treat the deviant behavior as a symptom to be remedied (Black 1976:47; Black 2011:148–49; Horwitz 1990:79–95; Tucker 1999). It is not surprising, then, that many signs of self-conflict—high levels of guilt, self-blame, and negative character judgments—are usually conceptualized as symptoms of a mental illness such as depression. A medical model tends to dominate discourse about what we here call self-conflict, just as it dominates most discourse on suicide. The result is that self-conflict is not often recognized as such. Even if we do recognize it as a form of conflict, it might seem so rooted in the human mind—often secret and invisible to outsiders—that it seems odd that a work of *pure* sociology would address it at all. But despite the extent to which self-conflict is a psychological problem, purely sociological theories can also help us understand it. For instance, following Black's notion that self-interaction obeys the same principles as all interaction, self-conflicts are sparked by the same social factors that spark other conflicts—overstratification, underintimacy, and other movements of social time. Its likelihood, severity, and odds of becoming self-destructive vary accordingly. The likelihood of these conflicts resulting in suicide also varies with their structure, such as the degree to which individuals are close to themselves and isolated from others. Indeed, therapists who seek to help suicidal people might be applying psychiatric knowledge, but to the extent they are successful, it is because their behavior also follows sociological principles. By intervening to help someone with his or her self-conflict, the therapist makes a crucial change to the conflict's social geometry: it now includes a third party, one whose social distance and social elevation will shape the course of the dispute.

The role of such third parties will be the focus of our next chapter. For now, note that the relationship between social closeness and the therapeutic style may also help explain why suicide is able to behave as external aggression. Therapeutic social control treats deviance as the result of forces beyond the deviant's control: the deviant is not an offender but a victim (Black 1976:5). The closer the aggressor and target of violence, the more likely the violence is to be treated as symptom. Self-inflicted violence is the closest of all, which is why in the modern world—where privacy and individuality make people especially close to themselves—it is usually discussed in psychiatric terms (Black 2011:148). That blame for the violence is deflected away from the one who inflicts it and onto forces beyond his or her control, such as mental illness, provides a clue to the behavior of *liability*—the degree someone is held accountable for wrongdoing or misfortune (Black 1998:49–50). Aside from blaming mental disorder, or such traditional analogues as spiritual possession, there is another way in which liability for suicide is displaced from the perpetrator: blaming other people, including the suicide victim's close associates—who are also prone to blame themselves. Whether placing the blame on mental illness, other people, or ourselves, we attribute responsibility for the violence to factors beyond the perpetrator's control and are more likely to do so for self-inflicted violence than for violence against acquaintances or strangers. The external displacement of liability is what allows suicide to be a weapon against one's associates: in the case of social sanctions because other people will hold them responsible, and in the case of psychological sanctions because they will hold themselves responsible.

Though some sociologists focus exclusively on status and inequality, these variables are not the whole of social space. Human relationships also vary in their degree of intimacy and interdependence, social networks in their degree of connectedness and solidarity, and individuals in the extent to which they are integrated or isolated. Whether we consider suicide in general or moralistic suicide in particular, we see the effects of social integration and social closeness. Suicide tends to concentrate at the margins of the network, among those who are distant from others but close to themselves. Whatever their current social location, further loss of close connections is dangerous, and so bereavement and abandonment are potent causes of suicide the world over. And while relationships with strong bonds of intimacy and interdependence can be a great source of support, they can also be the site of devastating conflicts. Should this be the case, the grievances that arise are more likely to result in suicide than would be true of a more distant dispute. This may be partly due to conflict itself representing a kind of disruption among intimates, a sort of normative distancing. It may also be relevant that some mechanisms that allow suicide to act as social control, such as causing guilt or remorse, are more likely with those who are close than with those who are distant. In the case of self-execution, it might even be a strange example of people's greater tendency to side with those who are socially close, such that, if the aggrieved is close enough, the offender will effectively side against himself. The details vary from case to case, and sensitivity to close conflict varies from person to person and culture to culture. And given the sheer frequency of intimate conflict, suicide is everywhere one of the rarer outcomes of it. But the relationships between closeness and suicide means that in the large majority of social settings, suicidal conflicts are overwhelmingly close conflicts.

4

Suicide and Support

Bolubese, wife of one of the previous paramount chiefs of Kiriwina, ran away from her husband to her own village, and threatened by her own kinsmen (maternal uncle and brothers) to be sent back by force, killed herself by lo'u [jumping from a palm tree]. (Malinowski [1926] 1976:97)

Popular discussions of suicide usually focus on it as an individual act explained by the characteristics of the individual actor. As previous chapters have argued, this view is incomplete. Suicide can also be understood as a social behavior, such as a way of handling or escaping from conflict. As such, it is a social interaction with two sides—a protestor and the state, a battered woman and her abusive husband, a jealous husband and his estranged wife. Taking account of both sides and the structure of their relationship—such as their degree of inequality, intimacy, and interdependence—thus allows us to better explain variation in suicide. But even when taking account of both sides, the aggrieved and his or her adversary, our description of the social structure is still incomplete. This is because social interactions are rarely limited to just two parties. Any behavior, such as a conflict or act of violence, may come to the attention of other people—third parties—whose presence and involvement can be fateful.

Imagine, for instance, that you are walking through a city at night and glance down an alleyway, where you see one man lying prone on the ground and another man standing and kicking him. What do you do? You may choose to keep walking and ignore the violence. Or you may choose to speak up and object to it. Or you may intervene more forcefully, physically restraining the assailant to protect his victim. Or you might call the police, hoping that they in turn will intervene—if not in time to stop the violence, perhaps to locate and punish the offender. Perhaps you recognize the victim as a hated enemy or notorious wrongdoer and cheer on the violence. Perhaps you join in. Whatever you choose to do, your presence has altered the social structure of the assault, and your behavior can have a drastic impact on the course of events. Such is also the case with suicide.

Aiding Survival, Abetting Suicide

Suicide is a peculiar form of violence in that, because it is self-inflicted, the assailant and the victim are one and the same. For sociological purposes, though, we can still think of anyone who witnesses or intervenes in another person's suicide as a third party. Perhaps the third party will passively watch the violence, or perhaps he or she will act to save a person from himself. Maybe a witness even encourages self-destruction. We can see all three reactions in a case from Germany:

> It was around noon on 12 August 1969 that 19-year old Jurgen Peters climbed the ladder on the outside of the water tower in the German city of Kassel. By the time he reached the top, a number of people were already gathering where the young man was at.
>
> It soon became clear that he intended to jump all the way down in an attempt to take his own life. . . . Bystanders called the police, who in turn called the fire department for assistance. A fire ladder was put out to the top of the tower, and one of the firemen tried to talk Jurgen out of his plan, without success, however. Then a girl he had been dating and liked very much was asked to talk with him. She succeeded in persuading him to give up the attempt.
>
> While stepping down from the water tower onto the fire ladder and starting his descent, a couple of young men watching the scene began yelling: "Hey, coward, you don't even have the guts to jump, do you?" and similar provocative remarks. One could observe Jurgen hesitating, interrupting his descent. Then all of a sudden he climbed up the ladder, hopped on the top of the tower and almost in one movement jumped off. He died on the spot. (Cutler, Glaeser, and Norberg 2001:221)

We see in this case the part that bystanders and other third parties can take in suicide. Some intervened to support Jurgen's survival, attempting to persuade him to spare himself. They might have succeeded had others not intervened to encourage his death. Third parties can play vital roles in self-inflicted violence, and we should consider these roles in more detail.

PREVENTION AND RESCUE

People usually seek to stop others from harming or killing themselves. Depending on the method of suicide being used, there may be a good deal of time in which people can learn about a suicide attempt and intervene to prevent the violence or rescue the victim from its effects. On the Polynesian island of Tikopia, for example, young people frequently attempt suicide by either swimming out to sea or setting out for the open ocean in a canoe. Both methods sometimes lead to fatalities, as swimmers eventually drown or are eaten by sharks, and canoes are eventually swamped with the same result. But there is often enough time for other people to intervene. If the departure is witnessed by other islanders, they immediately raise the alarm and dispatch a fleet of canoes on a search and rescue mission. These rescue canoes are crewed by a mixture of young, single men, who are the strongest rowers, older married men, there to keep the young men from being reckless, and sometimes women, there to persuade the lost person to turn back and cooperate with the rescuers (Firth 1967). Another island people, the Chuukese of Micronesia, also use swimming to sea as a method of suicide, and such swimmers are also frequently rescued. In one case, a man "had a bitter argument with his wife, finally walked out of the house, down to the beach, and swam off into the open sea," where he was soon rescued by his brother and father-in-law (Gladwin and Sarason 1953:145).

In these island societies, setting out to sea communicates suicidal intent and rouses others to intervene to prevent self-destruction. Other behaviors have a similar effect. Among the Chuukese, suicide sometimes involves jumping from tall palm trees, and so depending on the circumstances, climbing a tall tree can signal an impending suicide. Anthropologist Thomas Gladwin witnessed one such case, in which a young man "got into a trivial argument with his mother over the repair of a pillow. Voices rose and angry words were spoken; his father's sister, Rachel, was present and accused him of being a bad son to his mother" (Gladwin and Sarason 1953:145). The young man left the house with "an almost hysterical desperation on his face" and climbed a nearby tree with the apparent intention of committing suicide. "At this point," Gladwin reports, "I abandoned my observer role and stood under the tree" in order to prevent the man from jumping until an older relative succeeded in persuading him to climb down (Gladwin and Sarason 1953:146).

We can see similar interventions in modern cities, where tall buildings provide a means of jumping to one's death. "Jumpers," as they are sometimes called, often hesitate long enough to attract witnesses who might attempt to "talk them down" safely. We have already considered the case of Jurgen Peters, the young German who several people unsuccessfully tried to convince to climb down from a water tower. American boxing champion Muhammad Ali had better luck than Jurgen's would-be rescuers: in Los Angeles in 1981, Ali was cheered by onlookers after he successfully talked a man out of jumping from a ninth-floor window (Mann 1981:703). Police officers in cities with many tall buildings are commonly called upon to talk jumpers into not going through with the act. Such intervention is frequent enough that officers in some cities receive special training in dealing with jumper scenarios. Two veterans of such crisis intervention describe using tactics such as encouraging the jumper to talk, avoiding advice or judgmental language, and urging the jumper to just "put if off for a little while. . . . Take a little time to think about when things were good in your life, and how it could be good again" (Fowler and Maguire 2001:45–46).

We can observe persuasion in other circumstances as well. For example, someone threatening to shoot himself might be talked into putting the gun down. Or a verbal expression of intent to commit suicide might result in third parties trying to convince the potential self-killer to abandon the idea. In one case among the Netsilik Eskimo, "Irkrowatok, a blind woman [who had recently learned of her son-in-law's death] . . . said she wanted to kill herself. For about a year, her husband succeeded in dissuading her, telling her: 'Don't do it, so that the children may grow up near their mother'" (Balikci 1970:164–65). Many suicidal individuals are ambivalent about killing themselves and express not only a desire to die but a fear of this desire (Shneidman 1996:52). Remarkably, then, these potential perpetrators of violence actively recruit others to prevent them from committing it. In the United States and elsewhere, one form of suicide prevention is the "suicide hotline," an advertised phone service that people considering suicide can call to speak to a trained operator who will try to prevent their death. The very existence of this service is premised on the fact that suicidal people might mobilize third parties to help save them from themselves, just as people threatened by an external adversary might likewise seek help and protection.[1]

Help is not always welcome, however, and sometimes third parties intervene in ways that are more coercive. They might confiscate potential weapons that could be used for self-destruction. Both prisons and psychiatric hospitals sometimes take these steps with inmates they view as likely to commit suicide, confiscating items such shoelaces, belts, and other potential ligatures that could be used for self-strangulation. They might also confiscate eyeglasses, which could potentially be broken into dangerous shards (see, e.g., Kobler and Stotland 1964). Third parties might even forcibly restrain the potential self-killer. Sometimes police attempting to prevent someone from a fatal jump will use various ruses and distractions—such as offering a "last cigarette"—in order to get close enough to seize the jumper and pull him or her to safety (Fowler and Maguire 2001). Patients at psychiatric hospitals might be bound in straightjackets or locked in padded cells to prevent harm to both themselves and others. Those who threaten to passively bring about their own death by starvation might be forced to ingest food. During the eighteenth and nineteenth centuries, when African slaves attempted to starve themselves to death during the voyage from Africa to the Americas, the crew of the slave ships would pry open their jaws and supply them with nourishment against their will (Bly 1998). When inmates at the US Guantanamo Bay detention facility staged a hunger strike in 2005, their guards also resorted to forced feeding to prevent their hunger strike from becoming self-destructive (Lewis 2005).

The velocity of violence is variable, and the odds of rescue vary accordingly. Methods like fasting inflict damage very slowly, while methods like shooting oneself in the head inflict it almost immediately.[2] Hanging and strangulation are typically fast acting, but without a neck-breaking drop from a gallows these too allow time for rescue—in the New Guinea Highlands, for instance, hanging victims are sometimes discovered and saved before death (Berndt 1962:186–87). Some poisons act quickly, but many others act slowly enough to allow treatment if discovered in time, and so many victims of self-poisoning are discovered and successfully treated. Among the Dobe !Kung, a hunter-gatherer group in Africa's Kalahari Desert, people sometimes try to kill themselves with poisoned arrows, but "others will attempt to prevent this if they can, and will treat the injury with the usual procedure of drawing off as much blood and poison as possible from the injured limb if the person succeeds" (Howell 1979:61). Among the Trobriand islanders, many of those who attempt suicide in response to "lovers' quarrels" do so by ingesting a vegetable poison that can be cured with a dose of emetic, and so they are often saved (Malinowski [1926] 1976:94). Self-poisoners in modern urban settings often survive as well. For instance, rock musician Kurt Cobain's first suicide attempt, by intentional drug overdose, resulted in him being found and rescued by his wife, who ensured he received medical attention (Cross 2001:311–13). Studies of attempted suicide in the United States and elsewhere commonly find that unsuccessful attempts are several times more frequent than fatalities and that over 70 percent of attempters use self-poisoning (Mościcki 2001:315).

Prevention and rescue require that others be present and ready to act in a timely manner, and so surveillance is a component of suicide prevention. The Aguaruna Jívaro, knowing that the bereaved are likely to commit suicide, "keep close watch on distraught relatives to make sure that no poisons are within their reach and that they are not left alone long enough to hang themselves" (Brown 1986:315). Likewise, among the Tikopia, "when it is known that for any reason a man has become angry, a watch is kept upon him; if he says he is going somewhere, another man follows to prevent him from taking a canoe" (Firth 1967:134). Surveillance is also a component of suicide prevention in modern psychiatric facilities, where patients thought to be at risk of self-destruction are designated as such and put under more intense observation (see, e.g., Kobler and Stotland 1964). This might involve checks at regular intervals of time or even literally constant observation by a staff member dedicated solely to that purpose, sometimes for days on end (Shugar and Rehaluk 1990; Grant 2007). Inmates in jails and prisons may likewise be placed under "suicide watch" and given special attention to ensure they have fewer opportunities to harm themselves and greater chance of discovery and rescue if they do. In at least one facility, the inmate's peers are employed as observers (Junker, Beeler, and Bates 2005). The focus of surveillance may be even broader, seeking to identify potentially suicidal individuals within a larger population. Suicide prevention campaigns in modern America sometimes have this logic, seeking to educate both counselors and ordinary citizens on how to spot signs of suicidal intent. But just because a third party is present and aware of and impending attempt does not mean they will try to stop the violence. Some bystanders are content to do nothing at all.

INACTION, INSTIGATION, AND ASSISTANCE

Whether incredulous, indifferent, or hostile, third parties sometimes ignore or dismiss warnings and threats of suicide. In some cases, they even passively watch the violence unfold. When one elderly Netsilik Eskimo woman, reacting to her son's recent accidental death, set out to hang herself from a rock, "people saw her running with the thong and knew what she intended to do, but nobody tried to stop her" (Balikci 1970:165). The Eastern Highlanders of New Guinea believe that a woman has the ability to poison her husband with her menstrual blood, rendering him vulnerable to his enemies. Thus if a man dies in battle, suspicion might fall upon his wife, and so the suicide of a widow is usually met with either indifference or approval—something that either saves the clan the trouble of a vengeance killing or that is a way for the widow to prove her innocence and loyalty (Berndt 1962:182–88). One polygynous Highlander was killed in a raid by the family of one of his two wives. The other wife displayed her loyalty during his mortuary feast by slashing her cowife's throat and then hanging herself in front of her in-laws, who watched, waited until she was dead, buried her, and then resumed their feasting (Berndt 1962:183). In modern urban settings, those who threaten to jump from tall buildings sometimes attract large crowds of passive spectators who do nothing to stop the potential suicide. For instance, on July 27, 1938, "thousands of persons waited, some for 11 hours, until John Warden jumped from a 17th-floor hotel ledge" (Mann 1981:703).

While some third parties passively allow suicides to occur, others actively encourage them. As we have seen already, authorities sometimes command their subordinates to commit self-execution. People might also encourage suicidal altruism, especially if they stand to benefit from it, as when people charged with caring for the elderly or sick encourage them to kill themselves so as to eliminate the burden (e.g., Balikci 1970:165). Even bystanders who have no prior connection to the potential self-killer and no knowledge of the reasons for suicide might nonetheless encourage self-destruction. As in the case of the young German Jurgen Peters, the crowds who watch those poised to jump to their deaths might encourage them to do so, perhaps for the sheer spectacle. One study of suicides and attempted suicides described in news sources identified twenty-one cases in which crowds of onlookers urged an individual to jump, including three cases occurring in New York City between 1964 and 1979 (Mann 1981:704). More recently, in 2008, a seventeen-year-old British man, distraught over a recent breakup, climbed to the top of a city parking garage. While police negotiators attempted to talk him down, a crowd of three hundred other observers gathered underneath, some of them "shouting abuse at him and urging him to jump. One teenager even yelled: 'How far can you bounce?'" (Britten 2008). The young man eventually leapt to his death.

Beyond encouragement is rendering assistance. Elderly Eskimo seeking death often requested the assistance of their relatives in carrying out the act. In one case, "At Chesterfield Inlet a son-in-law helped his wife's mother, who was sick with tuberculosis, to hang herself. 'She felt that she was old, and having begun to spit up blood, she wished to die quickly, and I agreed. I only made the line fast to the roof, the rest she did herself'" (Hoebel 1976:77).

Among the St. Lawrence Eskimo, such suicides were highly ritualized affairs and often involved the participation of several persons who would accompany the suicidal individual to a designated "Destroying Place" where he would be hanged, shot, or stabbed by himself or by his assistants; in the case of hangings, several relatives would assist (Leighton and Hughes 1955:330). Depending on the degree of the relatives' involvement, these deaths could vary from relatively pure suicides to what might be classified as homicide with a willing victim. Such voluntary homicides were also common among the Chukchee of Siberia, where older men who wished to die might invoke their right to demand execution at the hands of a son or other junior relative (Sverdrup 1939). Similarly, on Fiji, the widow of a chief would often request that her relatives strangle her to death; according to sources, repeated requests were necessary before she was actually killed (Fisch 2005).

Assisting in self-destruction may itself be a kind of altruism or helping behavior—a therapy of last resort to end someone else's suffering. As such, it is controversial throughout much of the modern world, with some recognizing it as benevolence and others condemning it as murder. The activities of US physician Jack Kevorkian thus attracted a great deal of attention and debate. Kevorkian gained notoriety for assisting in the suicide of 130 people between 1990 and 1998, a practice that began with him advertising his services as a "death counselor" in a Detroit newspaper. To facilitate the suicide of his clients Kevorkian developed two devices—dubbed the "Thanatron" and "Mercitron"—that, respectively, injected lethal chemicals into the bloodstream and emitted lethal gas to be inhaled through a facemask (Jackson 2011). Kevorkian's role was to prepare the machines for use, though he left it to the client to activate them. The one known exception, in which Kevorkian administered a lethal injection while being videotaped, resulted in his being tried and convicted for murder despite the victim having provided informed consent to the procedure (Davey 2007).

Though assisted suicide, and suicide more generally, have long been condemned in the West, some Western countries increasingly tolerate the practice. In contemporary Switzerland, for instance, assisted suicide is legal in many circumstances, and hundreds of such suicides take place per year. Many of these involve foreign nationals from countries where the practice is more tightly policed coming to Switzerland to end their lives in a practice that has been dubbed "suicide tourism" (Wilson 2014). In the past decade, Belgium, Luxembourg, and the Netherlands have also decriminalized euthanasia and assisted suicide, as did Montana in the United States. Assisted suicide has been legalized in Vermont, and both Oregon and Washington allow doctors to prescribe lethal doses of drugs to terminally ill patients (Aviv 2015). While most cases of assisted suicide in these settings involve people with terminal illnesses, Belgium and the Netherlands also allow suicide for other reasons: "Although most of the Belgian patients had cancer, people have also been euthanized because they had autism, anorexia, borderline personality disorder, chronic-fatigue syndrome, partial paralysis, blindness coupled with deafness, and manic depression" (Aviv 2015).

Support, Settlement, and Suicide

The role of third parties in suicide goes beyond the act of suicide itself. Just as people might intervene in a particular act of violence, they might intervene in the conflict or other situation that produced the violence. Indeed, third parties play an important role in shaping conflict and thus in determining whether someone embroiled in a dispute will become suicidal in the first place. Should they intervene at all, third parties take on one of two major roles in a conflict: they are either *partisans*, supporting one side against the other, or *settlement agents*, handling the dispute in a relatively neutral fashion (Black 1998:95–143). As Black and Baumgartner (1983) note in their typology of third parties, support can range from providing encouragement and advice to being a champion who fights on another's behalf, and settlement can range from friendly peacemaking to a formal legal hearing. As Black (1998:125–43) discusses in his work on partisanship, taking sides can range from expressing a mild preference for one side to providing strong and uncompromising support for one coupled with extreme hostility toward the other. Even neutrality is variable, with some neutrals being mutually supportive peacemakers and other neutrals being completely indifferent and unwilling to get involved.

All this variation is relevant to how a conflict is handled, including whether or not it turns violent. In *Warriors and Peacemakers*, sociologist Mark Cooney (1998) traces several ways in which the presence and involvement of third parties affects the likelihood, nature, and severity of violence. Settlement, for instance, is an alternative to violent conflict, and so the presence of third parties who can act as settlement agents tends to reduce violence. This is one reason societies with developed legal systems, where people can take their grievances before police, judges, and jurors, tend to have lower rates of homicide (Cooney 1998:45–66). But one need not be a legal official to settle a conflict, and so informal peacemakers can also prevent violence.

Consider this example from the United States:

> Andrew's conflict with Vic arose out of a love triangle. Both men were dating the same woman, Beth. Each knew about the other, and the men had several arguments that almost came to blows. One night, Andrew and Vic happened to come to Beth's house at the same time. Both men were upset, and the rivals began to argue and push each other. However, several people intervened. Beth's two sisters, Karen and Helen, and Karen's boyfriend, Chris, were all at the house and separated the men. The men cooled off and then left the house at different times. A few hours later, however, Andrew walked past Vic's house, and Vic threw a beer bottle at him from the front porch. Andrew walked up to Vic's porch, and the two began to argue again, reigniting the conflict. This time the men fought unimpeded. Andrew beat Vic to death. (Phillips and Cooney 2005)

The case above comes from a study by Scott Phillips and Mark Cooney (2005) that compared matched pairs of conflicts, one of which ended in homicide and another that was resolved nonviolently. Their results show that conflicts in which a third party acted as a peacemaker were much less likely to end in violence. Even when conflicts do turn violent, the actions of third parties determine what form the violence takes. Strong partisanship toward both sides increases the odds of bilateral violence, like gang brawls or blood feuds (Cooney 1998:67–106; Campbell and Manning 2019). On the other hand, strong partisanship toward just one side increases the odds of unilateral violence, like lynch mobs that execute an alleged offender (Senechal de la Roche 1996, 2001). Third-party intervention thus alters the likelihood, nature, and severity of moralistic violence.

Suicide is no exception. Mutually supportive peacemaking can dampen or resolve a conflict before it escalates to the point where one side is willing to resort to such an extreme measure. Partisan support can also prevent suicide, depending on which side of the conflict attracts it. We saw in chapter 2 that suicide is more likely among those who face an adversary with superior status, such as greater wealth or power. But when an aggrieved inferior receives enough partisan support, it can help equalize the conflict, particularly if the partisans themselves are of higher status. This makes seeking help from others, whether particular individuals and organizations or "public opinion at large," an attractive option for many aggrieved inferiors and something that can be an alternative to suicide (Baumgartner 1984:316). Ready access to support levels the playing field and provides additional options, while a lack of support encourages suicide. Thus, in a conflict, *suicide varies inversely with third-party support* (Manning 2012).

DOMESTIC SUPPORT

We have already seen how patriarchal domination and violent discipline can lead wives to kill themselves. One factor that can temper such domination and deter domestic violence is third-party support for the wife. Drawing from numerous examples in the cross-cultural literature, sociologist M. P. Baumgartner (1992) describes how different patterns of residence, political alliance, and other social arrangements affect the amount of support available to wives and thus their vulnerability to domestic violence. Should conditions be conducive to support, even in an otherwise patriarchal society a woman might be able to count on the protection of her father, brothers, and other male kin, who will take offense and confront her husband if he treats her too badly. The mere knowledge of this might be enough to deter extremes of domestic violence. If kin are unwilling to intervene forcefully, they might provide support in other ways, such as by accepting a wife's decision to divorce and accepting her back into the family household. In societies where men tend to be the main breadwinners and a woman would be unable to live on her own, a simple willingness to provide food and shelter can be crucial in making divorce a viable alternative to suicide. On the other hand, an aggrieved wife might find no one, including her own family, will take her side, and if this is the case she is more likely to kill herself. Thus the frequency of suicide among Aguaruna Jívaro women is partly due to the fact that they "often find their relatives reluctant to defend them from abusive husbands" (Brown 1986:320).

Anthropologists and other observers report a similarly conspicuous lack of support for abused wives in other patriarchal settings with a high frequency of female suicide. In some cases an aggrieved woman's family will actively side with her husband, viewing her own complaints or attempts to end the relationship as the true deviance. Among the Mount Hageners of New Guinea, "the typical circumstance in which women act on a threat of suicide is dual alienation from both husband and home kin. After a marital quarrel the wife retreats; but far from taking her side, her brother or father try to dispatch her back with conciliatory gifts to placate the husband. A wife who is rebuffed in her demand for kinsmen's support against an injury done her by her husband may hang herself out of frustration and for revenge" (Strathern 1972:256). A wife's attempt to handle herself aggressively or use physical self-defense can also be treated as deviant by third parties who side with her husband and so become additional opponents. Anthropologist Dorothy Ayers Counts describes the case of a Lusi woman who, following such opposition, abandoned a strategy of self-defense for a strategy of self-destruction:

> I know of only one woman who consistently fought back when her husband beat her. This woman, the first of two wives, was finally beaten into unconsciousness by her angry husband. Fearing that, in a future rage, he might kill her, he called for kinsmen in a neighboring village to come to his village bearing a varku mask. This mask represents powerful ancestor spirits, and was a traditional instrument of social control. . . . It was announcing to all that the husband was now under the protection of the mask; if his wives struck him in the course of future quarrels, they would be required to pay a large fine to the mask. . . . After the next marital argument—during which the man struck his first wife, but she was prohibited from responding in kind—the woman attempted to commit suicide by drinking a concoction made from the [derris] plant. (Counts 1980:340)

If receiving support can reduce the effects of inequality, then facing opposition can exaggerate them. On the other hand, strong enough support for an abuse victim can effectively reverse the standing of the disputants, transforming the weaker side of the conflict into the stronger one. This in turn affects which of the disputants is likely to turn to suicide. Among the Mapuche (or Auracanian) people of Chile and Argentina, it is usually wives who turn to suicide in the face of domestic abuse, but if a woman's older sons side with her against her husband, it may be him who kills himself instead. One man's sons frequently sided with his wife during marital quarrels, and when, during one quarrel, one of the sons struck him with a hoe "the father took a lasso and . . . later he was found dead, hanging from a tree" (Hilger 1957:71). In modern societies legal officials can be powerful supporters who, if successfully mobilized, shift the balance of power against an abuser. In my study of suicidal conflicts in Louisville, over a dozen cases involved conflicts between family or intimate partners that escalated to suicide after the police showed up. The typical pattern was for a man to threaten or attack his partner, who then called the police, prompting the man to commit suicide upon their arrival. For example:

> The police were called to the decedent's residence on a domestic run. The decedent's wife said that her husband had beaten her, stripped her

partially nude, and then locked her out of the apartment. They called to the decedent, but he said that they would never get in without a warrant. The police then went with the wife and obtained an abuse and battery warrant from police court. They returned to the apartment. They showed the warrant to the decedent through the window in the door and told him to open up. He requested to see his wife. The officers refused, keeping her off to one side of the porch. He then yelled that if they wanted to come in, they would have to kick the door down. They kicked it in. After this, he put a pistol to his head and shot himself.

Family members and friends intervene as well. In one case, family members provided shelter to a woman whose husband had threatened to kill her, and they also encouraged her to contact the police. The husband then committed suicide while she was in hiding. In another case, a man who appeared poised to commit either homicide or homicide-suicide chose to commit suicide alone when a third party intervened. During the course of a violent argument, the man pointed a gun at his estranged girlfriend and told her he would kill her. At this point, the man's female coworker, there to give him a ride to work, placed herself in front of the gun by jumping on the ex-girlfriend's lap and refused to move when ordered. Being unwilling to kill his coworker as well, the enraged man relented, ordered them both out of the room, and shot himself in the head.

POLITICAL SUPPORT

Third parties also play an important role in political conflict. Indeed, most of what we call "politics" consists of recruiting and mobilizing partisans to support one side against another, whether through providing votes, money, or labor. Most strategies of political protest, while partly a tactic of communicating grievances to adversaries, are also a way of communicating them to bystanders who might be persuaded to support the cause. Activists read lists of grievances before crowds of onlookers, detailing the reasons for their demonstration and the wrongness of their adversary; some hand out written pamphlets and flyers aimed at persuading bystanders of the importance of their cause. Demonstrations and marches can advertise the nature of the grievance and convince others of its seriousness. If they are large enough, they might also signal the popularity of a cause, perhaps convincing potential partisans it is worth their time and effort to provide support or attracting those who wish to be on the winning side of a struggle. Other tactics of protest seek to demonstrate resolve or win sympathy by dramatizing the hardships faced by protestors and perhaps intentionally exposing them to violent retaliation from their adversaries. Protestors can thus use their own victimization as a means of attracting support (Campbell and Manning 2018:47–58).

This is the logic behind self-destructive acts of protest, such as hunger strikes and self-immolations: they are extreme and suicidal ways of attracting the support of third parties. In chapter 1 I discussed the example of Vietnamese monk Thich Quang Duc, who set himself on fire to protest the Catholic president's suppression of Buddhism. His death was part of a larger campaign of activism led by Buddhist monks, who were savvy enough to ensure that foreign reporters would be present and able to bring news of the self-immolation to the American public (LePoer 1989:61–64; Biggs 2005). Many others who commit protest suicide explicitly say that their death is meant to inspire third parties to get involved and support their cause. Between 1970 and 2004, South Korea experienced numerous protest suicides, mostly by burning, as activists campaigned for labor reforms and democratic government. An analysis of suicide notes left by self-immolators during the period found that most protestors killed themselves "in order to inspire movement activism among half-hearted activists and apathetic bystanders" (Kim 2008:573). For example, a college student who burned himself in protest of the Roh Tae-woo regime's repressive policies wrote: "I beg the activists of all persuasions. Throw away your own authoritarianism and obstinate egoism and immediately begin your work to accomplish the unification in practice. I beg with bloody tears this last time. Rise up. 1 million college students! Do not let my death and all the deaths of my predecessors be in vain" (quoted in Kim 2008:567). We see similar appeals in other countries as well. For instance a fourteen-year-old Kurdish girl who set herself on fire in London to protest the capture of a Kurdish leader later explained that "I wanted someone to stop and think about us" (quoted in Biggs 2008:25). Such desperate attempts to mobilize support are more likely where and when support is difficult to mobilize and where activists struggling against a superior adversary are failing to attract enough support to achieve any success.

The Social Structure of Third Parties

If the behavior of third parties shapes outcomes, then what is it that predicts the behavior of third parties? In pure sociology, this too is something we can explain with the structure and motion of social space. Third parties can be superior to one or both disputants or may be inferior to them. They might be relationally close to one or both disputants or distant from them. A third party is part of the overall structure of the conflict, and their place in this structure determines their behavior.

First, consider the likelihood that a third party will intervene at all. According to Black's theory of the third party, intervention is a direct function of the social distance between the disputants (Black 1995:835). The greater the relational and cultural distance between two adversaries, the more likely it is that third parties will get involved and the greater their involvement is likely to be. This principle helps explain both when disputants will try to recruit outsiders into the conflict and when outsiders will intervene of their own accord. People with grievances against intimates are more likely to treat them as private business, potentially embarrassing or shameful to share with outsiders. Even if they seek outside intervention, the closer they are, the more hesitant third parties are likely to be. For example, an experimental study found that bystanders were much more likely to intervene in a staged fight between a man and a woman if they were portrayed as strangers rather than as spouses (Shotland and Straw 1976; see also Rogers et al. 2019). Observational studies reveal that police are also hesitant to get involved in domestic disputes, and when called to the scene of domestic violence they are less likely to make an arrest than if the parties are more distant (Black 1980:114–15). The greater the distance, the more luck an aggrieved person will have in recruiting support and the less resistance a third party will meet when trying to offer it.

We have seen that third parties can take on different roles, intervening as neutral peacemakers or with varying degrees of partisanship toward one side and against the other. Social structure explains this as well. Black proposes that partisanship is a joint function of closeness to one and distance from the other side (Black 1998:126). Social closeness, including intimacy, interdependence, and cultural similarity, is conducive to support. All else being equal, a closer party is more likely to listen to the aggrieved person's complaints, accept his or her side of the story, and offer help in resolving the conflict in his or her favor. Someone equally close to both sides might try to help both at the same time, perhaps noting that both sides have a valid point or share blame for the problem and encouraging a mutually beneficial solution (Black 1998:135). Social distance, however, facilitates indifference or even hostility. Strangers and foreigners are often treated with suspicion, and their problems and complaints generally rouse less concern than those of friends and countrymen. Someone distant from both sides in the conflict is less likely to care much about what either side wants or even that the conflict has occurred. The greatest partisanship arises from the combination of closeness and distance, leading to strong and one-sided support: one side is totally right, a noble ally or innocent victim who deserves protection, assistance, and perhaps vengeance, while the other side is totally wrong, an offender or enemy who should be opposed, avoided, or punished.

We can see extremes of partisanship in many times and places. The ethnographic record contains numerous examples from tribal and traditional societies, where kinship is often the strongest predictor of support. This is why, in societies organized into clans, lineages, and other cohesive family units, a conflict between two individuals from different groups can easily escalate into a collective conflict between families, including blood feuds and other forms of collective violence (Black 1998:128–31; Cooney 1998; Diamond 2013:90). The back-and-forth cycles of vengeance killing between modern street gangs have a similar logic and similar social structure: a conflict between two clusters of people, each internally close—lifelong friends, neighbors, and often family members—but distant from the other (Cooney 1998). Tight-knit communities are generally more harsh and judgmental toward outsiders accused of victimizing insiders, which is why rural communities in the Jim Crow–era US South were more prone to lynch strangers and recent arrivals (Senechal de la Roche 2001). Even within the village or family, varying degrees of closeness predict who takes whose side. As the Bedouins of Arabia say, "Myself against my brother, my brother and I against my cousin, my cousin, my brother and I against the stranger" (Murphy and Kasdan 1959:20).

Social status is also relevant to taking sides. Black proposes that "partisanship is a joint function of the social superiority of one side and the social inferiority of the other" (Black 1998:127). Social superiors often find it easier to attract supporters. They may have subordinates for just that purpose, such as the military retainers of feudal societies or the legal staff of modern corporations. Or they may simply find many eager to get and stay on their good side, expecting future favors or repaying past ones. During nineteenth-century America's famous Hatfield-McCoy feud, feudist "Devil" Anse Hatfield was able to count on the support of not just kin but employees and tenants working his land (Waller 1988:78–85). On the other hand, people are often reluctant to oppose superiors. Slaves might inwardly sympathize when one of their own is subject to brutal punishment, but they are unlikely to take the risk of trying to stop it. As Black notes, "Social inferiors may not be subjectively tolerant of their superiors, but behaviorally they are exceptionally so" (Black 1998:89). Status inferiors, though, are usually safer to oppose and may be treated with more suspicion anyway—as moral inferiors as well as economic or hierarchical ones. When an inferior is accused of victimizing a superior, then, the third party is more likely to take the accusation seriously and act upon it. Lynch mobs in the US South tended to punish blacks for offending whites rather than the reverse, and if they did punish a white offender it was usually someone of particularly low status—such as an unemployed drunkard or notorious criminal—accused of victimizing an upstanding member of the community (Senechal de la Roche 1996, 1997, 2001).

Suicide is more likely when people have grievances against an intimate, and people with grievances against an intimate are also less likely to seek and receive third-party support. Suicide is more likely when people have grievances against a superior, and such grievances are also less conducive to third-party support. As Cooney observed in his work on the handling of homicide, the effects of a conflict's third-party structure often reinforce those of its core structure. But insofar as third-party structure can vary independently, its effects can run counter to those of the core structure and so help mitigate them (Cooney 2009:191–93). For instance, a third party very close to the aggrieved might be a strong partisan even in the most intimate conflict, or even against a superior adversary. Perhaps even small changes in the social location of third parties can shift the balance, making them more likely to intervene and more likely to take one side instead of the other. This in turn can have a major effect on the outcome of the conflict, including the likelihood of suicide. Consider an example from the history of Taiwan that shows how structural change can affect partisanship and suicide.

A CASE STUDY IN PARTISANSHIP

As in mainland China, the traditional family structure of rural Taiwan placed newly married women at the bottom. As described by anthropologist Margery Wolf (1972), based on information covering the early to mid-twentieth century, the most important social unit in Taiwanese society was the corporate patrilineage, an enduring kinship group, organized around the male line, which collectively held and managed property such as homes and farmland. The group dominated the individual, and within the family unit elder members commanded more authority and respect than younger members. Social organization was highly patriarchal: male children were preferred over female, and from a young age women were taught to defer to men, the main exception being a man's duty to respect his parents, including his mother. As we saw in chapter 2, parents acquired a new bride for their son as a way of continuing the family unit. The wishes of the respective spouses mattered little in this system. Marriage was an initially loveless affair, arranged by parents, between spouses who might have never interacted before their wedding day. The new bride entered the patriarchal family as an outsider and a questionable investment of family resources. Acquired to bear children and perform domestic labor, she had yet to prove her ability to do the former and was likely incompetent at the latter, not having been trained in these tasks by her own family because they knew she was destined to leave them and considered such training a waste (Wolf 1972:133). A young wife would likely be treated as an incompetent servant subject to constant criticism and insult, if not physical abuse.

Her options for dealing with this situation were limited. One might expect her own natal family to be the most likely source of support, but her marriage might well have resulted in her moving some distance away from them to a town or neighborhood filled with strangers. Even if her family might have agreed that she was being treated too harshly, they were unlikely to learn about it. Furthermore, her departure from them was not just physical but social, as her wedding day was marked by a ritual cutting of ties: they had formally bid her goodbye for life (Wolf 1972:34). They had also negotiated and accepted a payment of bride-price from her husband's family that they would have to return should they allow her to leave her husband and come back to them—something that would also be a source of stigma for all involved (Diamond 1969:59). The young bride was often on her own, with few options other than to endure the abuse and wait for age, experience, and childbearing to raise her stature within the family.

We have previously considered this sort of family structure as an example of patriarchy because of the dominance that husbands and their close kin could exercise over a wife. But within the patrilineal household it was often the husband's mother who was the bride's harshest taskmaster and critic. It was, after all, the mother-in-law who oversaw household chores, and many a mother ruled over the domestic sphere with an iron fist, subjecting her daughter-in-law to the same kind of abuse she herself had experienced when younger. To whom could a bride turn if her mother-in-law's abuse became too severe? With her own birth family unavailable or unwilling to intervene, she might turn to the member of her new family with whom she theoretically shared the closest connection: her husband. But in the earliest phases of marriage, this connection was not so close. The two might have never interacted before their wedding and, perhaps lacking any mutual attraction or rapport, have had little interaction since. Her husband's attentions to her might be limited to a grudging minimum of procreative sex, while he satisfied any remaining lust by visiting prostitutes. Distant from his wife, he was very close to his mother. She was not only an elder to be respected but someone he had known for his entire life. Under such conditions, the husband was unlikely to provide much help, even in cases of severe abuse.

The lack of support from within or without the martial family surely contributed to the number of young Taiwanese brides who resorted to suicide, an act that not only allowed them to escape but was also known to bring shame and supernatural curses upon their in-laws. According to Wolf, "Young women in their early and middle twenties, despairing at the cruelties of their mothers-in-law and desirous of revenge . . . drink poison or throw themselves off bridges or under trains, producing the highest rate of suicide of any age group" (Wolf 1972:163). Older women, on the other hand, tended to have much lower suicide rates. A woman who endured the early phases of marriage would see herself become an increasingly integral and respected member of her family and community. Her burgeoning ties with neighborhood women might make public opinion an avenue for curbing the worst excesses of domestic abuse, while with childbearing and increasing domestic skill she gained greater functional status within the family. Eventually she rose to the rank of a respected elder, receiving the affection and deference of her own adult children (Wolf 1975:123–47). Her relationship with her husband would surely grow closer, and though he still had authority over her, the support of her adult sons acted as a check on his abuse (Wolf 1975:123; see also Baumgartner 1992:27–28). In fact, should she outlive her husband, she might assume leadership of the family. By her old age, a woman had a high degree of social integration and a much greater level of social status than she had when she was first married. Female suicide rates reflected these changes and declined substantially with age.

This was the traditional pattern of marriage, conflict, and suicide in Taiwan. But during the middle of the twentieth century, the pattern began to change. Economic modernization disrupted old ways of life, including the importance and influence of the corporate patrilineage. The younger generation of men became increasingly reliant on paid employment and correspondingly less reliant on the collective resources controlled by their parents. With greater independence came greater autonomy: "Young men were no longer dependent on land held by their fathers to feed their wives. They could rebel and some did, at least enough of them to make parents pay more attention to their son's wishes" (Wolf 1975:126). One result of this new autonomy was that sons now exercised much more choice in whom to marry. Marriage became less an arrangement between families and more an affair between individuals, with young men seeking brides they personally found attractive. Though still formally a contract ratified by elders, marriage began to resemble courtship more than exchange. The result was greater closeness between spouses during the early phases of marriage.

During this period of Taiwan's transition to modernity the patterns of residency continued much as before, with brides leaving home to live among their husbands' families. And mothers-in-law still assumed authority over their new daughters, directed them in household tasks, and criticized their shortcomings. But the social location of husbands had changed—compared to the previous generation, they tended to be somewhat less subordinate to their parents and somewhat closer to their new brides. These two interrelated changes were enough to shift the winds of partisanship. When a bride objected to harsh treatment from her mother-in-law, it was now more common for a husband to take his wife's side. According to Wolf, the change was fateful:

> In generations past an emotional tie between husband and wife came later in life, if at all, and was not expected in the young strangers who were married at their parents' convenience. A young wife who enters as her husband's choice has emotional and sexual advantages over her mother-in-law from the outset. When the apparently inevitable conflicts arise between mother-in-law and daughter-in-law and the son intervenes on his wife's behalf, the effect on the older woman is stunning. . . . In despair over her powerlessness or in a fit of revengeful fury at her fickle son, the aging mother contemplates, threatens, or in some cases commits suicide. (Wolf 1975:127)

In one such quarrel, when the husband sided with his wife, "the mother-in-law threatened to kill herself and shouted bitterly, 'Then the two of you will be alone and won't have a mother in your way'" (Wolf 1972:159). As such situations became more frequent, the pattern of female suicide began to change. The age of first marriage became a less dangerous time for women, and so the suicide rates of young women declined. Older women, on the other hand—especially those around the age at which their sons first married—became more likely to kill themselves, and their suicide rates increased (Wolf 1975:125–26).

ISOLATION, INTEGRATION, AND THIRD PARTIES

We see in the example of traditional Taiwanese marriages how living arrangements can undermine a wife's ability to receive support from her natal family. This is a common feature of societies where a woman leaves her own kin group or homestead to live among strangers and one that makes her more vulnerable to domestic abuse. This is true of many of the patriarchal settings we considered in chapter 2, where it contributes to patriarchal domination and female suicide. In the New Guinea Highlands, for instance, women traditionally lived in a compound with their husbands' families and at a distance from their own (Berndt 1962; Johnson 1981). We see a similar combination of isolation and subordination among newly married women in rural India and Iran (Hadlaczky and Wasserman 2009:124; Aliverdinia and Pridemore 2009). The same has traditionally been the case in rural China, where a married woman might live at a distance from her own family. A case study of one Chinese woman's suicide emphasizes her marginality: "If Fang was depicted as a challenger [against her husband's family], she was a lonely one. She was socially isolated, without substantial support. . . . Her natal family lived far away and the lifestyle in her native village was totally different from that in her in-law family. . . . She spoke a dialect that sounded strange to the villagers in her new home. They nicknamed her 'mountain girl.' The nickname marked her as a non-local, an outsider" (Lui 2002:305).

Contrast this complex of subordination and isolation with situations where a new bride remains close to her kindred. Among the Cheyenne of North America, where married couples would usually reside in the immediate vicinity of the wife's mother, a married woman had ready access to support from her mother, father, and brothers. In one case, "a husband was beaten by members of his wife's family for his previous violence against the woman. The family then kept the woman with them for some time until her brother finally decided that the husband should be given another chance. He warned the man, however, that he himself would fight alongside his sister should there be further trouble in the marriage; the woman's mother also threatened the man. In fact, the couple thereafter lived in peace" (Baumgartner 1984:121–22, summarizing Llewellyn & Hoebel 1941:182–83).

In chapter 3, I discussed the evidence that suicide is often concentrated around the margins of social networks, rendering those with fewer and weaker attachments more vulnerable to self-destruction. There are several plausible psychological mechanisms for this relationship. Durkheim, for instance, posited a human need for attachment, and many readers will know from personal experience that loneliness is a source of psychological pain. Aside from these, there is also a major sociological mechanism: the effect of isolation on third-party support. All else being equal, someone with fewer and weaker ties is less likely to attract support and so is more likely to turn to suicide when faced with a conflict. We can see this in cases where marriage cuts women off from their closest ties and places them on the margins of a new social network, and we can see it in other scenarios as well. For example, among the Aguaruna Jívaro, men spend their lives cultivating political alliances, such that older males have a much wider network of potential supporters than do younger males. Men's tendency to commit suicide thus varies across the life course: "Adult men respond to conflict by redefining themselves socially through the mobilization of a supportive faction that can respond to opposition through public debate or, in extreme cases, violence," while "young single men" who "cannot back up their threats by mobilizing a group of kinsmen or spurring them to action" are much more likely to respond to conflict by committing suicide, especially if they are in conflict with an older man (Brown 1986:319).

Third-party behavior provides another reason why, as sociologist Wilfred Masumura (1977; see also chapter 3) suggested, isolation could have a greater impact in societies with higher overall social integration. In a setting where more people are enmeshed in networks of close ties, the most marginal people are more likely to find themselves in conflict with someone who is much more integrated; thus the isolate is likely to lack support, while also facing opposition from the supporters of his or her adversary. Indeed, a modern observer might be surprised by the gap between relational haves and have-nots in tribal and traditional settings, where widows, orphans, and other marginal people are sometimes treated with open contempt. Among the Maenge of New Guinea, orphans have no one to back them up in conflicts and so can be freely disrespected and are referred to as "rubbish men." While other men can organize supporters to aggressively pursue grievances, the rubbish men are likely to kill themselves (Panoff 1977).

CROSS-CUTTING TIES

Social isolation is not the only factor that undermines third-party support. Recall that the degree of partisan support that the aggrieved can expect to attract depends not only on the closeness of third parties to the aggrieved but also on their distance from the adversary. Even an aggrieved individual's close associates are unlikely to be strongly partisan if they also have close ties to the adversary. Thus even in settings where married women do not live at a distance from their own kin, they may find that the ties of interdependence between their kin and their husband rob her of their full support, especially if their husbands have high stature in the community. For example, among the Mount Hageners of New Guinea, fathers value exchange relationships with high-status individuals known as "big-men." In one case, "A woman returned to her parents to be met by an angry father, who expostulated: 'No! You must go back to your husband! I do not want to have a divorce and lose his goodwill—he is a neighbour and 'inside us' (the marriage was between two pairclans) and he is a big-man. I want to make [exchange] with and be friends with him'" (Strathern 1972:198). Similarly, Jívaro men use marriage to build alliances with one another for the purpose of defense and political advancement (Harner 1972:80–81; Taylor 1983:338; Brown 1985:42; Brown 1986). Given the high degrees of interdependence between male affines, fathers are reluctant to alienate a son-in-law by intervening on behalf of his wife. Among the Aguaruna Jívaro, "if a woman leaves her husband, he may simply ask her family to return her; they usually agree to do this unless he has treated her with the most extravagant brutality" (Brown 1985:137). And among the Bunyoro of Uganda, a father may fail to support his daughter if he has close ties to her husband. In one case, a young woman was forcibly married to one of her father's elderly friends: "She stayed with him for about a year, but as well as being old he was jealous and possessive and used to beat her, so at the end of the second year she began to run away from him. The first three times she did so her father ordered her to go back to him and she complied, weeping bitterly, my informants said. But on the fourth occasion she refused completely, and instead of returning to her husband she went into the bush and hanged herself on a tree" (Beattie 1960:150).

Social ties to both sides in a conflict lead third parties to qualify and soften their support, expressing concern for both the aggrieved and his or her adversary. This makes them prone to engage in mutually supportive peacemaking, which may be sufficient to soothe the conflict and prevent suicide. But if the aggrieved is disadvantaged in other ways, such as by facing a superior adversary, the efforts at conciliation are hard to distinguish from indifference or opposition.

SUPPORT AND SOCIAL TIME

That Jívaro kin will intervene given "extravagant brutality" illustrates another property of third-party behavior: whether third parties intervene, and whose side they will take, does not just depend on the social distance and social status of the adversaries. It also depends on the severity of the conflict (Campbell and Manning 2018:56–58). Not all conduct is equally offensive, and in any setting some actions are generally considered worse than others. As we have seen in previous chapters, Black's (2011) theory of conflict explains the severity of an offense with the degree to which it warps social space: actions that lead to sizable and rapid changes in inequality, intimacy, or other dimensions of social structure are more likely to be seen as serious deviance. His term for these changes is social time, and he proposes that the severity of a conflict is a direct function of social time.

Social time is relevant to explaining third-party reactions. Third parties are more likely to intervene when the conflict is more serious. This means that their intervention varies directly with social time, such that greater changes in status, intimacy, and so forth are more likely to provoke support for the aggrieved (Campbell and Manning 2018:56–58). The problem for many aggrieved people, especially those facing close and superior adversaries, is that structural conditions so mitigate against third-party support that it takes extreme escalation of the conflict to mobilize any intervention. Yet the third parties might inhabit a social location that, should such an extreme escalation occur, leads them to become fairly strong partisans after all. This helps explain why suicide itself can be a tool for mobilizing supporters against an adversary. For example, among the Aguaruna Jívaro, "the very kinsmen who may be unwilling to intervene on a woman's behalf when she is alive are galvanized into action when she kills herself" (Brown 1986:320). Beatings and abuse might lower someone's status, but suicide practically erases it; moving to a new homestead might weaken social ties, but suicide cuts them off entirely. Thus, while the family of an abused woman may be reluctant to intervene in a marital conflict if the offense is "merely" a beating, they may take more serious measures should the offense be driving their relative to attempt or commit suicide. It surely helps that her death also severs any marriage alliances that stayed her relatives' hand, though even without this factor suicide can succeed in mobilizing third parties—hence its sometimes successful use as a tactic of political protest. And because it provides a credible threat, a nonfatal attempt, or such gradual violence as a hunger strike, might produce the same reaction—though this requires a social structure conducive enough to intervention that lesser degrees of destruction can still mobilize supporters. Margery Wolf (1972, 1975), noting that the suicide attempts of young Taiwanese brides were mostly fatal, suggested that a nonfatal suicide attempt would be unlikely to improve the young bride's situation. Such was her degree of marginality and inferiority within the marital household, and isolation from her birth family, that anything less than death would fail to have an impact. Similarly, sociologist Michael Biggs (2005) notes that political self-immolations are rarely preceded by threats—perhaps because those attempting to rouse strangers against powerful enemies need to resort to more drastic steps to be taken seriously. To the extent that the conditions that make a behavior more effective also make it more likely, third-party location helps predict the lethality of suicidal conflict and perhaps of suicide in general.

Third Parties and Self-Conflict

Support does not only help prevent the suicide of the aggrieved; it can also help prevent the suicide of the accused. Self-execution, too, varies inversely with third-party support. For example, among the Tikopia, a man who volunteers to go on a suicide voyage because of some offense against the chief can be saved if "a man of rank" intervenes and orders him to stop, at which point the offender can "acquiesce in obedience to the command, yet with the dignity of having been prepared to expiate his offence with his life" (Firth 1967:138). Even self-executions ordered by the chief himself can be prevented if a ranking official steps in on behalf of the offender and pleads for mercy (Firth 1949:184–85).

Third parties might even intervene in conflicts between a person and his- or herself. As we saw in the last chapter, depressed and suicidal individuals often express guilt, worthlessness, and other negative evaluations of the self, and suicide can be a way of handling these grievances. And like any other conflict, people might turn to third parties for help. In the case of self-conflict, such help is likely to take the form of a healer, "a third party who intervenes in human conflict without seeming to do so at all" because their intervention "is defined as a kind of help, a treatment for someone suffering from an affliction beyond his or her control" (Black 1998:119). In many tribal and traditional settings, healers take the form of shamans, sorcerers, and witch doctors who diagnose these afflictions as the result of a supernatural curse or spiritual possession. Such supernatural healers are still common in many parts of the world today, but in wealthy industrialized countries healing is more often the province of psychiatric specialists, who understand the problem in terms of psychological disorder. Either way, the healer "combines elements of support and of settlement. Healers serve as friends to their patients, doing everything on their behalf, but at the same time they speak with authority about what is 'wrong' with the patient and what is necessary to achieve a 'cure' or 'adjustment'" (Black 1998:121).

Viewed in this light, much of what modern therapists do to help suicidal patients is a kind of conflict management, even if it is not often recognized as such. In some ways, professional therapy has a social structure similar to other forms of settlement behavior, such as legal hearings before a judge or tribal elder. Like other settlement agents, the therapist is equally distant from both "sides" of the conflict—in the case of self-conflict, because they are the same person. As educated professionals, claiming special expertise and often highly paid, modern psychiatrists and counselors usually have a social status similar to or somewhat higher than their patients. Settlement agents in general tend to have a status equal to or higher than the disputants—something important for encouraging disputants to listen to opinions and defer to their judgement (Black 1998:86). People rarely submit to the rulings of social inferiors. But therapists differ from many other settlement agents in that they are intervening in an extremely close conflict, the kind of conflict that tends to be most resistant to intervention. They also intervene in an unusually supportive way, avoiding overt moral judgments of any kind and seeking to help rather than punish. Both features are encouraged by closeness, and though professional therapists may start off as hired strangers, their work typically takes time and repeated interaction—often dozens or more sessions over a period of weeks or months, during which the patient exposes much of himself or herself to the therapist.

The help of a therapist can be an alternative to suicide and a means of preventing it. But the social structure of self-conflict creates obstacles to seeking and obtaining help. Again, extremely close conflicts tend to resist intervention, with grievances against oneself and one's closest intimates likely to be treated as private and potentially shameful matters to be hidden from other people. People with self-conflicts might not only avoid explicitly seeking or asking for help but also actively conceal their problems and hide signs of distress by maintaining a facade of normality (Heckler 1994:54–61). As one suicide attempter recalls, "There was something inside me that was just horrible or bad or needy or painful, and it didn't match the outside, because I'd always been so extroverted and everybody thought I was happy and normal and well-adjusted and I got straight A's. I was a good person, you know? I was just trying to pass for normal" (quoted in Heckler 1994:54). Many are repelled by the possible loss of stature involved in admitting to secret deviance or the need for help. Males are especially prone to this. According to one man who survived a highly lethal suicide attempt, "Did I tip anyone off as to how I was feeling? No, of course not! At six-feet-six and 240 pounds, could Big Ed admit to anyone, even himself, that he was going under?" (quoted in Heckler 1994:56). Compared to the tribal and village societies of the past, modern industrial societies are much more socially atomized places with much higher degrees of privacy. People interact as autonomous individuals and spend much greater amounts of time alone. People are generally less integrated into social networks and so are correspondingly closer to themselves. Such closeness means that their problems with themselves are more likely to attract a therapeutic style of social control, defined by themselves and others as illness and affliction rather than as wrongdoing (Black 1995:835n37; Tucker 2002). Yet the self-closeness presents a countervailing trend, reducing the likelihood that a given conflict will attract substantial intervention by therapists or other third parties. One's internal states are private, and to expose them is embarrassing—a possible source of lost respectability. Even when third parties want to help, they are often avoided.

The closeness of the conflict is not the only obstacle. It is compounded by the social distance between the aggrieved and the potential therapist. Professional therapists may grow closer to their patient during the course of therapy, but they begin as strangers, and usually it is up to the distressed individual to actively recruit their help. Prior network ties, such as a recommendation from a friend who has utilized the therapist, might be of crucial importance in bridging the social distance between a distressed individual and a potential healer. So too might other forms of support and urging. One study of suicidal college students who sought help reveals that many who did so cited the urging of friends and family—meaning that the first to intervene in their problems and define them in therapeutic terms were third parties who were much closer in social space (Downs and Eisenberg 2012). Informal therapy—the supportive helping behavior of friends and relatives—is often a prelude to formal therapy. To some extent formal and informal therapy can also be substitutes for one another. There is evidence that those with fewer supportive ties or those who live alone are more likely to utilize professional therapy, perhaps because they have few others to whom they can turn (Downs and Eisenberg 2012; compare Black 1995:835n37). But surely more self-conflicts in the modern world are handled through the intervention of friends, family, clergy, and other supporters than are handled by trained and paid therapists (Barnes, Ikeda, and Kresnow 2001). Loners might be more likely to turn to professional help rather than relying on informal help, but they are also more likely to receive no help at all and so are more likely to kill themselves.

The Structure of Survival

Let us return to the role of third parties in the act of suicide itself. Just as they might break up a fight or protect the target of an assault, people can save individuals from violence they threaten to inflict upon themselves. This is true of suicides that arise in the course of conflict as well as suicides that occur for any other reason. Third parties concerned with a potential victim's fate can prevent violence from happening, halt it once it begins, or provide medical attention to mitigate its effects. Yet third parties vary in their willingness and ability to do so, and the likelihood and lethality of suicide varies accordingly. The social location of the third party helps explain this variation as well and thus sheds light on patterns of prevention and rescue. Just as social distance facilitates indifference to someone's grievances, it can facilitate indifference to his or her life itself. When people in modern urban settings threaten to jump from tall buildings, the social distance between themselves and crowds of anonymous strangers surely contributes to the callous behavior by members of these crowds who mock the suicidal person and urge him or her to jump (Mann 1981). Marginal inferiors also attract less concern and effort relative to those with higher standing and stronger social ties. We have seen how in New Guinea's Central Highlands, members of the patrilineal kin group will do little to stop the suicide of a wife or widow. But should a man of their kin group attempt to hang himself, they will act swiftly to save him, so male hanging victims are commonly discovered and rescued before death (Berndt 1962:186–87).

Social distance and social isolation can also affect the ability of third parties to intervene even if they want to, making it less likely that they will learn that an individual is distressed, suspect that a suicide attempt is imminent, or know that an attempt has taken place. Among the !Kung San, the intense intimacy of the hunter-gatherer band means that someone else is almost always present during a suicide attempt, and because of their swift intervention suicide attempts are rarely fatal (Howell 1979:61; Lee 1979:375). The modern industrial world has much greater levels of seclusion and privacy. People routinely spend large chunks of time isolated behind closed doors, go for days without talking to close kin or friends, and come and go as they please according to idiosyncratic schedules. Even those who take slow-acting poisons may lie undiscovered by anyone who would be willing or able to help them. Some moderate the lethality of their attempt by taking steps to make it more likely they will be discovered—say, taking an overdose shortly before someone else is scheduled to arrive at their home. Others lack even this option. The effect of isolation on rescue is another mechanism contributing to the relationship between integration and suicide, and it helps explain sociologist Ronald Maris's finding that people who survive suicide attempts tend to be less isolated than those who die from them (Maris 1981:107, 114; but compare Beautrais 2001).

Pure sociology is premised on the fact that behavior varies with its social structure. Ways of managing conflict, conducting business, or exchanging information are not randomly distributed; rather, they differ in predictable ways depending on whether the people involved are equal or stratified, close or distant, interdependent or independent. The structure extends outward beyond victim and offender, buyer and seller, source and audience: it encompasses any who can learn of events and be drawn into them. Each interaction or relationship is situated within a larger network of social ties, and the social distance and social status of these people matters as well. Recognizing the role of third parties adds a level of complexity to our analysis. True, we are still able to identify simple principles that govern the behavior of third parties and thus predict the overall outcome. But when we begin to account for the variety of relationships that can contribute to conflict structure, we see more clearly the effort it can take to thoroughly and accurately describe any conflict or suicide in sociological terms. This is especially so if we recognize that various elements of a conflict structure might interact in various ways. I will consider these interactions in the conclusion.

Conclusion

Mundri, the wife of the headman Kaklur, frequently quarreled with her husband over the question of visiting her parents, and one day when she wished to go and her husband stopped her, she became so miserable that she hanged herself from a mango tree. (Elwin 1943:122)

The task of sociological theory is to identify the simple patterns underlying the rich complexity of human behavior. And a rich complexity it is. While at first glance suicide might appear to be a singular behavior, closer inspection reveals a great deal of variation, with the context and character of self-destruction differing across time and place and from one case to another. Within this variation we can discern several distinct patterns—different types and forms of suicide, at least some of which appear to be a self-destructive version of some larger family of social life.

That these larger families of social life can take on both suicidal and nonsuicidal forms is a testament to the plasticity of human behavior. However we define its most basic categories, we will see that they occur in myriad varieties—different ways of producing, mating, helping, competing, or whatever. If we take *conflict*—defining and responding to wrongs—as one of those basic categories, we see that people express their grievances in many ways, such as complaining to a superior, giving the cold shoulder, or delivering a bloody beating. All of these behaviors are instances of *conflict management*, also called *social control* (Black 1998:1–19). Conflict management can take on many other forms as well, including suicide. Suicide might be a kind of terminal withdrawal, sociologically similar to divorce or storming off in a rage. Or it may be an act of aggression, a way of using one's death to punish a wrongdoer. It may be a kind of protest, a desperate way of beseeching others for redress. It might display elements of all of these behaviors, perhaps combined with self-inflicted euthanasia. In any case, the question remains: Why did the conflict get handled in this way instead of another?

One way to answer this question is with *pure sociology*, a new strategy of explanation developed by sociologist Donald Black, a pioneer in the sociology of conflict. Pure sociology explains human behavior with the structure and motion of social space, as defined by the kinds and degrees of social distance between all people involved in an instance of social life. These vary from one conflict to the next, and their dynamic geometry predicts and explains different outcomes.

The foregoing chapters identified several features of social space that make it more likely that people involved in conflict will turn to suicide. Taken together, this is a theory of *moralistic suicide* that predicts and explains when people will handle their grievances with lethal violence against themselves. In addition to helping us explain suicide, this theory contributes to a larger body of principles that explain variation in how people handle conflict. It thus belongs alongside theories of law, lynching, genocide, terrorism, avoidance, and negotiation under the umbrella of a general theory of conflict and social control. This conclusion considers the theory of moralistic suicide in more detail, addressing how the different relationships it proposes interact with one another, how the theory helps explain related forms of conflict management, and the theory's larger implications for the study of suicide. Let us begin with a summary of the theory and the questions it answers.

The Structure of Suicide

Many suicides occur as part of a conflict. But what causes these suicidal conflicts to occur? As Black's (2011) theory of conflict tells us, conflicts erupt because of changes in social structure, such as fluctuating levels of inequality and intimacy in human relationships. People complain and fight about things like broken bonds and invasions of personal space, about being put down or having their authority undermined. These fluctuations, which Black calls *social time*, are a matter of degree. The larger and faster they are—the more drastically they alter relationships and warp the shape of social space—the more likely they are to cause conflict, and the more severe the conflict is likely to be.

Social time causes suicide as well (Black 2011:49, 76). Whatever factors predispose a person to suicide, it is often triggered by some event or series of events that alters patterns of inequality and intimacy (Manning 2015d). While any drastic change can spark conflict, only certain kinds of social time are commonly responsible for suicide, and it is these that cause most suicidal conflict. One of these dangerous fluctuations is when someone experiences downward mobility, which necessarily alters relationships of superiority and inferiority (chapter 2). When someone suffers a loss and falls below others, or when others rise to dominance, there is an increase in social stratification. Black (2011:59) calls this type of fluctuation *overstratification*, and it is particularly likely to cause suicide among the ones who experience an increase in their social inferiority—or as Black (2011:71) calls it, *overinferiority*. It might take the form of losing material wealth, like money and property, or of suffering a blow to one's reputation and losing the esteem of others, or of losing one's basic ability to function and perform various tasks. It might also come from being dominated and coerced by others. All of these kinds of downward mobility might occur independently, but they can also encourage and compound one another—for instance, losing wealth might lead to shame and loss of prestige. In any case, the greater and faster the loss, the more likely it is to cause suicide (chapter 2).

The second major cause of suicidal conflict, and of suicide in general, is the decline in intimacy that occurs when a close relationship drifts apart or ends altogether—a kind of social time that Black (2011:43) calls *underintimacy*. It too is a matter of degree, and the greater and faster the loss of intimacy, the more likely it is to cause suicide (chapter 3). The end of a marriage or intimate partnership is especially dangerous, as is the death of a spouse or close family member. The decline in closeness caused by a competing relationship, especially a competing romantic relationship, can be dangerous as well. A sudden increase in closeness, or *overintimacy* (Black 2011:21), can also cause suicide, but it seems to do so only when especially large and when combined with some kind of overstratification—as in cases of rape, forced marriage, or the sexual slavery that awaited women captured in ancient warfare (chapter 3).

These are the social events most likely to trigger suicide and are the issues most likely to be at stake in a suicidal conflict. But nothing in the social universe is influenced by a single variable alone. While the factors that spark a conflict help explain how it plays out, so too does the pattern of relationships among everyone involved in the conflict. That is, once a grievance arises, how it is handled will depend in part on its location, distance, and direction in social space. Is the grievance directed at a friend or a stranger? A superior or a subordinate? A foreigner or a countryman? Answering these questions allows us to describe the *social structure,* or *geometry,* of the conflict, and this in turn helps us explain why the same sort of grievance is sometimes handled in very different ways.

Suicide is more likely when the conflict is between people who are stratified rather than equal—that is, when the disputants have different levels of wealth, authority, reputation, and other forms of social stature. Within these conflicts it is a tool of the weak, whether a means of escape, protest, or punishment. Understood as an action directed at an adversary it is greater in upward directions than downward ones, and the greater the superiority of the adversary, the more likely suicide becomes. Suicide is not always a way of handling grievances against others, though—sometimes it is a response to an offense by the suicide victim, a kind of self-inflicted execution for one's own wrongdoing. This too is more likely in stratified conflicts and is more likely on the weaker side—as a reaction to offenses, it is more likely to punish upward ones rather than downward ones, and this disparity too grows greater as inequality increases.

The influence of the social world is not limited to the vertical relations between people—issues of status and inequality, superiority and inferiority. It also includes their horizontal relations—the distribution of intimacy and interdependence (chapter 3). Sociologists have long known that position in a social network matters, such that marginal or isolated people are at greater risk of killing themselves—whether in a conflict or over anything else. In conflict in particular, suicide is also more likely if the adversaries are socially close than if they are socially distant. *Social closeness* includes *relational closeness,* intimacy as defined by the frequency, scope, and history of interaction (Black 1976:40). Spouses and family members are generally much closer than acquaintances and strangers, and so conflicts between the former are more likely to produce suicide. This applies whether the suicide is expressing a grievance against someone else or is a reaction to the suicidal individual's own problematic behavior (chapter 3). Social closeness also includes *functional interdependence,* the degree of reliance and cooperation between people, and this too encourages conflict to turn suicidal. Whether mutual or one-sided, it hampers escape and avoidance, and where one-sided, it places the dependent in a weaker position and undermines more aggressive ways of pursuing grievances—all of which make suicide more likely.

The structure of a conflict also includes the social distance and social status of third parties (chapter 4). Third parties behave differently depending on their social location, and their actions can be fateful. As Black's (1998:125–40; Black 1995:835) theories tell us, third parties are more likely to intervene when they are closer to the disputants and when the disputants are more distant from one another. Those who do intervene are more likely to take sides when they are close to one side and distant from the other. They also tend to favor superiors over inferiors, though if the latter can successfully gain support, it will often help bolster their side and equalize the conflict. An adversary who receives support is less likely to commit suicide, but one who faces additional opposition is more likely to commit suicide. The role of supporters also goes beyond the conflicts that generate suicide to include the act of suicide itself, whatever its cause might be: the conditions that breed strong support, such as access to many close ties, often increase the chances that suicide will be prevented or suicide attempters rescued.

According to this theory, each variable—inequality, social closeness, third-party support, and social time—encourages a conflict to result in suicide. So far, we have mostly considered these relationships in isolation, looking at one factor at a time. But in reality the various influences on human behavior interact with one another. Consider the logic of these interactions in more detail.

If two factors each make suicide more likely, then when they occur together, suicide will be more likely still. While we do not have enough information to specify whether this effect is additive or multiplicative, the variables that encourage suicide are more dangerous in combination. Consider the movements of social time likely to cause suicide. One can readily find cases where suicide is preceded by both underintimacy and overstratification. For example, anthropologist Gordon M. Wilson writes of an East African man who "could see his whole world collapsing around him" when he was simultaneously subjected to marital infidelity, public humiliation, legal prosecution, and job loss (Wilson 1960:197). In his study of coroners' records in Chicago, sociologist Ronald Maris observes that self-killers commonly experienced a combination of problems like job loss, illness, and broken relationships (Maris 1981:40–69). According to Black, when multiple dimensions of social space fluctuate at once, the effect is "like one explosive substance added to another" (Black 2011:8). Extreme levels of both underintimacy and overstratification create a heightened risk of explosive violence that might involve both homicide and suicide. Consider the case of a man who committed suicide after first killing his ex-wife and eight of her relatives:

> [The killings] occurred six days after his wife finalized a divorce, which ended not only his relationship with his wife but with his stepdaughter and others in his wife's family. His wife also obtained a

court order requiring him to support her in the future, to make lump sum payments of ten thousand dollars to her, to allow her to keep the diamond wedding ring he had bought for her, and even to give her the family dog (his last remaining close companion). He had recently lost his job as well, making it difficult for him to meet expenses such as the support payments to his ex-wife, his legal fees, and his house payments. (Black 2011:8)

As Black proposes in his theory of conflict, fluctuations of social space can also interact with prior fluctuations to produce a cumulative effect: "Just as each puff of a cigarette does not result in lung cancer, so each movement of social time does not result in a conflict. And just as the likelihood of cancer increases if smoking continues, so the likelihood of conflict increases with each movement of social time" (Black 2011:5–6). This is also true of the effect of social time on suicide. Larger and faster losses are most dangerous, but risk increases with a continuous sequence of smaller ones. An investigator of suicide in early twentieth-century Seattle thus made a distinction between cases due to "immediate crises" and those due to "cumulative crises" involving "an accumulation of difficulties over a relatively long period of time" (Schmidt 1928:70). And Maris notes that it was common for self-killers in his Chicago sample to have a long history of vertical and relational losses stemming from injury, illness, addiction, and interpersonal conflicts—a pattern of gradual erosion that he refers to as a "suicidal career" (Maris 1981:xvii). Considering suicidal conflict in particular, we can see cases where the immediate cause was a relatively minor fluctuation, a grievance over something that most observers would find trivial.[1] Yet if we look deeper, we often find a history of grievances accumulating over time, the conflict growing in severity with each new offense. Writing of the "trivial" grievances that lead many young Chuukese to kill themselves, author Francis X. Hezel notes that "behind most of these single trivial incidents that immediately preceded suicides lies a tale of long-standing family tensions and conflicts" (Hezel 1984:197). Thus many apparently minor conflicts are but the latest in an ongoing series, with the most recent grievance being the straw that breaks the camel's back.[2] In this history of conflict, the aggrieved might employ several different forms of social control before turning to self-destruction. For instance, clinical psychologist David K. Curran reports that adolescent suicide in the United States typically follows a series of escalating conflicts with parents, in which the adolescent first engages in "rebellion" (i.e., argument and noncooperation) before turning to "withdrawal" (i.e., avoidance within the household), then perhaps "running away," and finally suicide (Curran 1987:64–65).

These ideas have testable implications. One is based on the notion that larger and faster movements of social time are more likely to be a sufficient cause of suicide, even in the absence of any other movements. We would thus expect cases stemming from more drastic losses of status—say, a wealthy investor's fortune is rapidly destroyed in a financial collapse—to be less likely to involve underintimacy as well and also less likely to follow a history of repeated small losses. The fatal fall might even occur after a prolonged period of upward mobility, marking a drastic reversal in fortune (Black 2011:74–76; Davies 1962). Contrariwise, cases where the immediate trigger was a smaller degree of downward mobility should be more likely to involve underintimacy and a prior history of downward movements. We can apply the same logic to cases where the suicide was sparked by a large degree of underintimacy versus those that appear to involve smaller degrees, expecting that suicide cases involving the latter are more likely to also involve downward mobility and a cumulative history of lost social connections.

Again, how a grievance is handled depends not just on the events that sparked it but also on the social environment in which it occurs. Each structural element conducive to suicide is a matter of degree, as conflicts can be more or less close, more or less stratified, and so forth. All else being equal, the greater the degree of each variable, the more likely suicide becomes. And as with social time, the risk is even greater when they occur in combination. Suicidal conflicts are concentrated in relationships that combine inequality, intimacy, and interdependence, such as relations between parents and children or between husbands and wives in patriarchal households. But since each factor can vary independently and each has its own influence on suicide, a sufficient degree of one might overshadow the influence of another. For instance, a high degree of inequality might counteract the effect of a low degree of social closeness, while a high degree of closeness might compensate for a low degree of inequality. Again, this has implications for the patterns of structure we would expect to observe in samples of suicidal conflict. Conflicts between adversaries that are more relationally distant will tend to involve higher levels of inequality than those between adversaries that are highly intimate. Likewise suicidal conflicts between social equals will tend to involve greater intimacy than those between people of drastically different ranks. And the more that a conflict structure is conductive to suicide—the more unequal, intimate, and so forth—the smaller the degree of social time needed to provoke a suicidal conflict. Contrariwise, suicidal conflicts with apparently minor causes are more likely to have multiple elements of the suicide structure present in high degrees.

Patterns of Suicidal Conflict

We can go beyond using the theory to address the overall risk of suicide, or which pattern of structure and motion we should expect to see when comparing suicide cases. We can also ask how different combinations of these variables affect the form and patterning of suicidal conflict. Even if they both produce suicide, conflicts between intimate equals and stratified strangers tend to differ in many ways. The exact patterning of suicidal conflict—the specific nature of the grievances, the history of moves and countermoves, and the particular form of self-destruction—will vary across different structural configurations. The possible combinations are endless, but in empirical reality some configurations of social space and time are much more common than others, and so are the patterns of suicidal conflict they produce. Consider three common scenarios.

DISTANT DOMINATION

The first pattern involves conflicts with a low amount of social closeness but a very high degree of social stratification. The aggrieved has no personal, face-to-face relationship with the adversary, who might be an organization rather than an individual or a political leader known only from news media. But the relational distance goes along with vertical distance, and the adversary is vastly superior—a powerful corporation, national government, or the leaders in charge of such.

Compared to close conflicts, distant conflicts are more likely to be collective affairs. They are more likely to produce many people taking sides and intervening as partisans, as well as the collective liability that holds an entire social group responsible for wrongdoing (Black 1998:56–57; Senechal de la Roche 1996, 2001). When they involve governments or other large organizations whose actions affect the lives of many individuals, they are also likely to produce widespread grievances shared by large numbers of people. Suicidal conflict with distant superiors thus tends to be part of a larger campaign of protest and political struggle that seeks justice on behalf of some social group. The grievances usually have to do with dominance and coercion and, compared to other suicidal conflicts, are more likely to also involve cultural grievances such as state suppression of religious expression.

Suicide is not usually the first resort in these conflicts. It tends to emerge after the adversary has taken steps to repress other protest activity, further exercising its dominance. For example, protest suicides by Vietnamese monks and nuns began after a series of demonstrations, including some in which protestors were killed by government forces (Biggs 2005, 2013). Prior to his self-immolation, Korean labor activist Jeon Tae-il attempted to organize a labor union, failing due to opposition from government and business owners. He also collected and disseminated information on brutal working conditions and hoped to further raise public awareness by staging a large public rally, but this effort too was quashed by the authorities—at which point he publicly burned himself. And the contemporary rash of Tibetan protest suicides began after the Chinese government successfully quelled anti-Chinese riots in Tibet and subjected Tibetan monasteries to increased surveillance and patriotic reeducation (Morrison 2013; Shakya 2012).

In collective conflict, protest suicide is not only an act of moralism, the protester expressing grievances against an adversary, but also an act of partisanship, with the protestor sacrificing his or her life on behalf of others (see Manning 2015c). Like other acts of partisanship, it is encouraged by closer ties to one side than the other (Black 1998:126). One implication is that there is an element of truth in Durkheim's theory of altruistic suicide: fatal self-sacrifice is an extreme act of partisanship and most likely on behalf of individuals and groups to whom one is closely tied. In this sense, social ties—and hence integration into a social group—do facilitate altruistic self-sacrifice. At the same time, however, the weight of evidence suggests that higher social integration generally make suicide less likely. The result of these two countervailing relationships is that suicidal protestors tend to be integrated in some ways but not in others (Manning 2015c). They are rarely social isolates and are usually members of organizations that provide the main basis for political protest, such as monasteries, labor unions, or student activist groups. Yet they are also relatively detached in other ways, tending to be single and childless and perhaps cloistered away from the rest of society. Many are monks, nuns, or college students. We might also expect most who sacrifice themselves to be relatively marginal within their activist organizations: the elderly Thich Quang Duc of Vietnam was initially ignored by the movement's younger leadership in part because he was, in the words of one leader, "just some bothersome old monk disturbing me in the middle of a hectic situation" (Chanoff and Van Toai 1986:141).

As sociologist Michael Biggs observes, based on his database of several hundred political self-immolations, suicide protest is least likely in both the most democratic and most autocratic regimes, being more frequent in authoritarian states somewhere between these two extremes (Biggs 2012:145).

It is rarer in more democratic regimes because domination is less severe than in more authoritarian ones, and protest suicide is encouraged by a highly superior adversary and the repression of other protest activity. But if the adversary is too dominant, protest activity of all kinds tends to decline. Protest by its nature is aimed at persuading, if not the adversary, then at least third parties. Protest and persuasion flourish where adversaries are not so superior, and their domination so complete, as to make partisanship against them nearly unthinkable (Campbell and Manning 2018:50–56). Too distant, too superior, and protest of any kind is as unlikely as it is ineffective. The machinations of genocidal dictators and imperial invaders might drive many to suicide, but such deaths are rarely part of a protest campaign. Protest suicide is most likely where status relations make collective action and popular partisanship difficult but not impossible. They are thus also encouraged by ready access to masses of spectators, strangers whose support is not automatic but who can witness the event and come to sympathize with the aggrieved. Protest suicide thrives in modern urban settings, especially in a world connected by modern mass media, where thousands or millions can learn of the sacrifice. Aimed as much at fellow members of the aggrieved group as at the adversary, protest suicides can inspire further activism and struggle, including further suicide. Thus protest suicides often occur in waves.

CLOSE RUPTURE

A second pattern of suicidal conflict involves a low degree of inequality but a very high degree of social closeness. Such a structure is increasingly common in marriages and cohabiting partnerships in the modern West. Both parties are extensively involved with one another: they live together, eat together, sleep together, and relax together. They have a monogamous sexual relationship and have been together for years. They usually have their own dwelling, separate from their respective families, shielding them from daily contact with other intimates who might compete for time and attention. Neither is much superior to the other. Perhaps one has greater income, but both have other resources to fall back on. One may be physically stronger and more aggressive, but neither has any substantial authority. Law and custom grant both equal rights, including the right to end the relationship. They are relationally close and vertically close as well.

Closeness does not necessarily mean harmony. Intimacy might encourage toleration of any given offense, but it also provides many more opportunities for offenses to occur. Conflict is inevitable, and grievances can accumulate over time. Furthermore, some offenses are less tolerable than others. The most severe conflicts among intimates tend to be those over intimacy it-self—the grievances that arise when closeness declines. Conflict itself might be the source of these declines, as an unhappy spouse handles marital prob-lems by reducing contact, perhaps terminating the relationship altogether. Yet an act of social control can also be deviance, and the end of a relationship leads to severe conflict. Abandoned partners rarely take the loss in stride: they might cry and complain or beg and plead. They might attempt to ne-gotiate an alternative or shout bitter recriminations, including accusations of betrayal and disloyalty. They might turn to third parties, gossiping and seeking consolation from friends and family. Defining their own reactions as deviant, or at least undesirable, they seek the help of a therapist or numb themselves with intoxicating drugs. Sometimes they become violent against the estranged partner who they see as wronging them. Sometimes they be-come violent against themselves. Sometimes they do both.

Violent reactions are not the most common outcome. Most breakups and divorces lead to neither homicide nor suicide. But though the extreme out-comes are rare, the rupture of a close relationship makes them much more likely than they would be otherwise and is a common scenario behind their occurrence. It accounts for most homicides in which men kill women and the vast majority in which a person commits homicide and suicide together. It lies behind a large proportion of all suicides—in some places, the large majority. And in places like modern America, where women are more likely to initiate separation and divorce, close rupture looms larger in the suicide of men.[3]

The nature of the suicide, the way it is carried out, the language and logic used by the self-killer—all of this varies from case to case. Some abandoned partners seem mostly concerned with ending their grief, and their suicides are behaviorally similar to those who kill themselves when mourning the death of a loved one. Perhaps they are also phenomenologically similar. But being actively rejected probably produces different subjective reactions, and it can certainly produce behavioral differences. Some who kill themselves in such circumstances express anger and hostility toward the one who left them. They may mix this with expressions of forgiveness or even guilt for their part in the decline of the relationship, or they may pour out one-sided blame and vitriol. In choosing their last words and manner of death, some take obvious steps to inflict guilt, shame, and horror upon the one who hurt them.

These suicides do not lead to much involvement by third parties. Even when hostile, the sanctions they inflict are mostly psychological rather than social. A close and exclusive relationship might be conducive to inflicting guilt, but it is not conducive to attracting high levels of outside involvement.

Nor are the scattered and anemic families of the modern West prone to collective action. And even if they were, the law gives them little option, deterring private vengeance and rarely concerning itself with suicides beyond confirming they are not murders. If the family of the deceased blames the surviving partner, they are unlikely to do much more than gossip or shun a person who would have had little future contact with them anyway. They may also blame themselves, wondering what they could have done to prevent the death. One way or another, liability for suicide extends beyond the perpetrator and ensnares others, contributing to the "special grief" of those who have lost intimates to suicide (Pangrazzi 2019).

CLOSE DOMINATION

A third pattern of suicidal conflict takes place in relationships that are intimate but highly unequal. Such is the case in highly patriarchal marriages, especially those in settings where law and custom formally grant the husband and his kin rights over his wife's person and property. The parties share many sources of closeness common to married couples—living together, having sexual intercourse, and sharing an enduring a socially recognized bond. But they are far from equal, and one party clearly dominates the other. The domination is often violent, as the husband, and perhaps members of his kin group, can use violence without fear of consequence. The wife has few resources of her own and little ability to live independently of her husband. She has few rights she can claim or supporters she can rally. She has little freedom to exit the relationship, just as she had little choice in entering it.

Inequality is a kind of social distance—vertical distance—and exists in tension with relational closeness. Highly stratified couples tend to be less intimate than egalitarian ones (Black 2018). In the most patriarchal societies, women and men spend most of their days apart in separate spheres and may even eat their meals separately. If it is an arranged marriage, the two might not have had much interaction prior to the wedding. In the tribal and traditional settings where this sort of relationship is most common, married couples live not in isolation but surrounded by at least one spouse's kin. In the most patriarchal settings this tends to be the husband's family, and their proximity and intimacy encourage their involvement in the marriage. Unfortunately for the wife, their involvement tends to further her subordination. In conflicts with her husband, they are likely to support his patriarchal rights and dismiss her complaints. The kindred may even be the main source of conflict, with her husband acting as a partisan supporter in favor of his kin.

Given the basic inequality of the relationship, acts of dominance are expected. Giving orders, imposing restrictions, verbally berating and physically punishing—these things do not arouse the same concern as if they had occurred among equals. Even the wife might agree in abstract that these are right and proper, though she objects when she views her own treatment as unfair or excessive. This is the main source of grievances that will lead to suicide. The conflict escalates, and suicide becomes more likely, as discipline and dominance become more frequent and extreme—excessive and capricious even by local standards. Such escalation can occur over a long period of time, but for most wives in hierarchical marriages, the risk is greatest early on, when they are first subjected to more domination than they experienced at home, and when changing households has left them with perhaps the lowest levels of social integration and social support that they will ever experience.

Suicide is not the first or only option. A wife might run away or try to rouse supporters to help her. But while these conflicts are more prone to outside intervention than are marital conflicts in atomized and egalitarian settings, in many ways they are still resistant. People outside the local kin group, including the wife's own natal family, are unlikely to forcefully intervene in the close hierarchy of the relationship. Family business is family business, wives ought to obey husbands, and mere marital problems are not worth hostility between family groups. It takes a large distortion of social space to convert potential partisanship into kinetic partisanship. Suicide offers the wife escape and also provides a means of escalating the conflict to the point where outsiders will step into action against her adversaries. It is escape and vengeance in one. In settings where her situation is common, the reaction will be common as well, and there may even be cultural rules about how it is to be carried out to make its moralistic nature clear to all witnesses.

Another version of this scenario occurs between youth and parents. Here the structure is similar—close hierarchy and imbalance of third-party ties— but the pattern of conflict differs. There is none of the shocking downward mobility that comes from entering a new and subordinate position. The youth has always been subordinate and is certainly no more inferior to the parent than earlier in childhood. Herein lies the source of conflict. Adolescence might not lead to greater parent-child conflict in every culture, but neither is it unique to the modern United States. Maturation means greater strength, skill, and knowledge, a rising position along several dimensions of social status. Acts of domination that were once accepted are now questioned, and this questioning is an offense that begets further dominance. So goes the cycle of discipline and rebellion, exacerbated by attempts to enforce or subvert independence. And where the hierarchy is strict, dependence is high, and outside supporters are unavailable, the escalating cycle of conflict is a common cause of youth suicide.

HYBRID PATTERNS

The three patterns described above are but common clusters of variation. They are not discrete entities but rather a range of values centered around the intersection of several continua. Thus we can see intermediate types that blend elements of more than one pattern. Sometimes these might be common enough to merit their own labels. For instance, in my Louisville study, several cases involving male victims combined elements of close domination and egalitarian rupture. In this pattern, which we might call *failed domination,* a man has a history of coercive violence toward his wife or girlfriend. But despite these attempts at coercive control, the abused partner retained enough social and economic resources to successfully defy him, leaving the relationship and perhaps mobilizing law and other third parties against her abuser—who then turns to suicide. We thus see a pattern of escalating abuse that culminates in the suicide not of the abused but of the abuser.

Each variable that encourages suicide is a matter of degree, and so too is each pattern of suicide described above. The fine-grained variation in suicidal conflict occurs both within and between each major pattern. There is also variation that cuts across all these categories, including variation in the nature and severity of moralism.

MORALISM AS A MATTER OF DEGREE

While we might use the term "moralistic" to refer broadly to any behavior that handles grievances, not every way of handling conflict puts an equal emphasis on the language and logic of morality. Social control varies in the extent to which it involves a concern with formal rules of conduct, decisive judgments about right and wrong, overt condemnation of deviance, and explicit appeals to justice. In this sense moralism is a variable, one that increases as social control grows more formalistic, decisive, punitive, and coercive (Black 1998:145–49). According to Black, moralism increases as social distance increases (Black 1998:144). Closer social control tends to be less concerned with condemning a violation of the rules than with resolving a problem and is more likely to involve a diffusion of blame rather than a clear-cut distinction between offender and victim.

Social closeness encourages moralism to take the form of suicide, but it also encourages the moralistic aspects of suicide to be relatively muted.

While more individuals kill themselves over egalitarian rupture than over distant domination, the moralistic aspects of the latter are more obvious than the former. People who kill themselves to express political grievances often articulate exactly what wrongdoing they wish to combat, what legal or ethical rules it violates, and what steps their adversaries and supporters should take to remedy the situation. The same goes for protestors who use less lethal kinds of self-destruction, such as hunger strikes or self-mutilation. They make the moralistic nature of their actions clear, though perhaps unsympathetic observers—including their adversaries—will deem their actions the result of mental disorder.

People who resort to self-destruction in intimate conflicts, on the other hand, are less likely to be so explicitly moralistic. They are less prone to framing their adversary's conduct as a violation of rules, are less likely to make explicit demands, and tend not to use the language of justice. Attempted suicide may function much like a protest and may succeed in winning concessions for the aggrieved. But it does so without employing the rhetoric of protest, and indeed attempters and their sympathizers may bridle at the notion that the attempt was "manipulative." Close conflicts attract the language and logic of therapy, so perhaps only an unsympathetic observer would attribute the action to anything *but* mental disorder.

Punishment—the infliction of pain and deprivation—is a variable feature of moralism and of suicide as well. Most who kill themselves, including many of those who kill themselves over conflicts, do not seem to be trying to punish anyone. Their words and deeds suggest rather that they are mostly concerned with fleeing an adversary or otherwise ending their own suffering. But we have seen that some people do express the notion that their death is a way of hurting someone, and some take steps to maximize the suffering it inflicts. Perhaps most extreme are cases in which committing suicide in a culturally stereotyped fashion can plausibly lead to vengeance killings, torture by legal officials, or banishment from the community.

Social distance is again relevant, but so too is inequality. Punishment increases with social distance but also declines in upward directions. The result is that the extremes of punishment are found neither in cases of distant domination (where there is maximal distance but also inferiority) nor in cases of egalitarian rupture (where this is minimal inferiority but also distance) but in cases of close domination. This is especially so because, empirically, this pattern of conflict tends to occur in tribal and traditional settings where marriage links together different kinship groups, such as clans or lineages, each internally solidary and correspondingly distant from outsiders

(Manning 2015a). The combination of closeness and distance is conducive to punitive suicide.

Across the universe of suicidal conflicts, both the most distant and the least distant tend to be less moralistic. The least distant tend to be less moralistic because closeness makes right and wrong lose their clarity. Even many of those who express blame and condemnation in their last words seem to be merely taking half-hearted parting shots, and they are likely to mix blame with absolution. The most distant tend to be less moralistic because they involve the most superior adversaries. As we move outward and upward, we find punishment increasing until it gives way to protest and beyond that to simple flight. Distant superiors such as invading empires might be able to provoke mass suicides, but they attract little in the way of suicidal protest or punishment. For those they conquer and target for extermination, death is mainly an escape. The same is true of many of the closest conflicts as well, including those in which someone dies to escape from him- or herself (Baumeister 1990).

SUICIDE ATTACKS

We have seen that suicide can be a moralistic action in its own right—that through various mechanisms, it can be a means of protest or punishment. As such, it can be an alternative to acts of interpersonal violence—to punishing an enemy by directly using force against him or her. But suicide can also occur alongside interpersonal violence, and acts of violent aggression against another person might involve more or less self-destruction.

In chapter 3 we considered cases of homicide-suicide, in which an aggrieved person kills both his adversary and himself. These involve a kind of joint reaction in which a conflict produces both homicide and suicide. Often both acts are planned in advance, and it may be useful in many cases to view the suicidal component as primary—having "been driven" to suicide, the suicidal individual first takes vengeance on the one he blames for this state. But there are other mixtures of suicide and homicide where self-destruction seems a secondary or indirect consequence of inflicting violence on another person. Consider such suicidal attacks as the suicide bombings of modern terrorists, who detonate explosives concealed on their bodies as a way of killing their enemies, or of Japan's kamikaze pilots in World War II, who flew explosive-laden airplanes into enemy ships at the cost of their own lives.

The theory of suicide in this book specifies a conflict structure in which suicide is more likely than alternatives. It can also help us understand when suicide becomes mixed with alternatives, such as when suicide and homicide occur together or when methods of attack involve an element of self-destruction. The key is to understand that when pure sociologists specify which conflict structures lead to this outcome or that, we are talking about the way in which patterns of behavior are distributed across a range of social conditions.

We can imagine a multidimensional space where each point is a different combination of inequality, intimacy, and so forth. This is the distribution of conflict structures. Within it conflicts that have similar structures are closer to one another, and those with very different structures are distant from one another. Blackian theory is premised on the idea that forms of conflict management are not randomly distributed across conflict structures: the more similar the structure of two conflicts, the more similar the behaviors they produce. Thus there will be a region in this distribution of structures where lynching is more frequent than it is elsewhere, a region where negotiated compromise is more frequent than it is elsewhere, and so forth. The key to explaining variation in conflict management is to map this distribution, and Blackian theories of lynching, negotiation, and so on do exactly that.

But remember that we are dealing with variables, and everything is a matter of degree. My theory of suicide specifies a region in the distribution of conflict structures where suicide is more likely than it is elsewhere. It is a region, not a point, and the different patterns of suicide described above concentrate at different areas within this larger region. As we approach its boundaries, we find social structures that are less and less conducive to suicide but more and more conducive to one or more of its alternatives. And like an estuary where fresh and saltwater mix, we will find a range of social structures conducive to hybrid behaviors that combine elements of self-destruction with some other kind of reaction, such as terrorist attacks. A theory that describes the structural habitat of suicide thus helps us map the location of related behaviors.

For example, somewhere between the conflict structures most conducive to pure homicide and those most conducive to pure suicide lies a range of structures where both their probabilities ebb, while the probability of homicide-suicide grows. In chapter 3, for instance, I argued that the conflicts leading to homicide-suicide between intimate partners are similar to those that produce either homicide or suicide alone but with an intermediate degree of relational closeness. Not all intimate partners are equally intimate, and the relative likelihood of these three behaviors varies accordingly. There are other ways in which the structural habitat of homicide and suicide can overlap. Increase the superiority of the aggrieved, and pure homicide becomes more likely and pure suicide less likely. Increase their inferiority, and the opposite occurs. Again, we should expect the hybrid behavior to be relatively more frequent in between the extremes—more common in cases of failed domination than in cases of extreme domination or egalitarian rupture.

Suicide attacks, including suicide terrorism, also involve conflicts that contain at least some features conducive to self-destruction, though combined with features that are much more conducive to interpersonal violence (Manning 2015c). For instance, suicide attacks tend to cross greater degrees of social distance than does the typical protest suicide. While protest suicide often involves grievances against domestic leaders, suicide terrorism (and terrorism more generally) tends to cross the vast distances between foreign populations that differ in language, ethnicity, and religion (Black 2004a). The same goes for suicide attacks in the course of warfare, such as Japan's kamikaze missions against the US Navy. On the other hand, suicide attacks share with protest suicide a stratified structure and upward direction. They too are a weapon of the weak, aimed at enemies with greater wealth, organization, and military capabilities (Manning 2015c).[4]

Again, everything is a matter of degree, and the structural distributions of different behaviors can overlap. Though protest suicide and suicide attack tend not to occur in the same conflicts, sometimes they do (Biggs 2005:183). Indeed, a large-scale conflict will usually generate multiple reactions, some peaceful and some violent, perhaps with varying degrees of self-destruction. This is especially so for a long-running conflict, where we can see the relative frequency of behaviors change as the dynamics of the conflict alter its social structure. For instance, as one side wins victories and gains a decisive advantage, its superiority grows and its adversary becomes increasingly inferior. Thus conventional attacks by the losers might give way to suicide attacks. Such was the case for Japan during World War II, which resorted to suicide attacks by planes, boats, and submersibles only after the destruction of its naval forces gave its enemies overwhelming military superiority (Hill 2005; Lewis 2012:59–60). Similarly, the Kurdistan Workers Party, or PKK, a Kurdish separatist group in Turkey, had long used nonsuicidal attacks but began to make more frequent use of suicide bombing after successful assaults by the Turkish government left it substantially weakened (Pedahzur 2005:89–91). A further blow to the organization, the capture of its leader, led to a rash of self-immolations by supporters. As the organization weakened, the progression was thus from attacks to suicide attacks to pure protest suicide.

The theory of moralistic suicide specifies a core range of conflict structures in which we are most likely to see the conflict handled by suicide as such. This range overlaps with that of other forms of social control: of protest, of homicide, of terrorism and violent rebellion. In this way my theory and other Blackian theories of social control dovetail together into a single body of ideas capable of predicting and explaining how conflicts are handled—a general theory of conflict (Black 1998:1). But the theory in this book serves a second master. As a theory of suicidal conflict, it is relevant not just to the sociology of conflict but also to the sociology of suicide.

The Pure Sociology of Suicide

The theory outlined in this book employs a distinctive strategy of explanation—the sociological paradigm known as Blackian or pure sociology (Black 1995). Because of this, it differs from conventional theories in several ways that allow it to explain kinds of variation that previous theories do not.

UNITS OF ANALYSIS

Consider first the unit of analysis of the theory. In social science methodology, a *unit of analysis* is the type of thing being compared—such as whether our theories and observations deal with differences between one person and another, one organization and another, or one interaction and another. For most conventional theories of suicide, the focus is on the individual person, and the main question is why some types of people are more likely to commit or attempt suicide. This is obviously so for psychological theories that explain suicide with depression, hopelessness, and other internal factors. Less often recognized is that the individual is also the main concern of much sociological thought as well. For all of Durkheim's insistence that he was explaining the "social suicide rate" rather than why individuals kill themselves, his theory of suicide is nonetheless individualistic in logic and application (Black 2000:344; compare Durkheim [1987] 1951:297–325; Berk 2006). Thus for each of his sociological variables he provides a psychological account of how it motivates the individual to commit suicide, whether this is due to an inability to justify one's life without attachment to something greater or the frustration of having one's passions overly stimulated or violently choked. And he uses these ideas to explain such things as why suicide varies according to marital status, parenthood, or organizational rank. Most subsequent applications of his theory are also concerned with such differences. True, some applications are concerned with differences across collectivities—such as predicting that nations or states with higher divorce rates have higher suicide rates—and this may appear to make the theory collectivistic, something that explains the properties of groups as such. But the locus of the explanation remains the individual, who is either too integrated or not integrated enough, too regulated or not regulated enough.

Pure sociological theories are different. Neither individualistic nor collectivistic, they explain behavior with the social structure of the behavior itself. Is social control upward or downward? Does it cross long distances or short ones? Thus the locus of explanation in Blackian theories of conflict management is neither the person nor the society but the conflict structure.

This allows pure sociological theories to explain variation that conventional approaches do not address. As Black (2004b) argues, not even the most violent people are violent all of the time, in every interaction. And if we look within even the most violent societies, we will see that violence happens only in certain times and places. This applies to self-inflicted violence as well. Whatever predisposes a person to handle a conflict with suicide, he or she does not handle every conflict in this manner. And even in societies where suicide is a culturally accepted way of handling conflict, only a fraction of conflicts lead to it. Only a theory focused on the properties of conflicts can explain variation across them.

Though the conflict structure is the locus of explanation, a theory of suicide structures can be applied to other units of analysis as well. Just as we might apply an individualistic theory to explaining group differences— for example, by expecting societies with more unintegrated people to have higher suicide rates—so too can we apply pure sociological theory. If we can infer something about the distribution of conflict structures across societies—say, that highly patriarchal societies tend to have more close, stratified conflicts—we can predict differences in the frequency and patterning of suicide. Similarly, if we can infer who is most likely to find him- or herself in certain conflict structures, we can make predictions about how suicide varies across certain types of individuals—such as women in patriarchal societies having elevated rates of suicide or marital conflict accounting for most female suicide in these settings or female suicide rates in these settings peaking at the age of first marriage.

Blackian theories are not necessarily incompatible with theories that use conventional approaches. A theory that explains variation across individuals and one that explains variation across conflicts could both simultaneously be true. For instance, if low integration encourages suicide, then—holding other elements of the conflict structure constant—suicide should vary inversely with the integration of the aggrieved. The same might be said for psychological or biological characteristics, such as a ruminating thought style or genetic predisposition to depression. It may well be that personal characteristics make some more sensitive than others to the structural conditions of suicide. But the reverse can also be true, and the right structural conditions can increase the likelihood of suicide when individual characteristics are held constant.

We might go even go further: some of what we usually consider individual characteristics can also be understood as elements of the conflict structure. In chapter 3, we addressed social integration as a location in social space, and this is indeed how Black conceptualizes it. In *The Behavior of Law*, he describes integration as location in radial space, with some closer to the center and others closer to the edge (Black 1976:48–49). In this conception, integration is not just a property of persons, or even of groups, but of social life. Conflicts can be more or less centrally located, depending on how integrated the parties are. And grievances can have a distance and direction in radial space: they might be inward, by a marginal person against a more integrated person, or outward, by an integrated person toward a more marginal one (Black 1976:49–53). Viewed in this light, the social integration of the aggrieved person is but a partial description of the conflict structure—we also need to consider the integration of his or her adversary. Differences in integration can behave like a form of social status, and like those facing wealthier or more reputable adversaries, those facing more integrated adversaries are often at a disadvantage. As we saw in chapter 4, one reason for this is differential closeness to third parties and the effects this can have on their intervention and support. Not only is pure sociology able to incorporate insights from Durkheimian theory, but in doing so it suggests new ways of understanding them and new avenues for research.

The same goes for other traditional sociological concepts. Sociologists have long studied vertical mobility, and Durkheim made its impact the centerpiece of his theory of anomic suicide. We might understand vertical mobility as a characteristic of individual persons, something one person experiences and another does not. For the sake of convenience, chapter 2 often discussed vertical mobility in these conventional terms. But we can also understand vertical mobility in Blackian terms as a fluctuation in social inequality, a change in the social structure of an interaction or relationship (Black 2011:59). The new conception focuses our attention on different sorts of variation—such as the situational changes in inequality that occur when one person rises over another—and suggests new hypotheses and avenues for study. The degree to which vertical mobility warps relationships of equality, superiority, and inferiority may prove crucial to a better understanding of its impact and making more specific predictions about its effects.

THE BEHAVIOR OF SOCIAL LIFE

Pure sociology does not only differ from conventional approaches in its explanatory variables. It also differs in how it conceives of the thing being explained. In pure sociology, what we might otherwise understand as the actions and decisions of individuals are reconceptualized as the behavior of some form of social life (Black 1995). For example, Black's (1976) theory of law predicts and explains the behavior of law as such—where and when governmental social control will be greater or lesser, more punitive or more compensatory. Law is treated as a natural phenomenon, like gravity or electricity, which predictably varies with its immediate environment. The actions and decisions of individuals are but aspects of the behavior of law. This is not merely a difference in labels. The conceptual leap is what allows a single proposition, such as Black's idea that *law varies directly with relational distance,* to predict and explain the actions of numerous individuals taking distinct roles in the application of law (Black 1976:40–46; Black 1989:12; Black 1995:832). Because calling the police is an increase in the involvement of law in a conflict, Black's principle explains why some crime victims (such as those victimized by strangers) are more likely than others (such as those victimized by intimates) to call the police. If we compare cases where police have been notified, the same principle predicts their behavior as well: in cases where the offender is present, it tells us when the police are more likely to make an arrest as opposed to merely providing a warning or ordering the offender to leave the scene. If we look at cases that result in arrest, the relational distance principle also helps predict when prosecutors will bring charges or when they will bring more severe ones. Among cases that go to trial, this principle explains when judges and juries will decide to convict and how much punishment they will apply. And it can even predict and explain the behavior of the accused, such as when they are likely to apply law to themselves by pleading guilty (Black 1998:65–72). Victim and offender, police and prosecutors, judges and juries—each might perceive the situation differently and have their own unique motives and reasons for making their decisions. But the beauty of pure sociology is that we do not need a separate theory of decision making for each of these actors—we only need a theory of the behavior of law (Black 1995:860).

The typical suicide does not involve the same number and diversity of social actors as does the typical legal case. But a theory of the behavior of suicide can also explain the actions of more than just the suicidal individual. For instance, the conditions that encourage self-execution explain not just when some offenders spontaneously choose to take their own lives but also when an aggrieved party will encourage or demand that they do so. And they explain when third parties will also allow or encourage them in this act, perhaps even praising it as the honorable thing to do. The structure is conducive to the pattern of social life itself, and that pattern is manifested in the behavior of various individuals.[5] It might also be manifested in the actions of organizations. Organizations can file lawsuits and bring criminal charges, and so Black's (1976) theory of law predicts their behavior as well as that of individuals. A pure sociology of suicide can similarly apply to violent self-destruction by organizations. The conflict structure conducive to suicide might lead an organization to sacrifice one or more of its members—as when activist monks in Vietnam helped plan and orchestrate the suicide of Thich Quang Duc, even tossing him matches when his gasoline-soaked lighter failed to ignite (Biggs 2005). Or it might lead to the destruction of the entire group in a mass suicide, such as when besieged rebels or religious cults slaughter one another when threatened with defeat or disbandment. Whether it involves organizations or individuals, the behavior of suicide obeys the same principles.

BEYOND CONFLICT

Because it uses a distinctive paradigm, my theory of moralistic suicide explains variation not addressed by previous theories, suggests new hypotheses in need of study, and points to new avenues for research. But the applicability of pure sociology is not limited to the study of conflict, and neither are its possibilities for the study of suicide. As a general framework or strategy of explanation, pure sociology can be applied to any topic. And suicide, as we have seen, is a diverse category of behavior. Self-destruction arises from a variety of social contexts, and a theory of suicidal conflict does not necessarily explain suicide due to bereavement or terminal illness. It is more useful for explaining suicidal social control than for explaining suicidal altruism. But while a theory of moralistic suicide is not a theory of all suicide, it suggests ways in which one can apply pure sociology to explaining other types, forms, and varieties of suicide.

It might seem odd that self-execution and protest suicide occur in approximately the same social structure: protesting someone else and punishing oneself are in some ways opposite things. But this pattern likely suggests both a deeper regularity and a useful heuristic. Black has proposed that *social life is isomorphic with its social field,* meaning that different types of behavior tend to converge in form when they occur in the same social structure (Black 1998:91; see also Campbell 2015a:322; Campbell and Manning 2018:73n5). For instance, Black argues that the conditions that encourage people to handle conflict with negotiated compromise also encourage them to negotiate economic exchanges and marriage contracts (Black 1998:90). Likewise, building on the insights of Mark Cooney (2006), Bradley Campbell (2015a) argues that the conditions that make moralism collective, unilateral, and violent also make predation collective, unilateral, and violent. This, he observes, is why perpetrators of genocide often loot and rape their victims while also going out of their way to make these hated enemies suffer from torturous punishments. We might similarly expect that conditions conducive to reciprocity apply equally to reciprocal altruism and reciprocal moralism, with the parties exchanging gifts during peace and violence during conflict. Clearly, we must explain differences as well as similarities and so find aspects of social space that explain why we get conflict or marriage, moralism or predation, altruism or vengeance. But still the principle of isomorphism provides a guide for extending structural theories of conflict management to other realms of social life and means that a theory of moralistic suicide can help us understand suicide of other kinds.

Consider, for instance, suicide in the context of funeral rituals. There are many ways that mourners might express grief, loyalty, or reverence in the wake of someone else's death, and some of these are suicidal. The custom of "following into death," as historian Joerg Fisch (2005, 2006) calls it, has been found in many cultures across history and around the world. We can see it in ancient Rome, where at the funeral of the Emperor Otho several of his Praetorian guards carried his body to the funeral pyre and then stabbed themselves to death next to it, "not from feelings of remorse, or fear of being punished . . . but out of pure love for their emperor, and in the hope of following his noble example. Similar suicides were later reported at other camps among soldiers of various ranks" (Rankin 2012:10–12). Similarly, a British medical officer writing in 1895 described the death of a widow in the Indian city of Baroda who had pledged to burn to death atop her husband's funeral pyre:

> The poor widow walked steadily and unassisted to the place of her sufferings, and seemed in no way shaken from her steadfastness of purpose. . . . I took one quiet opportunity, unobserved by her people, to whisper in her hear, that if she felt any misgivings, my presence

would prevent it from being too late, even at the supposed last moment. But her look of reply was quite sufficient; she had not come without counting the cost. . . . I saw her last lying down, and embracing the corpse, and I heard her voice to the last, as if she had never changed her position; and I confidently believe she did not change it. (quoted in Fisch 2006:1–3)

But of course not every death leads someone to voluntarily follow: even in societies where this sort of suicide is a socially sanctioned custom, it is far more likely in some cases than in others. Following death varies with its location and direction in social space. In fact, its structure looks familiar: it too is greater in upward directions, committed by social inferiors to display loyalty and reverence to their superiors. In Rome this took the form of soldiers, slaves, and servants killing themselves upon the death of their generals, emperors, or masters (Van Hooff 1990:18). In premodern Japan, samurai retainers would follow their feudal lords into death (Seward 1968:32–37).[6] Imperial Chinese retainers were likewise expected to kill themselves after or in anticipation of the death of their lords, as were warriors in traditional Tamil society (Rankin 2012; Subrahmanian 1983:41). Wives in patriarchal settings might also be expected to follow their husbands, as was the case in traditional India: in some cases the death of a high-ranking polygynous king resulted in the mass suicide of multiple wives and concubines (Fisch 2006:217–47; Subrahmanian 1983; Thakur 1963:126–27,160). Partly because it increases with the social elevation of the deceased, following death is generally greater at higher elevations, a practice of social elites and their immediate households and retainers. Widow burning was thus rare among low-caste Indians, and in places like Fiji and New Britain only the wives of chiefs or "big men" follow their husbands into death (Fisch 2005, 2006).[7] But women are not invariably inferior to men, and in times and places where nonelite men marry elite women it may be the man who is expected to follow his wife into death (Fisch 2005:307, 309).

Institutionalized following death might be rare in the contemporary world, but this seemingly exotic practice surely has modern analogues. Specifying the social structure of following death might be the starting point for explaining modern suicide pacts, suicides due to bereavement or grief, or why some suicidal individuals aim to take children or other close dependents with them when they die.[8]

We might approach other types of suicide in the same way. For instance, the elderly and infirm may turn to suicide to relieve potential caretakers of their burden, or during times of food shortages some may take their own lives to leave more resources for others. In some cultures the practice is institutionalized, accepted, and may even be carried out with the full assistance of one's family (see, e.g., Leighton and Hughes 1955).[9] This too might appear exotic to most contemporary readers, but it also has contemporary analogues in the suicide of elderly and disabled persons. As with suicidal moralism, we can approach the question of suicidal altruism by asking what fluctuations of social space spark altruistic acts, what social distances and directions produce the greatest altruism, and in what structural configuration altruism is most likely to take the form of self-destruction. And here too the principle of isomorphism may give us a starting point, though there is clearly more work to be done.[10]

Finally, remember that no one exists in a social vacuum, and neither does any act of suicide. Perhaps suicide in contemporary urban societies is indeed more self-focused than suicide in other times and places. Self-killers often express more concern with their own internal states than with their relationships to others, and it may be hard to classify their act as something directed at anyone but themselves. But the relationship to the self is variable too, and as Black argues, modern self-concern is the product of modern self-closeness (Black 2011:148). Self-closeness in turn is the product of distance from others, and the degree of this distance partly determines the probability of rescue and patterns of lethality. Whatever the details, self-killing is an action that unfolds in a multidimensional social structure.

The pure sociological approach to suicide suggests many new directions for research into both suicide and suicidal conflict. Mainstream sociology often focuses on individuals and their cultural identities; pure sociology reveals the importance of comparing situations and relationships (Black 1995:852). Ambitious studies by social scientists sometimes produce impressively large samples of people who might be compared with one another or tracked over time; pure sociology suggest the importance of creating samples of conflicts, divorces, funerals, and other instances of social life. Psychologists have put great effort into developing measures of mental characteristics like depression and hopelessness; pure sociology requires sociologists to develop more sophisticated measures of structural characteristics like relational closeness or overstratification.

Mainstream suicide research focuses on the suicidal individual, but pure sociology tells us that this individual is only part of the story. Conventional data sources will prove inadequate for the further development of this kind of theory. Official statistics tell us little about the events leading up to suicide or the way it is carried out; coroners' records give us few details about the other parties involved or their relationship to the deceased. The pure sociology of suicide requires enterprising researchers to find new ways to observe the phenomenon and suggests the new observations will be fruitful.

Finally, the pure sociology of suicide offers suggestions for those who wish to prevent suicide. It does not require us to deny the effects of brain chemistry or cognitive habits, the existence of genetic heritability or the efficacy of antidepressants. But it does remind us that they are not the only sources of variation in suicide, and for at least some subset of cases they are not the source that matters most. Preventing or reducing suicide thus goes beyond providing medical care or professional therapy. It can take the form of financial assistance or providing a place to stay, of taking someone's side or mediating a dispute, of helping save face or avoid dependence.[11] It can also involve trade-offs, reducing the risk for one pattern of suicide but increasing the risk for another. Exactly which strategies are best will vary across societies, social classes, and subcultures, depending on what patterns of suicide are involved. Like suicide itself, prevention must vary with the social structure in which it occurs.

APPENDIX A

On Methodology

This book has a long history. It began with an effort to classify patterns of suicide described in the ethnographic and historical literature and then grew into a project that extended Blackian theories of social control to create a new theory of suicide. The main goal of the project was to develop a theory that specified when people were more likely to handle grievances with self-destruction. That theory, with extension and revision, became the one advanced in this book.

On Developing Theory

Sociologists often lack consensus about the meaning of terms, and the word *theory* is no exception. It might refer to any abstract conception or typology, it might refer to epistemological arguments about the nature and goals of sociology, or it might refer to paradigms or frameworks for developing theory. The kind of theory I sought to develop was an explanation, one that tells us why some cases are handled differently than others. It was to be an explanation in the scientific sense of stating a quantitative relationship between suicide and other features of the social world. Such statements, variously called laws, principles, propositions, or hypotheses (depending on their level of generality and our confidence that they are true), are the core of any explanatory idea and what allow us to make testable predictions about how things will vary from one set of conditions to another (Braithwaite 1953; Hempel 1965; Homans 1967). My goal, then, was a set of propositions that were general (could explain behavior in many times and places); simple (parsimonious); testable (able in principle to allow observation of patterns opposite to what they would predict); and, I hoped, correct. (On these and other standards for judging theory, see Black 1995.)

Despite often expressing reverence for theory, relatively few sociologists specialize in crafting such general explanations or make developing one the central goal of their work. Thus theoretical methodology does not seem to get the same attention in the field as empirical methodology. Indeed, sometimes explanatory theory is not even recognized as such, and theoretical arguments might be inappropriately judged by standards more suited to judging sample surveys. One can imagine contemporary peer reviewers haranguing Charles Darwin for cherry-picking the examples in his *Origin of Species* (as if one could take a representative sample of all life-forms, past, present, and future) or complaining of the lack of data in Einstein's "On the Electrodynamics of Moving Bodies." Any standard that excludes those great scientific achievements probably is not a useful standard to apply to theory overall.

One might even doubt if there can *be* a theoretical method, since as philosopher of science Karl Popper ([1934] 2002) long ago observed, the logical induction of a theory is impossible (see also Black 2000:357; Hume [1748] 1955; Popper 1994:85–101). While we might continue to use the term *induction* to refer to a process of developing theory, the conclusion of this process, the theory, never logically follows from the premises, the facts it explains. Scientific theories take the form of generalizations that necessarily go beyond the specific instances we have observed. In the classic formulation, having observed many white swans does not logically imply that all swans are white. Perhaps less easily appreciated is that, for any set of facts we possess, there are potentially other explanations that would fit them just as well or better. Einstein's theory of general relativity explained all the same phenomena as Newton's theory of gravity—only it did so more precisely, and predicted new facts besides. Thus a theory that many contemporaries thought effectively proven true was supplanted by one that was truer still. And wise observers, including Einstein himself, admitted the possibility of his new theory being supplanted in turn. Reality does not tell us how to explain it, and there is no mechanical way to add up the facts to produce the correct theory. Explanation requires creativity and always involves some speculative leap. No method unburdens the theorist from having ideas, deciding which are most promising, and taking a risk by proposing them to others for criticism and empirical test.

Yet the observations the theorist makes on his or her way to developing the theory surely have some impact. If one has never learned anything about a phenomenon, the odds of creating an accurate explanation of it would seem low. Popper (1994:82–111) suggested the psychological process of theory development was something like the scientific method writ small, as the mind continually tests and revises expectations—from unconscious hunches up through intensely thought-out ideas—by comparing them to observations. Whatever the details, those who study scientific creativity note the importance of an incubation or saturation period where the thinker familiarizes himself or herself with his or her field of study and the problems he or she will eventually solve (e.g., Gardner 1993; Simonton 2004; Stephan and Levin 1992).

But there may be such a thing as too much familiarity. In his sociological theory of scienticity, Black (2000) proposes that the most scientific ideas—those that have the greatest testability, validity, generality, simplicity, and originality—tend to occur when source and subject are neither too socially close nor too socially distant. In the social sciences, where we study the behavior of fellow humans, being too close is the more common problem. Those who focus exclusively on subjects that are relationally and culturally close—their own social identity and activities, their own society or segment of society—tend to have ideas that are narrow rather than general, complex rather than simple, and untestable rather than testable. Even when work is empirical rather than ideological, it often lacks generality and explanatory power. Very close subjects repel scientific theory. One can counteract this scientific handicap by observing more distant subjects, such as the behavior of people in past and foreign societies (Black 2000:353, 360–61).

Attention to past and foreign societies—and to the wealth of information gathered by anthropologists and historians—has another benefit. It allows us to see how behavior varies across the widest possible variety of social conditions. Tribal societies can show us levels of solidarity and homogeneity completely absent in the modern world, while ancient civilizations expose us to degrees of social stratification that citizens of a modern democracy find almost inconceivable. We can see the full range of variation in the variables of interest, and by comparing extremes we can see empirical relationships thrown into sharp relief (Black 2002:108). For a nonexperimental science that relies mostly on observations of naturally occurring behavior, this is extremely valuable.

The sources of information that will prove most useful will also depend in part on one's strategy of explanation. The strategy I adopted was Black's pure sociology, and this paradigm directs our attention to the behavior itself and to the particular constellation of circumstances and relationships in which it occurs. Using this strategy, the most useful information one can find is descriptions of actual suicide cases, including descriptions of the events leading up to suicide, the way in which it was carried out, and the relationships between everyone involved. Here is another benefit of the ethnographic literature. While the official statistics produced by modern states have their uses, they are often blind to what suicide looks like at the level of the individual case. The kinds of "up close" accounts found in many ethnographic and historical documents are much more relevant to my theoretical aims.

The Ethnographic Literature

Developing this sort of theory required reading as widely as possible about variation in suicide, with a preference for sources that gave insights into the social structure of the case and for those that showed how suicide varied across a range of social conditions. If one wants to call this a sampling strategy, one can call it *theoretical sampling*. Though it would be just as accurate to say I read all I could find, beginning with searches of common scholarly databases (e.g., JSTOR) and the entire suicide sections of the University of Virginia and West Virginia University libraries.

I also made extensive use of the electronic Humans Relations Area Files (eHRAF), a database containing a vast number of ethnographic documents that are all indexed and searchable at the paragraph level. At the time I began my project it covered about 230 human cultures; since then, with the addition of new sources (digitized from microfiche files), it covers over 300. All material in the eHRAF is coded, at the paragraph level, into subject categories developed by anthropologist George Murdock (1987). I initially limited myself to the search results for code 762, "suicide," used for any discussion of the incidence and justifications of, motives and methods for, and attitudes regarding suicide. This method produced hundreds of matches for hundreds of the listed cultures. I selected the societies that produced the most detailed results (five paragraphs of information or more) and that addressed conflict as a reason for suicide, and then I used the database to locate additional sources (e.g., general ethnographies) that would allow me learn more about such aspects of the societies as their patterns of marriage and residence, parent-child relationships, dimensions of social inequality, and the like. In the years since, I have continued to consult the eHRAF (to which new documents are continually added) using search terms (e.g., "marriage and suicide" or "infidelity and suicide") relevant to particular theoretical problems I was working on. The eHRAF is perhaps the most valuable store of information on human behavior in all the social sciences, even if the nature of ethnographic sources make it difficult to produce precise quantitative measures for statistical hypothesis testing (for attempts to do this with the topic of suicide, see, e.g., Krauss and Krauss 1968; Masumura 1977; Naroll 1969; Palmer 1965, 1971).

Coroners' Records

Another useful source for observing individual cases of suicide, particularly in modern societies, are the records of coroners and medical examiners. A coroner (or, depending on the jurisdiction, a medical examiner) is a state official charged with investigating cases of violent or mysterious death. The qualifications, authority, and practices of such officials vary across jurisdictions, but all rely on some combination of forensic evidence and testimony by informants to establish both the cause of death (such as asphyxiation or gunshot wound) and the mode of death (such as accident, homicide, or suicide). Such decisions may be made entirely by the officials or may take the form of an inquest in which a jury of citizens is asked to judge the evidence and reach a verdict. Either way, the investigation will usually generate sociologically relevant evidence, including case descriptions and suicide notes.

Several previous sociological works on suicide have made use of such records to describe patterns of suicide and characteristics of self-killers (see Cavan 1928; Fincham et al. 2011; Hassan 1995; Holmes and Holmes 2005; Maris 1969, 1981). Coroners' investigations from past centuries are also a major primary source for historians of suicide (e.g., Bailey 1998; MacDonald and Murphy 1990). But few of these previous efforts gave much attention to the role of conflict, and none focused on social distance, inequality, or other purely sociological variables. I thus conducted my own study of coroners' files as part of my inquiry into suicide

After sounding out officials in several jurisdictions, I was granted access by Ronald Holmes, a suicide researcher who was then chief coroner of Louisville, Kentucky (see, e.g., Holmes and Holmes 2004). His office employed seven deputy coroners—mostly former homicide detectives—and had jurisdiction over the city and surrounding county, including suburban and rural areas. I conducted my research there in 2009.

At the office I had access to records from 2003 to 2009, organized in file folders by date and name of the deceased. The folders contained such documents as the coroner's investigative report, reports of homicide detectives, scene photos, copies of suicide notes, and newspaper clippings. Due to the vagaries of record keeping I could not get access to recent records prior to 2003, but I could find records from the 1950s and early 1960s stored at the city archives. These older files tended to lack a separate coroner's report but usually contained police homicide reports and, when applicable, suicide notes. For a few cases, both modern and historical, I was able to find supplementary information by searching newspaper archives.

To assess the causes of suicide in general and get an idea how much suicide was due to conflict, I started by taking a sample of all consecutive suicides from 2008 to 2009 and, from the town archives, from 1950 to 1952. Due to time constraints I could not record information on all the remaining cases, so I limited myself to those in which the reports or suicide notes indicated that an argument, interpersonal problem such as a breakup, or legal dispute contributed to the suicide, including all cases in which the deceased expressed complaints in a suicide note. I also included cases of homicide-suicide. The result was that after reading over a thousand suicide cases, I recorded information on 451 cases, 287 of them apparently precipitated by some kind of conflict.

The quantity and quality of information varied from case to case. Some case summaries were very terse; for example, one stated only that "the decedent shot herself in the mouth in front of her boyfriend after they had a domestic altercation." Others were several paragraphs long and delved into the decedent's social history and present circumstances. Only about 15 percent of victims left any note at all, something consistent with other studies of suicide notes (see Sanger and Veach 2008), and notes ranged in length from a few words to lengthy diaries and manifestos. Most files contained at least some information on what seemed to precipitate the suicide—ill health, family conflict, job loss, etc.—though for a few cases this was impossible to determine. Any numerical comparisons made in the text of this book exclude cases where the relevant information was missing, and so the reported total of cases varies accordingly.

A Note on Validity

Ever since sociologist Jack Douglas (1967) advocated skepticism of official suicide rates, sociologists have recognized the possibility that some bias in the way suicides are investigated, classified, or recorded might lower the accuracy of official records and the statistics calculated based on them. One potential source of bias is the fact that suicide has historically been a source of stigma in Western society and that suicidal deaths can potentially be more emotionally difficult for loved ones than, say, accidental deaths. Sociologists have studied the investigation of suicide and report that in cases where it is ambiguous whether death was intentional or accidental, officials tend to err on the side of classifying it as an accident (see generally Atkinson 1978; Timmermans 2005). The coroners I spoke with similarly professed that they followed a "51%" rule, not classifying something like a drug overdose as suicide unless they had some positive evidence that the latter was more likely than the former (such as reports that the deceased had expressed suicidal intent recently, or, for prescription drugs, if the dosage taken far exceeded the therapeutic dose).[1] Surely at least some cases of suicide are thus misclassified as accidents.

Still, there is little reason to think the errors are of sufficient magnitude and in the proper direction to invalidate commonly observed patterns of suicide. Recall that for some comparisons, such as divorce or employment status, rates for one group are double those of another—it would require an implausibly large population of misclassified suicides, nearly all of them for married and employed people, to erase this pattern. We also have empirical evidence on the accuracy of coroners' determinations in the form of sociological researchers who second-guess coroners by applying a more liberal standard to classifying cases as suicide rather than accident and find that the extra cases do not substantially change rates and patterns of suicide (see, e.g., Sainsbury and Jenkins 1982). Though critics might like to repeat the memorable anecdote of the Irish coroner who would never classify any death as suicide—"the gun accidentally went off while he was cleaning the barrel with his tongue"—there is little reason to think that most modern investigators are so biased or that their observations are fundamentally inaccurate. Rather, the main shortcoming of coroners' files as a data source for pure sociology is the lack of detail about important sociological variables. The records are mostly valid, but frustratingly incomplete.

APPENDIX B

On Suicide and Social Contagion

Readers familiar with the sociology of suicide might see a major lacuna in this book's discussion of social ties (chapter 3): the possibility that suicide can diffuse across networks through a process of social contagion.

People learn from one another, adopting technologies, techniques, and ideas from their fellows. Thus behaviors, including ways of dressing, ways of making a living, and beliefs about the nature of reality, can spread from one person or group to another. Social scientists study this phenomenon under a variety of names, including social contagion, the diffusion of innovations, social learning, socialization, and acculturation (Henrich 2016; Rogers 2003; Sorokin 1959). And they do so by examining the adoption and spread of many different things—rumors, technologies, religions, drug use, and even suicide.

Writing even before Durkheim's famous study, French sociologist Gabriel Tarde (1903; see also Abrutyn and Mueller 2014b) proposed that suicide could be spread by "imitation": having observed someone else engage in this behavior increases the odds that the observer will engage in it as well. People follow the example set by their fellows, and knowing other people who handled their problems with suicide makes it more likely that someone will also adopt this solution. Thus suicide can diffuse through social ties.

Researchers since have continued to explore this possibility and have used social contagion to explain why suicide sometimes clusters in time and place. Some studies indeed find that having a friend or acquaintance attempt suicide increases one's likelihood of attempting suicide in the future (e.g., Bearman and Moody 2004; Abrutyn and Mueller 2014a; Mueller and Abrutyn 2015). Others find that being exposed to other people's suicide via news media also has an effect, such that news coverage about the suicide of a celebrity leads to a spike in suicide rates in the region exposed to the coverage (Phillips 1974; Gould 2001; Stack 2000a, 2003). Even specific patterns of suicide, like the use of self-burning for political protest, appear to diffuse across populations, as an initial use of the tactic inspires protestors in similar situations to adopt it (e.g., Biggs 2005, 2013).

If suicide can spread by social contagion, then it is not alone: social influence can encourage the adoption of any behavior. And here is the main reason for not addressing social contagion in my chapter on suicide and relationships: the topic is properly understood as falling under the study of *diffusion* rather than the study of either suicide or of conflict. When we ask what makes people more likely to adopt the ideas and behaviors of others, we are studying the behavior of diffusion. And like any other form of social life, diffusion varies with its location and direction in social space.

For instance, Tarde proposed that that social influence was greater among those who were less distant from one another, with "distance" being "understood here in its sociological meaning" to include "numerous and daily relations" (Tarde 1903:224). We might quibble over exactly what he meant, but his conception of social distance can be easily translated into Blackian terms: *diffusion varies inversely with relational distance.* People are more likely to adopt the behaviors of intimates than of acquaintances and of acquaintances than of strangers. The more intimate people and groups become, the more likely they are to adopt one another's characteristics, becoming more similar in culture and behavior. Relational closeness facilitates cultural and functional closeness. This goes for everything from adopting new styles of clothing or modes of entertainment to joining social movements. For example, "By far the strongest predictor of going to Mississippi [to participate in the 1964 Freedom Summer civil rights project] was having strong network relationships with other participants or with a Freedom Summer activist. Having a close friend who withdrew from the project influenced others to withdraw" (Rogers 2003:93). People are more likely to adopt a new religion to the extent they form close ties with its adherents, while having fewer or weaker ties to those with competing beliefs (Loftland and Stark 1965; Heinrich 1977; Stark and Bainbridge 1980; Kox, Meetus, and Hart 1991). Criminological theorists note that a similar pattern governs the use of recreational drugs or participation in violent crime (Akers et al. 1979; Bandura 1978). And in his theory of the success of ideas, Black (2000:349) proposes that ideas from closer sources are more likely to be treated as true and important, something that usually involves adopting and repeating them.

Tarde also recognized the importance of inequality: imitation of social superiors is greater than imitation of social inferiors (Tarde 1903:213–15). Though a superior and inferior might both adopt some of one another's characteristics, Tarde argued, the inferior would generally adopt more and the superior less. Modern techniques of observation allow us to see this relationship playing out at the level of individual interactions. As evolutionary biologist Joseph Henrich writes, "Subordinates unconsciously mimic prestigious individuals more than vice versa. . . . One study of vocal mimicry involved CNN's longtime talk-show host Larry King. . . . As expected, when Larry was interviewing someone perceived to be highly prestigious, Larry shifted his vocal frequencies to match his guest's patterns. However, when he was interviewing those perceived to be of lower status than Larry himself, it was the guests who automatically and unconsciously shifted to match Larry's frequency" (Henrich 2016:125, citing Gregory and Webster 1996). We can see similar patterns play out on larger scales, as fashion, language, technology, and ideology are more likely to diffuse from upper class to lower class, from the capital to the hinterlands (Sorokin 1959:575–77; Tarde 1903:2013–2245). As Black proposes, the ideas of social superiors are taken more seriously—something that aides their spread (Black 1998:166–67; Black 2000:349). To restate Tarde's theory in Blackian terms: *downward diffusion is greater than upward diffusion.*

We can see the impact of both closeness and superiority in the diffusion of suicide. For instance, several have pointed to the influence of celebrity suicide, and celebrities combine closeness with superiority: they are wealthy and prestigious, and their fans develop a kind of one-sided closeness to them through frequent exposure to their activities and the details of their personal and professional lives. Their behavior is thus influential: for instance, when famed South Korean actress Choi Jin-sil—popularly known as "the nation's actress"—killed herself in 2008, it was followed by a month-long 70 percent increase in the nation's suicide rate (Harden 2010).

But note that a theory of diffusion is not a theory of suicide as such. Diffusion is no more or less relevant to explaining suicide than it is to explaining any other action that people might imitate. What it does not do is specify a set of social conditions that make people more likely to adopt suicide rather than the myriad other potential reactions they have also seen modeled by their fellows. Someone with a grievance might be more likely to handle it by burning themselves in protest if they are aware of previous cases—after all, innovation is rare and adopting a known technique is more likely than independently inventing it. But they are not likely to do so in reaction to every grievance they have. If, as Michael Biggs (2005, 2013) argues, the highly publicized self-burning of Thich Quang Duc in Vietnam was crucial in introducing this practice to various people around the globe and providing them with a model to imitate, we still need to explain why they imitate this example rather than some others and adopt it for some conflicts but not others. The answer is the same thing that explains why the innovation occurred in the first place: a conflict structure conducive to self-destruction. The same structural features encourage both the independent invention of a form of social control and its adoption if it is introduced from elsewhere. They provide the social habitat in which the behavior is likely to arise and also likely to thrive when introduced. The behavior of diffusion has some influence at the margins, but the social geometry of suicide is a topic of its own.

Notes

1. Before going to his death he uttered the famous final words: "I am just going outside and may be some time" (Wikipedia 2017e).

1. SUICIDE AND CONFLICT

1. In one national sample of 272 US attempters, "nearly half reported that their attempt was a 'cry for help'; 13% reported that they intended to die but knew the method was not foolproof; 39.3% reported that they intended to die and were saved only due to luck" (Mościcki 2001:314).

2. One might argue that widespread belief in an afterlife means that few adults accept the finality of death. Even without concrete ideas about an afterlife, nonexistence may be hard for many to grasp, and in my research I have seen a few suicide notes that included some variant of "I will miss you."

3. Thus, unless otherwise specified, I use the term "suicide" to refer to both fatal suicides and nonfatal attempts. Note, though, that suicide attempts can range in lethality from "serious" attempts that carry a high risk of death to those that carry almost no actual threat of death, only the superficial appearance of trying to kill oneself. Some scholars prefer to distinguish the latter with terms such as "parasuicide" or "suicidal gestures" (see, e.g., Kreitman 1977; compare Taylor 1982:140–60). Other kinds of self-inflicted violence have even lower lethality, and scholars use terms like "self-harm," "self-injury," and "self-mutilation" to refer to behaviors such as shallow skin-cutting, hair plucking, self-biting, and other mild forms of violence people inflict on themselves (see, e.g., Levenkron 1999).

4. One unusual case of public suicide occurred in Florida in 1974, when news reporter Christine Chubbuck fatally shot herself in the head on camera during a live news broadcast after announcing to viewers that "in keeping with Channel 40's policy of bringing you the latest in 'blood and guts,' and in living color, you are going to see another first—attempted suicide" (Pelisek 2016).

5. This definition of conflict differs from the way the term is used when discussing neo-Marxian "conflict theory" in the field of sociology. In the latter usage, *conflict* refers to opposing interests that inhere in social life, such as the opposing economic interests of business owners (who benefit from cheaper labor) and their employees (who benefit from higher wages). Also note that Black's (1998:xiii) definition of conflict does not require the grievance be contested: if one friend complains of another's being late to an engagement and the late friend immediately apologizes and no further action is taken, it still counts as a conflict. It would even count as a conflict if the offended friend did not complain directly to the offender but instead gossiped to a third friend. It is the grievance that makes the conflict.

6. The conceptual strategy used here is not usually seen in the empirical literature on suicide, but neither is it unique. Several theorists of suicide, such as Jean Baechler, Jack Douglas, Steven Taylor, and Ronald Maris, have recognized the diversity of suicidal behavior and have sought to classify suicide into different types based on some underlying kind of social behavior of which the suicidal act is but one self-destructive example. Jean Baechler (1975) recognizes a distinction between suicides that are a matter of escape (including escape from an enemy as well as from suffering in general), those that are a matter of aggression (including vengeance and appeal), "oblative suicides" that can involve sacrificing one's life for a higher value or seeking to attain a higher state of being, and "ludic suicides" that involve risking death to prove oneself to others (Baechler 1975:59–199). Jack Douglas argues that there are four distinct patterns of suicide, each with its own "social meaning": suicides meant to be an escape into the afterlife, suicides meant to transform others' views of the victim (including displays of sincerity or atonement for wrongdoing), suicide to attract sympathy from others, and suicides meant to get revenge on others (Douglas 1967:284–319). Steven Taylor distinguishes suicides based on whether they are primarily a self-imposed ordeal, a submissive seeking of death, or an appeal to other parties (Taylor 1982:140–93). And in his study of attempted and completed suicide, Ronald Maris (1981) proposes that most suicidal behavior can be divided into four categories: escape from unpleasant situations, aggression against others, changing or sacrificing the self for some higher purpose, and risking life in order to improve it (Maris 1981:291). These different conceptual schemes overlap in various ways, both with each other and with the categories employed in this book. For instance, all of these authors recognize categories of suicide that would fit into the concept of social control, such as suicides for vengeance, appeal, aggression, and atonement.

7. In feudal Japan, one of the earliest recorded instances of seppuku—suicide by disembowelment—was that of Minamoto-noTametomo following his defeat in the Hogen War in 1156: "Since death was slow in coming, he hastened its advent, before the enemy could catch and abuse him, by cutting into the nerve centers of the spinal column" (Seward 1968:25). Though disembowelment with a sword would eventually become a ritualized practice employed as a means of atonement, execution, protest, and honoring the dead, this early case appears to be an impulsive act of escape.

8. This and other cases reported in this book come from my study of the coroners' records of Louisville, Kentucky. Details of this study are reported in "Appendix A: On Methodology" (see also Manning 2015a).

9. Protest suicide may also occur alongside less lethal but still self-destructive tactics, such as acts of self-mutilation (Baumgartner 1984). During one protest by Vietnamese Buddhists during the 1960s, a monk cut off part of his finger before a crowd, while in another a monk roasted his own finger over a candle flame (Biggs 2005:194). Similarly, in 2001, twenty men from a South Korean nationalist group cut off their fingers to protest a visit by the Japanese prime minister to the controversial Yasukune shrine, said to house the spirits of Japanese soldiers who committed war crimes against Korea during World War II (*Telegraph* 2001). Fasts or hunger strikes, in which protestors refuse to consume food until their demands are met, are also typically nonlethal but can be carried to the point of being suicidal. Indeed, fasting might be unique in that it allows the protestors to continuously escalate their degree of self-destruction over a long period of time and so halt at the lowest level of lethality that will sway opponents and bystanders. Hunger strikes were famously used by Mohandas Gandhi and his supporters in their conflicts with the British Empire and have been commonly used (often with massive participation) in contemporary Israel (Waismel-Manor 2005; Silke 2006). An example of a fatal hunger strike is that of ten Irish Republican prisoners who starved to death in 1981 while protesting the British government's decision to treat Northern Irish militants as criminals rather than combatants (Lewis 2012:127–31).

10. The term "Maroon" refers broadly to several different ethnic groups descended from escaped slaves that share similar patterns of culture and social structure. These groups include the Paramaka (or Paramacca), the Aluku, the Ndyuka (or Djuka), and the Saramaka (Price, Price, and Skoggard 1999).

11. The Aguaruna are one of several subgroups of the Jívaro people. Other subgroups include the Shuar and Achuara (Beierle 2006).

12. One relevant statute read: "Whoever on account of a dispute intimidates or exerts pressure upon another person and causes his death shall be punished by 100 strokes of the heavy bamboo. . . . Whoever applies intimidation or pressure to a person in connection with fornication or theft and causes a person's death shall be beheaded" (Meijer 1981:290). Depending on the circumstances, cases could also result in banishment or strangulation. Note that the punishment for causing suicide varies according to the status of the offender in the way predicted by Black's (1976:21–27) theory of law: "When the family relationships are involved punishments increase when the offender is a junior member and decrease when he is senior" (Meijer 1981:299; see also Tucker 2015).

13. Baechler distinguishes such acts of "private vengeance" from "public vengeance" involving social sanctions (Baechler 1975:123–26).

14. That this is so is likely an important clue about the behavior of liability—a condition of being held accountable for misfortune or wrongdoing (Black 1998:47–64; see also chapter 3).

15. In some cases, self-killers might go out of their way to have others discover their bodies simply because they are concerned about allowing their body to be found and buried in a timely manner. For this reason people who live alone sometimes invite over an acquaintance shortly before dispatching themselves.

16. Black (2004b:146) coined the term *moralistic violence* to refer to the larger category of violent social control. Moralistic suicide is one type of moralistic violence.

17. Compared to older people, younger people—especially adolescents—are more likely to commit nonfatal attempts. If youth suicide is both more likely due to conflict and more often nonfatal, it may be because moralistic suicides—at least in the modern Western context—tend to have lower lethality. Lower levels of lethality would seem to indicate that moralistic suicide among youth is more often a matter of interpersonal protest or appeal. We might also suspect the same is true of US women, who are far more likely than US men to survive their suicide attempts (Mościcki 2001). But note that these patterns are not universal, and in some societies I will consider in this book female and youth suicide has much higher average lethality.

18. Sociologist Alan V. Horwitz and psychiatrist Alan Wakefield (2007) argue that there has been a tendency among practitioners and the public to stretch the original clinical definition of depression to what was once considered ordinary grief or sadness, and they view this as part of a larger trend to medicalizing personal and social problems. Similarly, psychologist Nick Haslam (2016) argues that concepts related to harm and dysfunction—such as depression, abuse, and trauma—have undergone a process of inflation over the years, such that they now cover a much wider range of behavior, including those that are much less extreme (see also Campbell and Manning 2018:86–93).

19. In the words of psychiatrist Scott Alexander (2017), "The problem with depression research isn't that we don't have any leads on what causes depression. It's that we have so many leads on what causes depression that we don't know what to do with all of them."

20. Note that most suicide victims in the United States use firearms and that shooting oneself in the head usually leads to an instant death. It is not clear why building up a tolerance to physical pain would be relevant to this common method of suicide.

21. Some claim that nearly all who kill themselves suffer from a mental disorder. For instance, the American Foundation for Suicide Prevention (2017) reports that "90% of people who die by suicide have a potentially treatable mental disorder," most commonly "major depression" and other "mood disorders." Such claims seem to rely on an expansive definition of "depression" or "disorder" that includes what might otherwise be considered "normal" sadness over stressful life events, such as the death of a loved one or painful physical illness (Haslam 2016; Horwitz and Wakefield 2007). It also stems from a tendency to medicalize any and all deviant behaviors associated with self-destruction, such as heavy use of alcohol, frequent displays of anger, or a tendency to seek attention from others.

22. Suicide rates in the contemporary world also vary dramatically from one country to another. For example, in 2015 the US rate was 12.4, the South Korean rate was 24.1, and the Italian rate was 5.4 (World Health Organization 2017).

23. Black's terminology might seem strange and confusing, but it has an analogue in contemporary physics, where space and time are considered part of a single construct known as *space-time*. All time is measured by some change in physical position—such as the motion of a clock's hands—and when time speeds up or slows down (something predicted by Einstein's theory of general relativity and confirmed by experiments), it means that physical changes happen more or less quickly (relative to some other frame of reference). Hence the notion that time *is* change, and Black's conception of social change as social time (Black 2011:5).

2. SUICIDE AND INEQUALITY

1. Education is an example of *cultural status*, determined by the quantity of culture one possesses (Black 1976:63–67). This is the type of status that makes experts superior to nonexperts and those with extensive knowledge superior to those with limited knowledge. In contemporary societies it is often measured with educational credentials, but we can also observe it in times and places without formal education systems. In tribal societies it is a form of status possessed by shamans and other ritual specialists and accounts for much of the deference given to elders in general. *Organization* is the capacity for collective action, and varies with a group's size, division of labor, and degree of centralized leadership (Black 1976:85). It is the type of status that gives a gang an advantage over a lone individual and a disciplined army and advantage over a disorderly mob. *Conventionality* is the frequency of a cultural characteristic, such as a religion, language, or ethnic identity (Black 1976:67–73). It is the form of status that gives majorities an advantage over minorities.

2. American blacks are, on average, lower on numerous dimensions of social status. For instance, the average white family has a net worth several times greater than the average black family (see, e.g., Conley 1999). There are corresponding aggregate differences in education. Blacks Americans are more likely to have criminal records (and thus lower respectability) and, as minorities, have lower conventionality as well. Racial differences in status were greater earlier in history, particularly in the US South. During the era of Jim Crow laws, blacks were expected to defer to whites, producing a strict caste system in which nearly all blacks were hierarchically inferior to nearly all whites. The high prevalence of beliefs about black moral inferiority also meant much lower respectability, even for those with good reputations as individuals. Indeed, viewed in terms of Blackian theory, much of what is called "racism" is social control marked by *collective liability* that treats all members of a social category as deviant (Black 1998:xv–xvi, 56).

3. Suicide data can describe the properties of a collectivity (such as the suicide rate of a nation) or of individuals (such as the characteristics of people who commit suicide). In methodological terms, collectivities and individuals are different *units*

of analysis, and the strongest arguments draw on evidence from the same unit of analysis as their conclusion. For instance, the strongest evidence that poverty makes individuals likely to kill themselves would be data telling us that poor individuals have higher suicide rates than do rich individuals. While data showing that poor countries have higher suicide rates does count as evidence for the effect of poverty on which individuals kill themselves—in that it is something we would expect to be the case if poverty did have that effect—it is weaker evidence because we do not know for certain who within the poor country is committing suicide. It is thus possible that wealthy people are more prone to suicide and that this difference is even greater in poor countries where wealthy people are rarer, but where their suicides are frequent enough to raise the national rate. If this were the case and we firmly concluded otherwise, we would be making an error that sociologists refer to as the *ecological fallacy,* which refers to incorrect conclusions about individuals based on data drawn from collectivities. There is also an opposite error, sometimes called the *part-to-whole* fallacy, where incorrect conclusions about collectivities are drawn from data on individuals.

4. Note that the loss of a job is more than a reduction in social status. It is also the loss of a source of social involvement and connections and thus a reduction in social integration. In chapter 3 we will consider the importance of social integration in preventing suicide and the role of lost relationships in causing it.

5. Notably, these were highly paid and skilled workers who experienced a high degree of downward mobility when they lost their jobs. Low-wage, unskilled textile workers, who regularly experienced seasonal unemployment, were less likely to kill themselves because of it (Watt 2001:185–86).

6. Sexual attractiveness is another physical resource that declines with age. Thus one American woman, described as "brazen about her beauty," killed herself because "at 34 . . . she felt she was going downhill" (Breed 1967:194).

7. To the extent physical pain is the main cause of suicide, effective painkillers may reduce the probability of it. For example, among the Vaqueiro pastoralists of Spain, suicide due to illness declined after the introduction of morphine (Cátedra 1992:161–71). According to one informant, "Before many people hanged themselves because those who had cancer had to suffer pain like fire; there wasn't any alternative. Now they give you morphine and you have no more pain" (quoted in Cátedra 1992:170). But to the extent that illness is also a social loss, painkillers will not totally eliminate the association between illness and suicide. They can even provide those with debilitating illnesses an effective and efficient means of killing themselves and thus increase the risk of suicide.

8. The authors of the cited research explain their findings with a selection effect: in times of high employment, those who remain unemployed are probably a more strongly selected population and thus more likely to have conditions (such as mental illness or physical disability) that simultaneously prevent them from getting jobs

and make them more likely to commit suicide. More research is necessary to test whether the selection hypothesis or the overstratification hypothesis explains the pattern. Given that the two hypotheses are not mutually exclusive, it is also possible that both selection and overstratification effects exist and contribute to the pattern.

9. Summarizing the literature on sex relations in the New Guinea Highlands, anthropologist Marilyn G. Gelber (1986) concludes that relations between the sexes in this region are not merely unequal but positively antagonistic.

10. Mount Hagen is an administrative district in the Central Highlands that contains a mixture of linguistic groups (Strathern 1972:3–5).

11. Marriages in this society are contracts between families in which the husband pays a sizable "bride-price" to his bride's kin group. Divorce requires the return of the bride-price to the husband's family. Many families are therefore reluctant to accept their daughter's return, which would mean the loss of a substantial amount of wealth.

12. The main exception is women of unusually high status, such as the first-born daughters of community leaders (Big Men), who are more assertive and aggressive than other women (Counts 1980:341).

13. Some of the cases reflected in these statistics may actually be homicides—so-called "honor killings" and "dowry deaths"—disguised as suicides (Aliverdinia and Pridemore 2009:316). But such killings are typically disguised as accidents, which are even less eye-raising than a suicide.

14. It is not always women who find themselves in the position of being a low-status outsider within a new marital family. Among the Bison Horn Maria, a tribal people of India, the position is sometimes reversed. Young men who wish to marry a woman sometimes perform "bride service" for a period of time during which they live near and labor under the authority of their future in-laws. Such men—known as *Lamhadas*—often come into conflict with their in-laws, and these conflicts can lead them to suicide. For example: "Akali Modi had served three years for his wife, to whom he was married four months before his death. As is often the case he was continuing to serve his father-in-law until the payment of the bride-price was completed. On the night before his suicide, two cows broke their tethering cords and damaged the crops. On such occasions it is almost routine to blame the Lamhada, and the father-in-law doubtless bewailed his mistake in giving his daughter to such a fool and made offensive remarks about the boy's mother. Modi, who is said to have been a sensitive, quick-tempered youth, waited till the rest of the family went into the fields and then hanged himself from a tree outside of the village" (Elwin 1943:131).

15. Though we can characterize these relationships as patriarchal—the new bride is subordinate to the patrilineage—it is not necessarily the relationship between husband and wife that is the main locus of conflict. As we shall see in chapter 4, the relationship between daughter-in-law and mother-in-law was often the main

fault line, and the husband's role in precipitating suicide was often more a matter of indifference than abuse.

16. Based on his fieldwork in norther China, anthropologist Wu Fei (2005) argues that family complexity leads to a higher level of family conflict in rural areas and that this plays a bigger role in causing suicide than inequality as such. Indeed, some informants attribute elevated rates of family conflict and suicide to the fact that age and sex hierarchies are less stable than in the past, meaning that attempts by parents and husbands to exercise dominance are more likely to cause serious conflict. This is consistent with Black's (2011:139) theory that overstratification causes more severe conflict in relationships that are less stratified. It also suggests that the total volume of moralistic suicide is not necessarily greatest where inequality is greatest, as the total volume depends both on the rate and severity of conflict as well as the likelihood that a given conflict will be handled with suicide rather than some other means.

17. Mataco society is ambilineal, meaning an individual can choose to affiliate with either his or her father's or mother's kin group, and in cases of divorce due to infidelity or abuse custody of both children and living quarters go to the injured party (Alvarsson 1988:138).

18. The Iroquois are sometimes described as a "matriarchy" because of their matrilineal clans and the prominent role that female clan elders played in tribal politics. The term probably exaggerates the dominance of women in day-to-day life, but it is true that women's standing was higher among these people than in many other premodern societies.

19. Note that the Iroquois were actually a confederacy of six nations—the Cayuga, Mohawk, Odondaga, Oneida, Seneca, and Tuscarora—and that while all were culturally similar, in traditional times there was some variation in social organization from nation to nation. For example, matrilocality was more typical of the Mohawk than of the Seneca (Randle 1951; see also Noon 1949:32). And of course patterns of social organization changed over time due to the influence of European-American civilization. For instance, between the colonial period and contemporary times, residence in communal longhouses increasingly gave way to residence in nuclear households.

20. Despite cultural change, these patterns persisted into the twentieth century (Fenton 1986).

21. Also notable is that the women most vulnerable to suicide were not the young and newly married, as is true in patriarchal cultures, but women approaching the age of menopause, whose husbands were prone to leave them for someone younger (Fenton 1941:123). Of course suicide was not the only option for an abandoned woman: writing of his fieldwork in early twentieth century, Fenton recalls "one or two cases of women beating their husbands or consorts" (Fenton 1986:450). But he also cites the case of a woman who attempted to assault her husband and then killed herself after he successfully restrained her, noting that Iroquois generally

find any kind of restraint "intolerable" (Fenton 1986:450). Even in a relatively sex-egalitarian culture the greater physical strength of men affects patterns of vengeance and punishment.

22. Marriages in any large and diverse society are going to vary substantially, and one can of course find cases of extreme patriarchal domination in the United States, the United Kingdom, and elsewhere. But these extremes are unusual, legally prohibited, and outside of certain subcultures (including recent immigrants from more patriarchal societies) widely condemned. Overall, marriages in the contemporary West tend to range from mildly patriarchal to highly egalitarian. The former Black (2018:6) calls *soft hierarchy* and is what many Americans might think of as "traditional marriage," with a male breadwinner who might take the lead in household decisions but is expected to consult with and respect his spouse. The latter Black divides into two types: the *close democracy*—what many Americans might call a "modern marriage"—involves spouses who are equal partners in everything, very close, and who might describe each other as their "best friend," while the *loose anarchy* refers to a relatively ill-defined and unstable partnership that includes many unmarried cohabiting partners and what some people call "serial monogamy" (Black 2018:3–6). Close democracy is increasingly common among the educated and professional classes, the loose anarchy among the lower and working classes.

23. Furthermore, both structural position and rate of conflict can vary across children within the same family. Interviews with suicide attempters and their parents suggest that the attempters were the least favorite of their parents' children, being subject to more criticism and discipline and receiving less affection (Wagner 2009:89–90).

24. Between 1991 and 2007 the percentage of adolescentLatinas attempting suicide each year varied between 11 and 21 percent (Zayas 2011:36).

25. It might seem obvious that this is so—perhaps even inconceivable that it would be otherwise. But it is not logically impossible for, say, the president of an international corporation to kill himself to protest misconduct by one of his line workers. What it may be is sociologically impossible.

26. In 1736, one samurai woman killed her husband after finding out that he was having an affair with his lord's wife, a shameful crime against his superior. Though the penalty for husband killing was strangulation followed by crucifixion, she requested the opportunity to commit seppuku instead: "I may be a woman . . . but I am a samurai woman. I will die by cutting my stomach" (quoted in Rankin 2012:140). Her request was granted, and she killed herself in front of two witnesses with horizontal and vertical cuts to the abdomen.

27. The day after a ceremony congratulating project head Hirate Yukie for successful completion of the task, he committed seppuku as well, an act understood by his contemporaries as taking responsibility for the men who died under his watch (Rankin 2012:146).

28. The note begs forgiveness for "the great crime"—which may be a reference to the outcome of the war or to an abortive coup attempt that took place just before the surrender.

3. SUICIDE AND RELATIONSHIPS

1. He called suicides that occur under conditions of low integration "egoistic suicide," a term that reflects the notion that these deaths arise from "excessive individualism," which occurs when "the individual ego asserts itself to excess" (Durkheim [1857] 1951:209).

2. Researchers since Durkheim tend to find that the protective effects of marriage are greater for males than for females. In more patriarchal societies it may not protect women at all, as the effects of domination and abuse outweigh any protection offered by greater social integration (see chapter 2). And for new brides in these settings, marriage might initially mean a net decline in integration, since residential patterns in these societies often mean a wife leaves her family and community to live among strangers (see chapter 4). The former possibility, that overinferiority overshadows the effect of integration, illustrates the necessity of holding other relevant factors constant when trying to understand the relationship between two variables. The latter possibility, that marriage is not always a source of integration, points to the importance of distinguishing between a general sociological concept and the specific indicators we use to measure that concept.

3. Such timing is also evidence that the relationship is not entirely due to selection effects—that is, people with characteristics that predispose them to suicide also have characteristics that predispose them to divorce.

4. What about those who become more distant from everyone, withdrawing from social intercourse altogether? They become more intimate with themselves and perhaps also more intimate with nonhuman companions such as cats or dogs. Black's (2011:21) zero-sum conception of intimacy rests on the idea that people can be more or less intimate with anyone or anything.

5. More precisely, adultery is both underintimacy and overintimacy, since it increases closeness in one relationship and decreases it in another. But in such cases it is in the relationship that grows more distant where the conflict is likely to erupt.

6. According to anthropologist Raymond Firth, the possibility of being kept from their chosen mate "not infrequently" leads to threats of suicide by Tikopia girls, who might tell their parents, "Of all the men that go about, I see only one; if you object I will swim out to sea." He adds that "this announcement is usually intended seriously and, as the natives say, parental affection concedes her desire. It is unpleasant for a Tikopian, as for any other father, to contemplate the certain prospect of his daughter being devoured by sharks" (Firth 1933:237).

7. Consider that tribal people typically spend their lives enmeshed in stable networks of kin who form their entire circle of social relations, with whom they share a wide range of activities from production to ritual to defense. Their family,

friends, neighbors, and coworkers are all the same people. Privacy is virtually unknown, and everyone knows everything about one another's activities (see Black 2011:140–43).

8. The Gainj of New Guinea, for example, have a rate of about 30 per 100,000 people, nearly three times the current US rate of around 12 per 100,000, though about the same as the rate of contemporary South Korea. Other New Guinea societies have rates ranging from 14 to 66 per 100,000 (Johnson 1981:326; Berndt 1962:182; Healey 1979:95; Smith 1981–82:242). The Tikopia of Polynesia, studied between 1929 and 1952, had a rate of about 53 per 100,000 (Firth 1967). And the Aguaruna Jívaro of the Peruvian Amazon, during the period 1977–81, had a rate of about 180 per 100,000 (Brown 1986:314).

9. Suicide is a dramatic behavior, and one that ethnographers tend to notice. For instance, the electronic Human Relations Area Files (eHRAF) database contains ethnographic studies of over three hundred societies, and a search of the term "suicide" produces results for over two hundred. For most of these the results only amount to a few paragraphs noting that suicide sometimes occurs for this reason or that, either specifying that it is rare or else giving no indication that it is frequent. While anthropologists are rarely able to give precise rates, it stands to reason that if a society that has been described by several independent observers had a comparatively high rate of suicide, one of them likely would have commented on it or written more extensively on the topic. Thus we might use the number of paragraphs written about suicide in a society as a rough proxy measure of suicide frequency (Naroll 1969). Of the three hundred societies in the eHRAF database, only forty produce ten paragraphs or more of results.

10. For example, Senechal de la Roche (1996, 1997) argues that community outsiders are much more susceptible to lynching than are community insiders—given the same offense, community members are less likely to kill those with whom they share strong ties. Similarly, a common scenario for genocidal extermination is when colonization and conquest bring two mutually alien societies into contact, allowing violence to cross a chasm of social distance (Campbell 2009; Campbell 2015b). Where different ethnic groups already live side by side, genocide is more likely when there is more distance between them, as measured by such indicators as low rates of intermarriage (Campbell 2009; Campbell 2015b). In both rioting and genocide, individuals from the aggressor group are less likely to participate if they have ties to the victim group, and individuals from the victim group are more likely to be spared if they have ties to the aggressor group. Terrorism too almost always targets strangers, especially strangers from foreign societies who do not even share indirect network links with their attackers (Black 2004a).

11. Male suicides, on the other hand, are typically caused by the loss of status (Wilson 1960:194; see also chapter 2).

12. Specifically, Black (2011:139) proposes that *"underintimacy conflict is a direct function of intimacy,"* meaning that the closer the relationship, the more likely it is

that a given reduction of intimacy will cause conflict and the more severe the conflict is likely to be. Underintimacy conflicts are thus more frequent and more severe in close relationships than in distant ones.

13. According to Black (2011:51–52), secrecy is also a kind of underintimacy conflict—a conflict over lack of exposure—though in this case it was surely compounded by downward mobility.

14. The case is similar to that of a Chukchee girl who hanged herself "out of anger because her mother refused to take her along to a feast in a neighboring camp" (Bogoras 1909:46).

15. To be more precise, about 16 percent of these suicidal conflicts involved family members, whereas about 7 percent involved disputes with friends or coworkers, and none involved strange individuals. Conflicts with nonfamily included the case of a middle-aged typesetter who was reportedly despondent because he believed his coworkers did not like him and the case of a man who had actually been living with a family for some time, despite not being a blood relative, and who killed himself after "falling out" with them. While no people killed themselves over grievances against strange individuals, three (cited in the previous chapter) killed themselves over conflicts with organizations, and fifteen killed themselves when threatened with arrest and imprisonment.

16. For instance, one abusive Florida man asked his wife—who had ceased having intercourse with him and was planning on leaving the relationship—if they could "work out their problems." When she laughed at the suggestion, he killed her by drowning her in the bathtub (Websdale 1999:83). As Black notes, such killings are effectively private executions for "the crime of saying goodbye" (Black 2011:46; see also Black 2018; Manning 2015b).

17. One disadvantage of the Hong Kong study is that it does not explicitly limit the comparison to cases stemming from conflict rather than predation (e.g., killing a spouse for insurance money) or altruism (e.g., "mercy killing" a dependent spouse before proceeding with a planned suicide), though the latter cases are a minority of the sample. While my West Virginia study (Manning 2015b) suffered from a small sample of cases with relevant information, it was entirely limited to cases stemming from interpersonal problems such as arguments, jealousy, and breakups. Future studies looking to test these relationships should also purify their samples in this way so as to provide the most relevant comparisons.

18. The importance of material independence in encouraging avoidance was a major conclusion of sociologist M. P. Baumgartner's (1988) study of social control in suburbia. Black (1998:80) includes this variable in his theoretical model of the avoidance structure, along with individuation, relational fragmentation, absence of hierarchy, and social fluidity.

19. The Chuukese socialization process is marked by stages in which the parents abruptly withdraw affection and support, effectively encouraging the youth to rely

on a widening circle of associates outside of the nuclear family. This is especially so for males, who were traditionally expected to leave the house at puberty because of a custom demanding brothers and sisters keep their distance from one another. Ethnographer Donald Rubinstein (1992; compare Rubinstein 2002) proposes that rapid social change has left parents without a "cultural script" for raising children under modern economic conditions and that this culture lag results in higher rates of family conflict.

20. It is not clear, however, why only males in this culture are so likely to kill themselves, a pattern that dates back to traditional times (Rubinstein 1992).

21. It is consistent with this hypothesis that some studies find rates of domestic violence, including homicide, to be greater in interracial or interethnic relationships (see, e.g., Mercy and Saltzman 1989; Chartier and Caetano 2012).

4. SUICIDE AND SUPPORT

1. Attempts to obtain the help and protection of third parties do not always take the form of explicit requests. Psychologist Edwin Shneidman (1996:51–53) notes that many of the "clues" given by those who are considering suicide are subtle and cryptic. They sometimes take the form of an indirect goodbye, such as "This is the last time I'll be in your office" or "You won't see me again" (Shneidman 1996:52). Behavioral clues might also be more subtle than brandishing weapons or climbing tall structures. Less dramatic indicators of suicidal intent include suddenly giving away prized possessions or putting one's legal and financial affairs in order through such actions as making a will (Shneidman 1996:52).

2. The concept of violence and social control having a "velocity" was suggested by Donald Black.

CONCLUSION

1. There were several cases in my Louisville study that were sparked by what most would consider minor issues. For example, one man shot his wife and then committed suicide because she would not eat a bowl of soup as he had ordered. Another man shot himself following an argument that grew from a disagreement over where to spend an evening out. Another argument that culminated in suicide was sparked by the prolonged crying of a baby and yet another by a wife's refusal to lend her husband the car so that he could buy beer.

2. Research and theory by pure sociologists of conflict often point to the role of relational closeness in encouraging tolerance and restraint, thus moderating the severity of social control (Black 1998:88–90, 153–54; Campbell and Manning 2019). But sustained relationships are not always peaceful and sometimes allow for an accumulation of grievances that produces more severe conflict overall. Such was the pattern observed by M. P. Baumgartner (1985, 1988) in her study of social control in a US suburb, where middle-class residents tended to be move frequently and have

shallow relationships with their neighbors, while working-class residents tended to have more stable ties. One result was that for middle-class people, a conflict with neighbors was likely to be a one-time affair, a first offense from someone with no prior history of enmity, and thus more easily tolerated. Members of the working class were more likely to have conflicts with people who were, from their point of view, repeat offenders, and thus more inclined to take action (Baumgartner 1985; 1988:87–95). In her theoretical work on lynching, Roberta Senechal de la Roche (2001) similarly observes the importance of repeat offending in predicting when an offender will be lynched. She proposes that repeat offenses are typically behind what she calls *communal lynchings*—when members of a tight-knit community lynch one of their own. While strangers and new arrivals are commonly viewed with suspicion and might be lynched for a single alleged offense, the deviance of insiders receives more toleration and usually only results in lynching when repeated offenses cause someone to achieve "the status of the finally intolerable" (Senechal de la Roche 2001:133, quoting Llewellyn and Hoebel 1941:49).

3. Black (2011:49) attributes greater male vulnerability to suicide following divorce to men having few close ties outside of marriage. Owing to the zero-sum nature of relational distance, this lack of competing relationships makes men closer to their wives than vice versa, and so their loss of intimacy is greater following a divorce.

4. Another major structural difference between protest suicide and suicide attacks is the organization of the perpetrators. Suicide attacks tend to be carried out by formally organized groups with a central leadership and advanced division of labor, including such long-standing terrorist groups as Al-Qaeda, Hamas, the Kurdistan Workers Party (or PKK), and the Liberation Tigers of Tamil Elam (or Tamil Tigers). In some cases, they are even carried out by nation-states, such as Japan during World War II. Suicide protestors might belong to monasteries, workers' unions, or student activist organizations, but these groups typically have lower capacity for collective action, and the suicide itself tends to be a spontaneous individual action rather than something planned and orchestrated by the organization as such (Manning 2015c).

5. As a call to the police, or even a threat to do so, is an increase in the quantity of law, then the demand to commit self-execution is an increase in the quantity of suicide. We can thus apply my theory to explaining cases where demands are made but not met. In one such case, when Adolph Hitler decided to eliminate Ernst Röhm, chief of staff of the storm troopers and "one of his oldest comrades," he "was keen to give his old friend the opportunity to kill himself" by seeing that he was provided with a pistol. Röhm, however, refused to commit suicide and was executed (Goeschel 2009:85, see also 140). The structure was similar to other cases in which Hitler gave such orders and they were obeyed.

6. For example, in 1607 two of ruler Tokugawa Ieyasu's sons, Tadayoshi and Hideyasu, died of illness: "Two of Tadayoshi's friends cut open their bowels; a third, who was in banishment on a remote island, returned to Edo and killed himself at

Zojoji Temple" (Rankin 2012:96–98). The practice was common enough that the Japanese even had a special name for it: junshi, or "suicide through fidelity" (Wikipedia 2017d).

7. Lusi widows of high-ranking men would request that others kill them following the death of their husbands, perhaps even taunting kin who were reluctant to carry out their wishes (Counts 1980:343). Similarly, among the Fijins in traditional times, the widows of chiefs would demand to be strangled, and according to custom the request was only granted if it was repeated several times (Fisch 2005).

8. The tendency to gravitate toward close superiors can also lead to collective suicide. Anthropologist Raymond Firth recounts the case of a Tikopian chief's daughter who, shamed to be illegitimately pregnant with a commoner's child, swam out to sea to die. She was followed in this endeavor by several of her companions among the island's unmarried girls, partly due to "the peer-group attachment which obtains among young men or young women" and partly due to the local attitude that "a person of high status should have a following when entering upon a new and critical experience" (Firth 1967:130). In this and other ways, the collectivization of suicide resembles the collectivization of other sorts of violence, which involves third parties gravitating toward a close superior (for relevant theory, see Black 1998:126–27; Senechal de la Roche 2001).

9. Among the Eskimo of St. Lawrence Island, "Once having decided to do away with himself, the individual initiated the process by asking his relatives to kill him or at least help in the suicide," and having obtained their consent, "he would then dress himself in his house as one already dead, i.e., with his clothing turned inside out. Presently a group of relatives would arrive and carry him seated on a reindeer skin to the 'Destroying Place,'" where several relatives might assist in his hanging (Leighton and Hughes 1955:330–33).

10. Again, relational closeness appears fateful: altruism is generally greater toward those who are socially closer, and so we might expect suicidal altruism—an extreme sacrifice to help others—to be so as well. One implication is that physical and financial dependence upon intimates is more likely to generate such suicide than is comparable dependence upon strangers. If such altruistic suicide by the elderly is a less prominent feature of contemporary societies than of many past societies, it is partly because state welfare systems have shifted dependence away from intimates and toward a faceless bureaucracy funded by strangers. People are unlikely to commit suicide to spare the government the cost of helping them. This is one reason financial assistance to the elderly is a feasible strategy of suicide prevention, especially in rapidly modernizing societies where until quite recently elder care was the primary responsibility of children (see, e.g., Kim 2019).

11. Officials in one Japanese city, recognizing that economic losses were a major reason for suicide, made financial assistance a major part of its suicide prevention efforts: "Instead of treating suicidal people only for depression, as has long been the practice, the city offers financial and legal counseling, along with 'nozomi' (hope

loans) to get the needy out of debt. The suicide rate in [the city] fell from 48.6 per 100,000 people in 2005 to 27.5 in 2007, and city officials expect it to decline again this year, even as the rate rises nationwide" (Hosaka 2009).

APPENDIX A. ON METHODOLOGY

1. Note that at that time, deaths by drug overdose in the United States were less common than they are at the time of this writing. Rising overdose rates may mean more ambiguous cases and more classification errors in recent times.

References

Abouzeid, Rania. 2011. "Bouazizi: The Man Who Set Himself and Tunisia on Fire." *Time,* January 21. http://content.time.com/time/magazine/article/0,9171,2044723 ,00.html.

Abrutyn, Seth, and Anna S. Mueller. 2014a. "Are Suicidal Behaviors Contagious in Adolescence? Using Longitudinal Data to Examine Suicide Suggestion." *American Sociological Review* 79(2): 211–27.

———. 2014b. "Reconsidering Durkheim's Assessment of Tarde: Formalizing a Tardian Theory of Imitation, Contagion, and Suicide Suggestion." *Sociological Forum* 29(3): 698–719.

Abu-Lughod, Lila. 1986. *Veiled Sentiments: Honor and Poetry in a Bedouin Society.* Berkeley: University of California Press.

Adeboye, Olufunke. 2006. "'Death Is Preferable to Ignominy': Politically Motivated Suicide, Social Honor, and Chieftaincy Politics in Early Colonial Ibadan." Unpublished presentation, Harriet Tubman Seminar, Harriet Tubman Resource Centre on the African Diaspora, York University, vol. 24.

Adinkrah, Mensah. 2012. "Better Dead Than Dishonored: Masculinity and Male Suicidal Behavior in Contemporary Ghana." *Social Science & Medicine* 74(4): 474–81.

Ahmadi, Alireza, Reza Mohammadi, David C. Schwebel, Naser Yeganeh, Ali Soroush, and Shahrzad Bazargan-Hejazi. 2009. "Familial Risk Factors for Self-Immolation: A Case-Control Study." *Journal of Women's Health* 18(7): 1025–31.

Akers, Ronald L., Marvin D. Krohn, Lonn Lanza-Kaduce, and Marcia Radosevich. 1979. "Social Learning and Deviant Behavior: A Specific Test of a General Theory." *American Sociological Review* 44(4): 636–55.

Alexander, Scott. 2017. "What is Depression, Anyway? The Synapse Hypothesis." *Slate Star Codex,* June 13. http://slatestarcodex.com/2017/06/13/what-is-depres sion-anyway-the-synapse-hypothesis/.

Aliverdinia, Akbar, and William Alex Pridemore. 2009. "Women's Fatalistic Suicide in Iran: A Partial Test of Durkheim in an Islamic Republic." *Violence against Women* 15(3): 307–20.

Alvarsson, Jan-Ake. 1988. *The Mataco of the Gran Chaco: An Ethnographic Account of Change and Continuity in Mataco Socio-Economic Organization.* Uppsala and Stockholm: Almqvist and Wiksell International.

American Foundation for Suicide Prevention. 2017. "Treatment." https://afsp.org /about-suicide/preventing-suicide/.

Anderson, Olive. 1987. *Suicide in Victorian and Edwardian England.* Oxford: Clarendon.

Araki, Shunichi, and Katsuyuki Murata.1987. "Suicide in Japan: Socioeconomic Effects on Its Secular and Seasonal Trends." *Suicide and Life-Threatening Behavior* 17(1): 64–71.

Atkinson, J. Maxwell. 1978. *Discovering Suicide: Studies in the Social Organization of Sudden Death.* London: Macmillan.

Aviv, Rahel. 2015. "The Death Treatment." *New Yorker,* June 22. https://www .newyorker.com/magazine/2015/06/22/the-death-treatment.

Baechler, Jean. 1975. *Suicides.* Translated by Barry Cooper. New York: Basic Books.

Bailey, Victor. 1998. *"This Rash Act": Suicide across the Life Cycle in the Victorian City.* Stanford, CA: Stanford University Press.

Balikci, Asen. 1970. *The Netsilik Eskimo.* Prospect Heights, IL: Waveland.

Baller, Robert D., and Kelly K. Richardson. 2002. "Social Integration, Imitation, and the Geographic Patterning of Suicide." *American Sociological Review* 67: 873–88.

Bandura, Albert. 1978. "Social Learning Theory of Aggression." *Journal of Communication* 28(3): 12–29.

Barnes, Lauren Seymour, Robin M. Ikeda, and Marcie-jo Kresnow. 2001. "Help-Seeking Behavior Prior to Nearly Lethal Suicide Attempts." *Suicide and Life-Threatening Behavior* 32(1): 68–75.

Barr, Ben, David Taylor-Robinson, Alex Scott-Samuel, Martin McKee, and David Stuckler. 2012. "Suicides Associated with the 2008–10 Economic Recession in England: Time Trend Analysis." *BMJ* 345: e5142.

Baudelot, Christian, and Roger Establet. 2008. *Suicide: The Hidden Side of Modernity.* Translated by David Macey. Cambridge: Polity.

Baumeister, Roy F. 1990. "Suicide as Escape from Self." *Psychological Review* 97(1): 90–113.

Baumgartner, M. P. 1984. "Social Control from Below." Pp. 303–45 in *Toward a General Theory of Social Control,* vol. 1, *Fundamentals,* edited by Donald Black. Orlando: Academic.

———. 1985. "Law and the Middle Class: Evidence from a Suburban Town." *Law and Human Behavior* 9(1): 3–24.

———. 1988. *The Moral Order of a Suburb.* New York: Oxford University Press.

———. 1992. "Violent Networks: The Origins and Management of Domestic Conflict." Pp. 203–31 in *Violence and Aggression: The Social Interactionist Perspective,* edited by Richard B. Felson and James Tedeschi. Washington, DC: American Psychological Association.

References

Bearman, Peter S., and James Moody. 2004. "Suicide and Friendships among American Adolescents." *American Journal of Public Health* 94(1): 89–95.

Beattie, J. H. M. 1960. "Homicide and Suicide in Bunyoro." Pp. 130–53 in *African Homicide and Suicide*, edited by Paul Bohannon. Princeton, NJ: Princeton University Press.

Beauchamp, William M. 1900. "Iroquois Women." *Journal of American Folklore* 13(9): 81–89.

Beautrais, Annette L. 2001. "Suicides and Serious Suicide Attempts: Two Populations or One?" *Psychological Medicine* 31(5): 837–845.

Beck, Aaron T., Gary Brown, and Robert A. Steer. 1989. "Prediction of Eventual Suicide in Psychiatric Inpatients by Clinical Ratings of Hopelessness." *Journal of Consulting and Clinical Psychology* 57(2): 309–10.

Becker, Jillian. 2003. *Giving Up: The Last Days of Sylvia Plath*. New York: St. Martin's.

Beierle, John. 2006. "Culture Summary: Jivaro." Human Relations Area Files. New Haven, CT: HRAF. https://ehrafworldcultures-yale-edu.www.libproxy.wvu.edu /document?id=sd09–000.

Berk, Bernard B. 2006. "Macro-Micro Relationships in Durkheim's Analysis of Egoistic Suicide." *Sociological Theory* 24(1): 58–80.

Berman, Alan L. 1979. "Dyadic Death: Murder-Suicide." *Suicide and Life-Threatening Behavior* 9(1): 15–23.

Berndt, Ronald M. 1962. *Excess and Restraint: Social Control among a New Guinean Mountain People*. Chicago: University of Chicago Press.

Biggs, Michael. 2005. "Dying without Killing: Self-Immolations, 1963–2002." Pp. 173–208 in *Making Sense of Suicide Missions*, edited by Diego Gambetta. Oxford: Oxford University Press.

———. 2008. "Dying for a Cause—Alone?" *Contexts* 7(1): 22–27.

———. 2012. "Self-Immolation in Context, 1963–2012." *Revue d'Études Tibétaines* 25: 143–50.

———. 2013. "How Repertoires Evolve: The Diffusion of Suicide Protest in the Twentieth Century." *Mobilization: An International Quarterly* 18(4): 407–28.

Bilby, Kenneth M. 1990. *The Remaking of the Aluku: Culture, Politics, and Maroon Ethnicity in French South America*. Ann Arbor: University Microfilms.

Black, Donald. 1976. *The Behavior of Law*. San Diego: Academic.

———. 1980. *The Manners and Customs of the Police*. New York: Academic.

———. 1989. *Sociological Justice*. New York: Oxford.

———. 1995. "The Epistemology of Pure Sociology." *Law and Social Inquiry* 20(3): 829–70.

———. 1998. *The Social Structure of Right and Wrong*. San Diego: Academic.

———. 2000. "Dreams of Pure Sociology." *Sociological Theory* 18(3): 343–67.

———. 2002. "The Geometry of Law: An Interview with Donald Black." *International Journal of the Sociology of Law* 30: 101–29.

———. 2004a. "The Geometry of Terrorism." *Sociological Theory* 22(1): 14–25.

———. 2004b. "Violent Structures." Pp. 145–58 in *Violence: From Theory to Research,* edited by Margaret A. Zahn, Henry H. Brownstein, and Shelly L. Jackson. Newark, NJ: LexisNexis/Anderson.

———. 2011. *Moral Time.* New York: Oxford University Press.

———. 2018. "Domestic Violence and Social Time." *Dilemas: Revistas de Estudos de Conflicto e Controle Social* 11(1): 1–27.

Black, Donald, and M. P. Baumgartner. 1983. "Toward a Theory of the Third Party." Pp. 84–114 in *Empirical Theories about Courts,* edited by Keith O. Boyum and Lynn Mather. New York: Longman.

Blakely, Tony A., Sunny C. D. Collings, and June Atkinson. 2003. "Unemployment and Suicide: Evidence for a Causal Association?" *Journal of Epidemiology and Community Health* 57(8): 594–600.

Block, Carolyn Rebecca, and Antigone Christakos. 1995. "Intimate Partner Homicide in Chicago: Over 29 Years." *Crime & Delinquency* 41(4): 496–526.

Bly, Antonio T. 1998. "Crossing the Lake of Fire: Slave Resistance during the Middle Passage, 1720–1842." *Journal of Negro History* 83(3): 177–86.

Bogoras, Waldemar. 1909. *The Chukchee.* New York: E. J. Brill.

Bohm, David. 1959. *Causality and Chance in Modern Physics.* Philadelphia: University of Pennsylvania.

Bosworth, Patricia. 1984. *Diane Arbus: A Biography.* New York: Alfred A. Knopf.

Braithwaite, Richard Bevan. 1953. *Scientific Explanation: A Study of the Function of Theory, Probability and Law in Science.* New York: Free Press.

Breault, K. D. 1986. "Suicide in America: A Test of Durkheim's Theory of Religious and Family Integration, 1933–1980." *American Journal of Sociology* 92(3): 628–56.

Breed, Warren. 1963. "Occupational Mobility and Suicide among White Males." *American Sociological Review* 28(2): 179–88.

———. 1967. "Suicide and Loss in Social Interaction." Pp. 188–201 in *Essays in Self-Destruction,* edited by Edwin S. Shneidman. New York: Jason Aronson.

Brent, David A., Joshua A. Perper, Grace Moritz, Marianne Baugher, Claudia Roth, Lisa Balach, and Joy Schweers. 1993. "Stressful Life Events, Psychopathology, and Adolescent Suicide: A Case Control Study." *Suicide and Life-Threatening Behavior* 23(3): 179–87.

Bridges, F. Stephen, and David Lester. 2011. "Homicide–Suicide in the United States, 1968–1975." *Forensic Science International* 206(1–3): 185–89.

Britten, Nick. 2008. "Suicide Teenager Urged to Jump by Baying Crowd." *Telegraph,* September 30. https://www.telegraph.co.uk/news/uknews/3108987/Suicide-teenager-urged-to-jump-by-baying-crowd.html.

Brown, Judith K. 1970. "Economic Organization and the Position of Women among the Iroquois." *Ethnohistory* 17(3/4): 151–67.

Brown, Martin, and Brian Barraclough. 1999. "Partners in Life and in Death: The Suicide Pact in England and Wales 1988–1992." *Psychological Medicine* 29: 1299–1306.

Brown, Michael F. 1985. *Tsewa's Gift: Magic and Meaning in an Amazonian Society.* Washington: Smithsonian Institution Press.

———. 1986. "Power, Gender, and the Social Meaning of Aguaruna Suicide." *Man* 21(2): 311–28.

Cain, Geoffrey. 2014. "South Koreans Blame Themselves for Ferry Tragedy." *PRI,* April 17. https://www.pri.org/stories/2014-04-17/south-koreans-blame-themselves -ferry-tragedy.

Campbell, Bradley. 2009. "Genocide as Social Control." *Sociological Theory* 27(2): 150–72.

———. 2015a. "Genocide as Predation." *International Journal of Law, Crime, and Justice* 43(3): 310–45.

———. 2015b. *The Geometry of Genocide: A Study in Pure Sociology.* Charlottesville: University of Virginia Press.

Campbell, Bradley, and Jason Manning. 2018. *The Rise of Victimhood Culture: Microaggressions, Safe Spaces, and the New Culture Wars.* New York: Palgrave Macmillan.

———. 2019. "Social Geometry and Social Control." Pp. 50–62 in *The Handbook of Social Control,* edited by Mathieu Deflem. Hoboken, NJ: Wiley-Blackwell.

Campbell, Elizabeth, and Isabelita Guiao. 2004. "Muslim Culture and Female Self-Immolation: Implications for Global Women's Health Research and Practice." *Health Care for Women International* 25(9): 782–93.

Cátedra, María. 1992. *This World, Other Worlds: Sickness, Suicide, Death, and the After-life among the Vaqueiros de Alzada of Spain.* Translated by William A. Christian Jr. Chicago: University of Chicago Press.

Cavan, Ruth Shonle. 1928. *Suicide.* Chicago: University of Chicago Press.

Centers for Disease Control. 2006. "Homicides and Suicides—National Violent Death Reporting System, United States, 2003–2004." https://www.cdc.gov /mmwr/preview/mmwrhtml/mm5526a1.htm.

Chan, Aris C. Y., Philip S. L. Beh, and Roderic G. Broadhurst. 2010. "To Flee or Not: Postkilling Responses among Intimate Partner Homicide Offenders in Hong Kong." *Homicide Studies* 14(4): 400–418.

Chan, Wincy S. C., Paul S. F. Yip, Paul W. C. Wong, and Eric Y. H. Chen. 2007. "Suicide and Unemployment: What Are the Missing Links?" *Archives of Suicide Research* 11(4): 327–35.

Chandler, Charles R., and Yung-Mei Tsai. 1993. "Suicide in Japan and in the West." *International Journal of Comparative Sociology* 34(3/4): 244–59.

Chang, Shu-Sen, David Gunnell, Jonathan A. C. Sterne, Tsung-Hsueh Lu, and Andrew T. A. Cheng. 2009. "Was the Economic Crisis 1997–1998 Responsible for Rising Suicide Rates in East/Southeast Asia? A Time-Trend Analysis for Japan, Hong Kong, South Korea, Taiwan, Singapore and Thailand." *Social Science & Medicine* 68(7): 1322–31.

Chang, Shu-Sen, David Stuckler, Paul Yip, and David Gunnell. 2013. "Impact of 2008 Global Economic Crisis on Suicide: Time Trend Study in 54 Countries." *BMJ* 347: f5239.

Chanoff, David, and Doan Van Toai. 1986. *Portrait of the Enemy.* New York: Random House.

Chartier, Karen G., and Raul Caetamo. 2012. "Interpersonal Violence and Alcohol Problems in Interethnic and Intraethnic Couples." *Journal of Interpersonal Violence* 27(9): 1780–1801.

Chen, Eric Y. H., Wincy S. C. Chan, Paul W. C. Wong, Sandra S. M. Chan, Cecilia L. W. Chan, Y. W. Law, Philip S. L. Beh, K. K. Chan, Joanne W. Y. Cheng, Ka Y. Liu, and Paul S. F. Yip. 2006. "Suicide in Hong Kong: A Case-Control Psychological Autopsy Study." *Psychological Medicine* 36(6): 815–25. Cohen, Dov, Richard E. Nisbett, Brian F. Bowdle, and Norbert Schwarz. 1996. "Insult, Aggression, and the Southern Culture of Honor: An 'Experimental Ethnography.'" *Journal of Personality and Social Psychology* 70(5): 945–96.

Conley, Dalton. 1999. *Being Black, Living in the Red: Race, Wealth, and Social Policy in America.* Berkeley: University of California Press.

Cooney, Mark. 1998. *Warriors and Peacemakers: How Third Parties Shape Violence.* New York: New York University Press.

———. 2003. "The Privatization of Violence." *Criminology* 41(4): 1377–1406.

———. 2006. "The Criminological Potential of Pure Sociology." *Crime, Law, and Social Change* 46(1–2): 51–63.

———. 2009. *Is Killing Wrong? A Study in Pure Sociology.* Charlottesville: University of Virginia Press.

Cooney, Mark, and Scott Phillips. 2002. "Typologizing Violence: A Blackian Perspective." *International Journal of Sociology and Social Policy* 22: 75–108.

———. 2017. "When Will Academics Contest Intellectual Conflict?" *Socius* 10:1–15.

Counts, Dorothy Ayers. 1980. "Fighting Back Is Not the Way: Suicide and the Women of Kaliai." *American Ethnologist* 7(2): 332–51.

———. 1987. "Female Suicide and Wife Abuse in Cross-Cultural Perspective." *Suicide and Life-Threatening Behavior* 17(3): 194–204.

———. 1990. "Beaten Wife, Suicidal Woman: Domestic Violence in Kaliai, West New Britain." *Pacific Studies* 13(3): 151–69.

Cross, Charles R. 2001. *Heavier Than Heaven: A Biography of Kurt Cobain.* New York: Hyperion.

Curran, David K. 1987. *Adolescent Suicidal Behavior.* New York: Hemisphere.

Cutler, David M., Edward L. Glaeser, and Karen E. Norberg. 2001. "Explaining the Rise in Youth Suicide." Pp. 219–70 in *Risky Behavior among Youths: An Economic Analysis,* edited by Jonathan Gruber. Chicago: University of Chicago Press.

Daly, Martin, and Margo Wilson. 1988. *Homicide.* New York: Aldine de Gruyter.

Danigelis, Nick, and Whitney Pope. 1979. "Durkheim's Theory of Suicide as Applied to the Family: An Empirical Test." *Social Forces* 57(4): 1081–1106.

Dantzer, Robert, Jason C. O'Conner, Gregory C. Freund, Rodney W. Johnson, and Keith W. Kelley. 2008. "From Inflammation to Sickness and Depression: When the Immune System Subjugates the Brain." *Nature Reviews Neuroscience* 9(1): 46–56.

Davey, Monica. 2007. "Kevorkian Speaks after His Release from Prison." *New York Times,* June 4. http://www.nytimes.com/2007/06/04/us/04kevorkian.html?ref=jack_kevorkian.

Davies, James E. 1962. "Toward a Theory of Revolution." *American Sociological Review* 27: 5–19.

Dawson, Myrna. 2005. "Intimate Femicide Followed by Suicide: Examining the Role of Premeditation." *Suicide and Life-Threatening Behavior* 35(1): 76–90.

Dean, John. 2013. "Dealing with Aaron Swartz in the Nixonian Tradition: Overzealous Overcharging Leads to a Tragic Result." *Verdict: Legal Analysis and Commentary from Justia,* January 25. https://verdict.justia.com/2013/01/25/dealing-with-aaron-swartz-in-the-nixonian-tradition.

Demarco, Megan, and Alexi Friedman. 2012. "Live Blog: Dharun Ravi Sentenced to 30 Days in Jail."NJ.com, May 21. http://www.nj.com/news/index.ssf/2012/05/dharun_ravi_sentenced_for_bias.html.

Diamond, Jared. 2013. *The World until Yesterday: What Can We Learn from Traditional Societies?* New York: Penguin.

Diamond, Nora. 1969. *K'un Shen: A Taiwan Village.* New York: Holt, Rinehart, and Winston.

Dillon, Nancy, and Rachel Desantis. 2018. "'Glee' Star Mark Salling Dead at 35 in Suspected Suicide by Hanging." *New York Daily News,* January 30. http://www.nydailynews.com/entertainment/glee-star-mark-salling-dead-35-suspected-suicide-article-1.3788124.

Dobbs, David. 2006. "A Depression Switch?" *New York Times Magazine,* April 2.

Douglas, Jack D. 1967. *The Social Meanings of Suicide.* Princeton, NJ: Princeton University Press.

Downs, Marilyn F., and Daniel Eisenberg. 2012. "Help Seeking and Treatment Use among Suicidal College Students." *Journal of American College Health* 60(2): 104–14.

Duberstein, Paul R., Yeates Conwell, Kenneth R. Conner, Shirley Eberly, J. S. Evinger, and Eric D. Caine. 2004. "Poor Social Integration and Suicide: Fact or Artifact? A Case-Control Study." *Psychological Medicine* 34(7): 1331–37.

Dublin, Louis I. 1963. *Suicide: A Sociological and Statistical Study.* New York: Ronald Press.

Duff, R. A. 1982–83. "Socratic Suicide?" *Proceedings of the Aristotelian Society* 83: 35–47.

Duman, Ronald S. 2014. "Neurobiology of Stress, Depression, and Rapid Acting Antidepressants: Remodeling Synaptic Connections." *Depression and Anxiety* 31(4): 291–96.

Durkheim, Emile. [1897] 1951. *Suicide: A Study in Sociology.* New York: Free Press.

Edwards, Adrian C. 1962. *The Ovimbundu under Two Sovereignties: A Study of Social Control and Social Change among a People of Angola.* London: Oxford University Press.

Elwin, Verrier. 1943. *Maria Murder and Suicide.* Bombay: Oxford University Press.

Ennis, Merlin W., and Albert Bates Lord. 1962. *Umbundu: Folk Tales from Angola.* Boston: Beacon.

Exline, Julia Juola, Lise Deshea, and Virginia Todd Holeman. 2007. "Is Apology Worth the Risk? Predictors, Outcomes, and Ways to Avoid Regret." *Journal of Social and Clinical Psychology* 26(4): 479–504.

Fahim, Kareem. 2011. "Slap to a Man's Pride Set Off Tumult in Tunisia." *New York Times,* January 21. http://www.nytimes.com/2011/01/22/world/africa/22sidi.html.

Falk, Richard. 2011. "Ben Ali Tunisia Was Model U.S. Client." Al Jazeera, January 25. http://www.aljazeera.com/indepth/opinion/2011/01/20111231453041972.html.

Fang, Chao-ying. 1943. "Ch'i-ying (Kiying)." Pp. 131–34 in *Eminent Chinese of the Ch'ing Period (1644–1912),* vol. 1, edited by Arthur William Hummel. Washington: US Government Printing Office.

Farberow, Norman L., and Edwin S. Shneidman. 1957. "Suicide and Age." Pp. 40–46 in *Clues to Suicide,* edited by Edwin S. Shneidman and Norman L. Farberow. New York: McGraw-Hill.

Faria, Neice Müller Xavier, Cesar Gomes Victora, Stela Nazareth Meneghel, Lenine Alves de Carvalho, and João Werner Falk. 2006. "Suicide Rates in the State of Rio Grande do Sul, Brazil: Association with Socioeconomic, Cultural, and Agricultural Factors." *Cadernos de Saude Publica* 22(12): 2611–21.

Fava, Maurizio, and David Mischoulon. 2009. "Folates in Depression: Efficacy, Differences in Formulations, and Clinical Issues." *Journal of Clinical Psychiatry* 70(5): 12–17.

Fei, Wu. 2005. "'Gambling for Qi': Suicide and Family Politics in a Rural North China County." *China Journal* 54: 7–27.

Fenton, William N. 1941. "Iroquois Suicide: A Study in the Stability of a Cultural Pattern." Washington: Smithsonian Institution.

———. 1986. "A Further Note on Iroquois Suicide." *Ethnohistory* 33: 448–57.

Fergusson, David M., Joseph M. Boden, and John Horwood. 2007. "Unemployment and Suicidal Behavior in a New Zealand Birth Cohort: A Fixed Effects Regression Analysis." *Crisis* 28(2): 95–101.

Filipovic, Milenko S. 1982. *Among the People, Native Yugoslav Ethnography: Selected Writing of Milenko S. Filipovic.* Ann Arbor, MI: Michigan Slavic Publications, Deptartment of Slavic Languages and Literatures.

Fincham, Ben, Susanne Langer, Jonathan Scourfield, and Michael Shiner. 2011. *Understanding Suicide: A Sociological Autopsy.* New York: Palgrave Macmillan.

Firth, Raymond. 1933. *We the Tikopia: A Sociological Study of Kinship in Primitive Polynesia.* New York: American Book.

————. 1949. "Authority and Public Opinion in Tikopia." Pp. 168–88 in *Social Structure: Studies Presented to A. R. Radcliffe-Brown*, edited by Meyer Fortes. Oxford: Clarendon.

————. 1967. "Suicide and Risk-Taking." Pp. 116–40 in *Tikopia Ritual and Belief*. Boston: Beacon.

Fisch, Jörg. 2005. "Dying for the Dead: Sati in Universal Context." *Journal of World History* 16(3): 293–325.

————. 2006. *Burning Women: A Global History of Widow Sacrifice from Ancient Times to the Present*. London: Seagull Books.

Fisher, Bonnie S., Leah E. Daigle, Francis T. Cullen, and Michael G. Turner. 2003. "Reporting Sexual Victimization to the Police and Others: Results from a National-Level Study of College Women." *Criminal Justice and Behavior* 30(1): 6–38.

Flanagan, Damian. 2014. *Yukio Mishima*. London: Reaktion Books.

Fock, Niels. 1963. "Mataco Marriage." *Folk, Dansk Ethnografisk Tidsskrift* 5: 91–101.

Foley, Denis. 1975. *An Ethnohistoric and Ethnographic Analysis of the Iroquois from the Aboriginal Era to the Present Suburban Era*. Ann Arbor: University Microfilms International.

Fowler, W. Rodney, and James V. Maguire. 2001. "Dealing with Defenestrators: Immediate Interventions." *Journal of Police Crisis Negotiations* 1(2): 41–51.

Freeman, Derek. 1983. *Margaret Mead and Samoa: The Making and Unmaking of an Anthropological Myth*. Cambridge, MA: Harvard University Press.

Friedl, Erika. 1994. "Sources of Female Power in Iran." Pp. 151–57 in *In the Eye of the Storm: Women in Post-Revolutionary Iran*, edited by Mahnaz Afkhami and Erika Friedl. New York: I. B. Taurus.

Fullerton, Jamie. 2009. "Dave Grohl: 'I Knew Kurt Cobain Was Destined to Die Early.'" *NME*, November 10. http://www.nme.com/news/music/nirvana-163 -1310748.

Gardner, Howard. 1993. *Creating Minds: An Anatomy of Creativity Seen through the Lives of Freud, Einstein, Picasso, Stravinsky, Eliot, Graham, and Gandhi*. New York: Basic Books.

Gelber, Marilyn G. 1986. *Gender and Society in the New Guinea Highlands: An Anthropological Perspective on Antagonism Toward Women*. Boulder, CO: Westview.

Giannini, Margaret J., Brian Bergmark, Samantha Kreshover, Eileen Elias, Caitlin Plummer, and Eileen O'Keefe. 2010. "Understanding Suicide and Disability through Three Major Disabling Conditions: Intellectual Disability, Spinal Cord Injury, and Multiple Sclerosis." *Disability and Health Journal* 3(2): 74–78. Gibbs, Jack P., and Walter T. Martin. 1964. *Status Integration and Suicide: A Sociological Study*. Eugene: University of Oregon Books.

Gladwin, Thomas, and Seymour B. Sarason. 1953. *Truk: Man in Paradise*. New York: Wenner-Gren Foundation for Anthropological Research.

Goeschel, Christian. 2009. *Suicide in Nazi Germany.* New York: Oxford University Press.

Goffman, Erving. 1974. *Frame Analysis: An Essay on the Organization of Experience.* Boston: Northeastern University Press.

Gorer, Geoffrey. 1967. *Himalayan Village: An Account of the Lepchas of Sikkim.* 2nd ed. London: Nelson.

Gould, Madelyn S. 2001. "Suicide and the Media." *Annals of the New York Academy of Sciences* 932(1): 200–224.

Gouldsbury, Cullen, and Hubert Sheane. 1911. *The Great Plateau of Northern Rhodesia.* London: Edward Arnold.

Granados, José A. Tapia, and Ana V. Diez Roux. 2009. "Life and Death during the Great Depression." *Proceedings of the National Academy of Sciences* 106(41): 17290–95.

Grant, Jon E. 2007. "Failing the 15-Minute Suicide Watch: Guidelines to Monitor Inpatients." *Current Psychiatry* 6(6): 41–43.

Graser, R. R. 1992. *A Study of Selected Cases of Family Murder in South Africa.* Pretoria: Human Sciences Research Council.

Greenberg, Jeff, and Tom Pyszczynski. 1986. "Persistent High Self-Focus after Failure and Low Self-Focus after Success: The Depressive Self-Focusing Style." *Journal of Personality and Social Psychology* 50(5): 1039.

Gregory, Stanford W., Jr., and Stephen Webster. 1996. "A Nonverbal Signal in Voices of Interview Partners Effectively Predicts Communication Accommodation and Social Status Perceptions." *Journal of Personality and Social Psychology* 70(6): 1231–40.

Griffin, Miriam. 1986a. "Philosophy, Cato, and Roman Suicide: I." *Greece & Rome* 33(1): 64–77.

———. 1986b. "Philosophy, Cato, and Roman Suicide: II." *Greece & Rome* 33(2): 192–202.

Gyatso, Sangye. 2017. "Tibetan Monk Sets Himself Ablaze in Qinghai in 150th Self-Immolation." Radio Free Asia, May 19. http://www.rfa.org/english/news/tibet/ablaze-05192017121758.html.

Haarr, Robin N. 2010. "Suicidality among Battered Women in Tajikistan." *Violence against Women* 16(7): 764–88.

Hadlaczky, Gergo, and Danuta Wasserman. 2009. "Suicidality in Women." Pp. 117–38 in *Contemporary Topics in Women's Mental Health: Global Perspectives in a Changing Society,* edited by Prabha S. Chandra, Helen Herrman, Jane Fisher, Marianne Kastrup, Unaiza Niaz, Marta B. Rondon, and Ahmed Okasha. Hoboken, NJ: Wiley-Blackwell.

Halbwachs, Maurice. [1930] 1978. *The Causes of Suicide.* Translated by Harold Goldblatt. London: Routledge and Kegan Paul.

Hannan, Michael T., Nancy Brandon Tuma, and Lyle P. Groeneveld. 1977. "Income and Marital Events: Evidence from an Income-Maintenance Experiment." *American Journal of Sociology* 82(6): 1186–1211.

———. 1978. "Income and Independence Effects on Marital Dissolution: Results from the Seattle and Denver Income-Maintenance Experiments." *American Journal of Sociology* 84(3): 611–33.

Harden, Blaine. 2010. "In Prosperous South Korea, a Troubling Increase in Suicide Rate." *Washington Post,* April 18. http://www.washingtonpost.com/wp-dyn /content/article/2010/04/17/AR2010041702781.html?noredirect=on.

Harner, Michael J. 1972. *The Jívaro: People of the Sacred Waterfalls.* Garden City: Anchor Books.

Harper, Dee Wood, and Lydia Voigt. 2007. "Homicide Followed by Suicide: An Integrated Theoretical Perspective." *Homicide Studies* 11(4): 295–316.

Haslam, Nick. 2016. "Concept Creep: Psychology's Expanding Concepts of Harm and Pathology." *Psychological Inquiry* 27(1): 1–17.

Hassan, Riaz. 1995. *Suicide Explained: The Australian Experience.* Carlton: Melbourne University Press.

Hawkes, David, ed. 2011. *Songs of the South: An Ancient Anthology of Poems by Qu Yuan and Other Poets.* London: Penguin Books.

Healey, Christopher. 1979. "Women and Suicide in New Guinea." *Social Analysis* 2: 89–106.

Heckewelder, John Gottlieb Ernestus. 1819. *An Account of the History, Manners, and Customs, of the Indian Nations Who Once Inhabited Pennsylvania and the Neighboring States.* Philadelphia: Abraham Small.

Heckler, Richard A. 1994. *Waking Up, Alive: The Descent, the Suicide Attempt, and the Return to Life.* New York: G. P. Putnam's Sons.

Heinrich, Max. 1977. "Change of Heart: A Test of Some Widely Held Theories about Religious Conversion." *American Journal of Sociology* 83(3): 653–80.

Hempel, Carl G. 1965. "Aspects of Scientific Explanation." Pp. 331–496 in *Aspects of Scientific Explanation and Other Essays in the Philosophy of Science.* New York: Free Press.

Henrich, Joseph. 2016. *The Secret of Our Success: How Culture Is Driving Evolution, Domesticating Our Species, and Making Us Smarter.* Princeton, NJ: Princeton University Press.

Henry, Andrew F., and James F. Short Jr. 1954. *Suicide and Homicide: Some Economic, Sociological and Psychological Aspects of Aggression.* Glencoe: Free Press.

Hezel, Francis X. 1984. "Cultural Patterns of Trukese Suicide." *Ethnology* 23(3): 193–206.

Hilger, M. Inez. 1957. *Araucanian Child Life and Its Cultural Background.* Washington, DC: Smithsonian Institution.

Hill, Peter. 2005. "Kamikaze, 1943–5." Pp. 1–42 in *Making Sense of Suicide Missions,* edited by Diego Gambetta. Oxford: Oxford University Press.

Hintikka, Jukka, Pirjo I. Saarinen, and Heimo Viinamäki. 1999. "Suicide Mortality in Finland during an Economic Cycle, 1985–1995." *Scandinavian Journal of Social Medicine* 27(2): 85–88.

Hjelmeland, Heidi, Keith Hawton, Hilmar Nordvik, Unni Bille-Brahe, Diego de Leo, Sandor Fekete, Onja Grad, Christian Haring, Ad J. F. M. Kerkhof, Jouko Lönnqvist, Konrad Michel, Ellinor Salander Renberg, Armin Schmidtke, Kees van Heeringen, and Danuta Wasserman. 2002. "Why People Engage in Parasuicide: A Cross-Cultural Study of Intentions." *Suicide and Life-Threatening Behavior* 32(4): 380–93.

Hoebel, E. Adamson. 1976. *The Law of Primitive Man: A Study in Comparative Legal Dynamics.* New York: Atheneum.

Hoffer, Tia A., Joy Lynn E. Shelton, Stephen Behnke, and Philip Erdberg. 2010. "Exploring the Impact of Child Sex Offender Suicide." *Journal of Family Violence* 25(8): 777–86.

Hollan, Douglas. 1990. "Indignant Suicide in the Pacific: An Example from the Toraja Highlands of Indonesia."^ *Culture, Medicine and Psychiatry* 14(3): 365–79.

Holmes, Ronald M., and Stephen T. Holmes. 2005. *Suicide: Theory, Practice, and Investigation.* Thousand Oaks, CA: Sage.

Homans, George C. 1967. *The Nature of Social Science.* New York: Harcourt, Brace and World.

Hopkins, Mary T. 1971. "Patterns of Self-Destruction among the Orthopedically Disabled." *Rehabilitation Research and Practice Review* 3(1): 5–16.

Horwitz. Alan V. 1984. "Therapy and Social Solidarity." Pp.211–250 in *Toward a General Theory of Social Control*, vol. 1, *Fundamentals*, edited by Donald Black. Orlando: Academic.

———. 1990. *The Logic of Social Control.* New York: Plenum.

Horwitz, Alan V., and Jerome C. Wakefield. 2007. *The Loss of Sadness: How Psychiatry Transformed Normal Sorrow into Depressive Disorder.* Kindle ed. Oxford: Oxford University Press.

Hosaka, Tomoko A. 2009. "Using Financial Aid to Curb Suicides." *Japan Times,* December 23. https://www.japantimes.co.jp/news/2009/12/23/national/using -financial-aid-to-curb-suicides/#.XajGFehKi7o.

Howell, Nancy. 1979. *Demography of the Dobe !Kung.* New York: Academic.

Hume, David. [1748] 1955. *An Inquiry Concerning Human Understanding,* edited by Charles W. Hendel. Indianapolis: Bobbs-Merril.

Hunt, Katie, and Shen Lu. 2015. "China: Former Official Jumps to His Death after Deadly Landslide." CNN, December 28. http://www.cnn.com/2015/12 /28/asia/china-landslide-suicide/index.html?sr=twcnni122915china-landslide -suicide0410AMVODtopLink&linkId=19957050.

Hurault, Jean Winchell. 1961. *The Boni Refugee Blacks of French Guiana.* Dakar: IFAN.

Iga, Mamoru.1986. *The Thorn in the Chrysanthemum: Suicide and Economic Success in Modern Japan.* Berkeley: University of California Press.

Jackson, Nicholas. 2011. "Jack Kevorkian's Death Van and the Tech of Assisted Suicide." *Atlantic,* June 3. https://www.theatlantic.com/technology/archive/2011/06 /jack-kevorkians-death-van-and-the-tech-of-assisted-suicide/239897/.

Jang, Sang-Hwan. 2004. "Continuing Suicide among Laborers in Korea." *Labor History* 45(3): 271–97.

Jeffreys, M. D. W. 1952. "Samsonic Suicide or Suicide of Revenge among Africans." *African Studies* 11(3): 118–22.

Johnson, Barclay D. 1965. "Durkheim's One Cause of Suicide." *American Sociological Review* 30(6): 875–76.

Johnson, Patricia Lyons. 1981. "When Dying Is Better Than Living: Female Suicide among the Gainj of Papua New Guinea." *Ethnology* 20(4): 325–34.

Joiner, Thomas E. 2005. *Why People Die by Suicide.* Cambridge, MA: Harvard University Press.

Junker, Gary, Art Beeler, and Jeffrey Bates. 2005. "Using Trained Inmate Observers for Suicide Watch in a Federal Correctional Setting: A Win-Win Solution." *Psychological Services* 2(1): 20.

Kameda, Masaaki. 2015. "Emperor's WWII Surrender Aired amid Turmoil in Wartime Regime." *Japan Times,* August 14. https://www.japantimes.co.jp/news/2015 /08/14/national/history/emperors-wwii-surrender-aired-amid-turmoil-wartime -regime/#.WnzTNOjwaM8.

Karman, James. 2001. *Robinson Jeffers: Poet of California.* Ashland, OR: Story Line.

Kelly, Joan B., and Michael P. Johnson. 2008. "Differentiation among Types of Intimate Partner Violence: Research Update and Implications for Interventions." *Family Court Review* 46(3): 476–99.

Kemp, Joe, Clare Trapasso, and Larry McShane. 2013. "Aaron Swartz, Co-founder of Reddit and Online Activist, Hangs Himself in Brooklyn Apartment, Authorities Say." *New York Daily News,* January 12. http://www.nydailynews.com/new-york /co-founder-reddit-hangs-brooklyn-apartment-article-1.1238852.

Khan, Murad M. 2002. "Suicide on the Indian Subcontinent." *Crisis: The Journal of Crisis Intervention and Suicide Prevention* 23(3): 104–7.

Kim, Hyojoung. 2008. "Micromobilization and Suicide Protest in South Korea, 1970–2004." *Social Research* 75(2): 543–78.

Kim, Jaewon. 2019. "No Country for Old Koreans: Moon Faces Senior Poverty Crisis." *Nikkei Asian Review,* January 29. https://asia.nikkei.com/Spotlight/Asia -Insight/No-country-for-old-Koreans-Moon-faces-senior-poverty-crisis.

King, Sallie B. 2000. "They Who Burned Themselves for Peace: Quaker and Buddhist Self-Immolators during the Vietnam War." *Buddhist-Christian Studies* 20: 127–50.

Kobler, Arthur L., and Ezra Stotland. 1964. *The End of Hope: A Social-Clinical Study of Suicide.* London: Free Press of Glencoe.

Koch, Klaus-Friedrich. 1974. *War and Peace in Jalémo: The Management of Conflict in Highland New Guinea.* Cambridge, MA: Harvard University Press.

Kox, Willem, Wim Meeus, and Harm 't Hart. 1991. "Religious Conversion of Adolescents: Testing the Loftland and Stark Model of Religious Conversion." *Sociological Analysis* 52(3): 227–40.

Koziol-McLain, Jane, Daniel Webster, Judith McFarlane, Carolyn Rebecca Block, Yvonne Ulrich, Nancy Glass, and Jacquelyn C. Campbell. 2006. "Risk factors for Femicide-Suicide in Abusive Relationships: Results from a Multisite Case Control Study." *Violence and Victims* 21(1): 3–21.

Kposowa, Augustine J. 2000. "Marital Status and Suicide in the National Longitudinal Mortality Study." *Journal of Epidemiology and Community Health* 54(4): 254–61.

———. 2001. "Unemployment and Suicide: A Cohort Analysis of Social Factors Predicting Suicide in the US National Longitudinal Mortality Study." *Psychological Medicine* 31(1): 127–38.

Krauss, Herbert H., and Beatrice J. Krauss. 1968. "Cross-Cultural Study of the Thwarting-Disorientation Theory of Suicide." *Journal of Abnormal Psychology* 73: 353–57.

Kreitman, Norman, ed. 1977. *Parasuicide.* New York: Wiley.

Kreps, Daniel. 2014. "Korean Safety Official Commits Suicide Following Concert Tragedy." *Rolling Stone,* October 18. https://www.rollingstone.com/music /news/south-korean-safety-official-commits-suicide-following-k-pop-concert -tragedy-20141018.

Knuth, Margot O. 1978. "Civil Liability for Causing or Failing to Prevent Suicide." *Loyola of Los Angeles Law Review* 12: 967–87.

La Fontaine, Jean. 1975. "Anthropology." Pp. 77–91 in *A Handbook for the Study of Suicide,* edited by Seymour Perlin. New York: Oxford University Press.

Lacasse, Jeffrey R., and Jonathan Leo. 2005. "Serotonin and Depression: A Disconnect between the Advertisements and the Scientific Literature." *PLoS Medicine* 2(12): e392.

Lalich, Janja. 2004. *Bounded Choice: True Believers and Charismatic Cults.* Los Angeles: University of California Press.

Laloe, Veronique, and M. Ganesan. 2002. "Self-Immolation a Common Suicidal Behaviour in Eastern Sri Lanka." *Burns* 28(5): 475–80.

Lee, Ricard B. 1979. *The !Kung San: Men, Women, and Work in a Foraging Society.* New York: Cambridge University Press.

Leighton, Alexander H., and Charles C. Hughes. 1955. "Notes on Eskimo Patterns of Suicide." *Southwestern Journal of Anthropology* 11(4): 327–38.

Lenoir, John D. 1973. *The Paramacca Maroons: A Study in Religious Acculturation.* Ann Arbor: University Microfilms International.

LePoer, Barbara Leitch. 1989. "Historical Setting." Pp. 1–76 in *Vietnam: A Country Study,* edited by Richard J. Cima. Washington, DC: Federal Research Division.

Leung, Angela K.-Y., and Dov Cohen. 2011. "Within- and between-Culture Variation: Individual Differences and the Cultural Logics of Honor, Face, and Dignity Cultures." *Journal of Personality and Social Psychology* 100(3):507–26.

Levenkron, Stephen. 1999. *Cutting: Understanding and Overcoming Self-Mutilation.* New York: W. W. Norton.

Lewis, Jeffrey Williams. 2012. *The Business of Martyrdom: A History of Suicide Bombing*. Annapolis, MD: Naval Institute Press.

Lewis, Neil. 2005. "Guantánamo Prisoners Go on Hunger Strike." *New York Times*, September 18. https://www.nytimes.com/2005/09/18/politics/guantanamo -prisoners-go-on-hunger-strike.html.

Lickerman, Alex. 2010. "The Six Reasons People Attempt Suicide." *Psychology Today*, April 29. https://www.psychologytoday.com/blog/happiness-in-world/201004 /the-six-reasons-people-attempt-suicide.

Liem, Marieke, and Paul Nieuwbeerta. 2010. "Homicide Followed by Suicide: A Comparison with Homicide and Suicide." *Suicide and Life-Threatening Behavior* 40(2): 133–45.

Linge, Heinz. 2009. *With Hitler to the End: The Memoirs of Adolf Hitler's Valet*. New York: Skyhorse.

Llewellyn, Karl N., and E. Adamson Hoebel. 1941. *The Cheyenne Way: Conflict and Case Law in Primitive Jurisprudence*. Norman: University of Oklahoma Press.

Loftland, John, and Rodney Stark. 1965. "Becoming a World-Saver: A Theory of Conversion to a Deviant Perspective." *American Sociological Review* 30: 862–75.

Lorant, Vincent, Anton E. Kunst, Martijn Huisman, Matthias Bopp, Johan Mackenbach, and EU Working Group. 2005a. "A European Comparative Study of Marital Status and Socio-Economic Inequalities in Suicide." *Social Science & Medicine* 60(11): 2431–41.

Lorant, Vincent, Alton E. Kunst, Martijn Huisman, G. Costa, and Johan Mackenbach. 2005b. "Socio-Economic Inequalities in Suicide: A European Comparative Study." *British Journal of Psychiatry*, 187(1): 49–54.

Lowenthal, Bennett. 1987. "The Jumpers of '29." *Washington Post*, October 25. https:// www.washingtonpost.com/archive/opinions/1987/10/25/the-jumpers-of-29 /17defff9-f725-43b7-831b-7924ac0a1363/?utm_term=.8fc350e09c64.

Lui, Meng. 2002. "Rebellion and Revenge: The Meaning of Suicide of Women in Rural China." *International Journal of Social Welfare* 11(4): 300–309.

Luo, Feijun, Curtis S. Florence, Myriam Quispe-Agnoli, Lijing Ouyang, and Alexander E. Crosby. 2011. "Impact of Business Cycles on US Suicide Rates, 1928–2007." *American Journal of Public Health* 101(6): 1139–46.

Macdonald, Charles J.-H. 2007. *Uncultural Behavior: An Anthropological Investigation of Suicide in the Southern Philippines*. Honolulu: University of Hawaii Press.

MacDonald, Michael, and Terence R. Murphy. 1990. *Sleepless Souls: Suicide in Early Modern England*. Oxford: Clarendon.

Macpherson, Cluny, and La'Avasa Macpherson.1987. "Towards an Explanation of Recent Trends in Suicide in Western Samoa." *Man* 22(2): 305–30.

Mäki, Netta, and Pekka Martikainen. 2012. "A Register-Based Study on Excess Suicide Mortality Among Unemployed Men and Women During Different Levels of Unemployment in Finland." *Journal of Epidemiology & Community Health* 66(4): 302–7.

Malinowski, Bronislaw. [1926] 1976. *Crime and Custom in Savage Society.* Totowa, NJ: Littlefield, Adams.

———. [1929] 1962. *The Sexual Life of Savages in North Western Melanesia.* New York: Harcourt Brace Jovanovich.

Mann, Leon. 1981. "The Baiting Crowd in Episodes of Threatened Suicide." *Journal of Personality and Social Psychology* 41(4): 703.

Manning, Jason. 2012. "Suicide as Social Control." *Sociological Forum* 27(1): 207–27.

———. 2015a. "Aggressive Suicide." *International Journal of Law, Crime, and Justice* 43(3): 326–41.

———. 2015b. "The Social Structure of Homicide-Suicide." *Homicide Studies* 19(4): 350–69. (Published online before print, August 2014. DOI: 10.1177/1088767914547819.)

———. 2015c. "Suicide Attacks and the Social Structure of Sacrifice." Pp. 151–71 in *Terrorism and Counterterrorism Today,* edited by Mathieu Deflem. Bingley, UK: Emerald.

———. 2015d. "Suicide and Social Time." *Dilemas: Revistas de Estudos de Conflicto e Controle Social* 8(1): 97–126.

Maris, Ronald W. 1969. *Social Forces in Urban Suicide.* Homewood, IL: Dorsey.

———. 1981. *Pathways to Suicide: A Survey of Self-Destructive Behaviors.* Baltimore: Johns Hopkins University Press.

Marshall, Mac, and Leslie B. Marshall. 1990. *Silent Voices Speak: Women and Prohibition in Truk.* Belmont: Wadsworth.

Martikainen, Pekka T. 1990. "Unemployment and Mortality among Finnish Men, 1981–5." *BMJ* 301(6749): 407–11.

Marttunen, Mauri J., Hillevi M. Aro, and Jouko K. Lönnqvist. 1993. "Precipitant Stressors in Adolescent Suicide." *Journal of the American Academy of Child & Adolescent Psychiatry* 32(6): 1178–83.

Marzuk, Peter M., Kenneth Tardiff, and Charles S. Hirsch. 1992. "The Epidemiology of Murder-Suicide." *JAMA* 267(23): 3179–83.

Masumura, W. T. 1977. "Social Integration and Suicide: A Test of Durkheim's Theory." *Behavior Science Research* 12(4): 251–69.

Meijer, M. J. 1981. "The Price of P'Ai-Lou." *T'oung Pao* 67(3–5): 288–302.

Mercy, James A., and Linda E. Saltzman. 1989. "Fatal Violence among Spouses in the United States." *American Journal of Public Health* 79(5): 505–99.

Métraux, Alfred. 1943. "Suicide among the Matako of the Gran Chaco." *American Indigena* 3: 199–209.

Metsä-Simola, Niina, and Pekka Martikainen. 2013. "The Short-Term and Long-Term Effects of Divorce on Mortality Risk in a Large Finnish Cohort, 1990–2003." *Population Studies* 67(1): 97–110.

Michalski, Joseph H. 2003. "Financial Altruism or Unilateral Resource Exchanges? Toward a Pure Sociology of Welfare." *Sociological Theory* 21(4): 341–58.

Michel, Konrad, and Ladislav Valach. 1997. "Suicide as a Goal-directed Action." *Archives of Suicide Research* 3(3): 213–21.

Miethe, Terrance D., and Wendy C. Regoeczi. 2004. *Rethinking Homicide: Exploring the Structure and Process of Deadly Situations.* New York: Cambridge University Press.

Milner, Allison, Matthew J. Spittal, Jane Pirkis, and Anthony D. LaMontagne. 2013. "Suicide by Occupation: Systematic Review and Meta-Analysis." *British Journal of Psychiatry* 203(6): 409–16.

Milroy, C. M. 1998. "Homicide Followed by Suicide: Remorse or Revenge?" *Journal of Clinical Forensic Medicine* 5(2): 61–64.

Ministry of Public Health. 2014. "Ministry of Public Health, Ministry of Women's Affairs and UN Call for Efforts to Strengthen Suicide Prevention in Afghanistan." https://reliefweb.int/report/afghanistan/ministry-public-health-ministry -women-s-affairs-and-un-call-efforts-strengthen.

Mishra, Srijit. 2006. *Suicide of Farmers in Maharashtra.* Mumbai: Indira Gandhi Institute of Development Research.

Misono, Stephanie, Noel S. Weiss, Jesse R. Fann, Mary Redman, and Bevan Yueh. 2008. "Incidence of Suicide in Persons with Cancer." *Journal of Clinical Oncology* 26(29): 4731–38.

Mohandie, Kris, J. Reid Meloy, and Peter I. Collins. 2009. "Suicide by Cop among Officer-Involved Shooting Cases." *Journal of Forensic Science* 54(2): 1–7.

Mohanty, Bibhuti B. 2005. "'We Are Like the Living Dead': Farmer Suicides in Maharashtra, Western India." *Journal of Peasant Studies* 32(2): 243–76.

Mor, Nilly, and Jennifer Winquist. 2002. "Self-Focused Attention and Negative Affect: A Meta-Analysis." *Psychological Bulletin* 128(4): 618–62.

Morrell, Stephen, Richard Taylor, Susan Quine, and Charles Kerr. 1993. "Suicide and Unemployment in Australia, 1907–1990." *Social Science & Medicine* 36(6): 749–56.

Morrison, Chas. 2013. "Tibetan Self-Immolation as Protest against Chinese State Repression." Pp. 102–18 in *Conflict, Violence, Terrorism, and Their Prevention,* edited by Arthur J. Kendall, Chas Morrison, and J. Martin Ramirez. Newcastle upon Tyne: Cambridge Scholars.

Mościcki, Eve K. 2001. "Epidemiology of Completed and Attempted Suicide: Toward a Framework for Prevention." *Clinical Neuroscience Research* 1(5): 310–23.

Moser, Kath A., A. John Fox, and D. R. Jones. 1984. "Unemployment and Mortality in the OPCS Longitudinal Study." *Lancet* 324(8415): 1324–29.

Mueller, Anna S., and Seth Abrutyn. 2015. "Suicidal Disclosures among Friends: Using Social Network Data to Understand Suicide Contagion." *Journal of Health and Social Behavior* 56(1): 131–48.

Murdock, George P., Clellan S. Ford, Alfred E. Hudson, Raymond Kennedy, Leo W. Simmons, and John W. M. Whiting. 1987. *Outline of Cultural Materials.* 5th rev. ed. Human Relations Area Files. New Haven, CT: HRAF.

Murphy, Terence R. 1986. "'Woful Childe of Parents Rage': Suicide of Children and Adolescents in Early Modern England, 1507–1710." *Sixteenth Century Journal* 17(3): 259–70.

Murphy, George E., John W. Armstrong, Stephen L. Hermele, John R. Fischer, and William W. Clendenin. 1979. "Suicide and Alcoholism: Interpersonal Loss Confirmed as a Predictor." *Archives of General Psychiatry* 36(1): 65–69.

Murphy, Robert F., and Leonard Kasdan. 1959. "The Structure of Parallel Cousin Marriage." *American Anthropologist* 61(1): 17–29.

Murray, Alexander. 1998. *Suicide in the Middle Ages.* Vol. 1, *The Violent against Themselves.* Oxford: Oxford University Press.

Naroll, Raoul. 1969. "Cultural Determinants and the Concept of the Sick Society." Pp. 128–53 in *Changing Perspectives in Mental Illness,* edited by Stanley C. Plog and Robert B. Edgerton. New York: Holt, Rinehart and Winston.

Noon, John A. 1949. *Law and Government of the Grand River Iroquois.* New York: Viking Fund.

Noueihed, Lin. 2011. "Feature—Peddler's Martyrdom Launched Tunisia's Revolution." *Reuters,* January 19. http://www.reuters.com/article/tunisia-protests-bouazizi-idAFLDE70G18J20110119.

Novelly, Thomas. 2017. "Autopsy Finds Kentucky Lawmaker Died from Self-Inflicted Gunshot Wound." *Louisville Courier Journal,* December 14. https://www.usatoday.com/story/news/politics/2017/12/14/kentucky-lawmaker-dan-johnson-autopsy/951377001/.

Nuijten, Michèle B., Marie K. Deserno, Angélique O. J. Cramer, and Denny Borsboom. 2016. "Mental Disorders as Complex Networks: An Introduction and Overview of a Network Approach to Psychopathology." *Clinical Neuropsychiatry* 13(4/5): 68–76.

O'Meara, J. Tim. 2002. *Samoan Planters: Tradition and Economic Development in Polynesia.* Belmont: Wadsworth/Thomson Learning.

Otterbein, Keith F. 1986. *The Ultimate Coercive Sanction: A Cross-Cultural Study of Capital Punishment.* New Haven, CT: HRAF Press.

Page, Andrew, Stephen Morrell, Richard Taylor, Greg Carter, and Michael Dudley. 2006. "Divergent Trends in Suicide by Socio-Economic Status in Australia." *Social Psychiatry and Psychiatric Epidemiology* 41(11): 911–17.

Palmer, Stuart S. 1965. "Murder and Suicide in Forty Non-Literate Societies." *Journal of Law, Criminology, and Police Science* 56: 320–24.

———. 1971. "Characteristics of Suicide in 54 Nonliterate Societies." *Suicide and Life-Threatening Behavior* 1: 178–83.

Pangrazzi, Arnaldo. 2019. "Bearing the Special Grief of Suicide." Survivors of Suicide Loss. https://www.soslsd.org/resource/bearing-the-special-grief-of-suicide/#.XL0Ao-hKi70.

Panoff, Michel. 1977. "Suicide and Social Control in New Britain." *Bijdragen: Tot de Taal-land-en Volkenkunde* 133(1): 44–62.

Park, B. C. Ben. 2004. "Sociopolitical Contexts of Self-Immolations in Vietnam and South Korea." *Archives of Suicide Research* 8: 81–97.

Park, B. C. Ben, and David Lester. 2009. "Protest Suicide among Korean Students and Laborers: A Study of Suicide Notes." *Psychological Reports* 105: 917–20.

Park, Soo Kyung, Chung Kwon Lee, and Haeryun Kim. 2018. "Suicide Mortality and Marital Status for Specific Ages, Genders, and Education Levels in South Korea: Using a Virtually Individualized Dataset from National Aggregate Data." *Journal of Affective Disorders* 237: 87–93.

Patton, Christina L., and William J. Fremouw. 2016. "Examining 'Suicide by Cop': A Critical Review of the Literature." *Aggression and Violent Behavior* 27: 107–20.

Pearson, Veronica, Michael R. Phillips, Fengsheng He, and Huiyu Ji. 2002. "Attempted Suicide among Young Rural Women in the People's Republic of China: Possibilities for Prevention." *Suicide and Life-Threatening Behavior* 32: 359–69.

Pedahzur, Ami. 2005. *Suicide Terrorism.* Malden, MA: Polity.

Pelisek, Christine. 2016. "Colleagues Recall Shock and Horror after Journalist Committed Suicide on Live TV: 'I Didn't See the Gun.'" *People,* February 10. http://people.com/crime/christine-chubbuck-colleagues-recall-shock-after-on-air-suicide/.

Peréz, Louis A., Jr. 2005. *To Die in Cuba: Suicide and Society.* Chapel Hill: University of North Carolina Press.

Perlin, Seymour, and Chester W. Schmidt Jr. 1975. "Psychiatry." Pp. 147–64 in *A Handbook for the Study of Suicide,* edited by Seymour Perlin. New York: Oxford University Press.

Pescosolido, Bernice A., and Sharon Georgianna. 1989. "Durkheim, Suicide, and Religion: Toward a Network Theory of Suicide." *American Sociological Review* 54(1): 33–48.

Pfeffer, Cynthia R. 1986. *The Suicidal Child.* New York: Guilford.

Phillips, David P. 1974. "The Influence of Suggestion on Suicide: Substantive and Theoretical Implications of the Werther Effect." *American Sociological Review* 39(3): 340–54.

Phillips, Herbert P. 1965. *Thai Peasant Personality: The Patterning of Interpersonal Behavior in the Village of Bang Chan.* Berkeley: University of California Press.

Phillips, Scott, and Mark Cooney. 2005. "Aiding Peace, Abetting Violence: Third Parties and the Management of Conflict." *American Sociological Review* 70: 334–54.

Pierce, Albert. 1967. "The Economic Cycle and the Social Suicide Rate." *American Sociological Review* 32(3): 457–62.

Piersen, William D. 1977. "White Cannibals, Black Martyrs: Fear, Depression, and Religious Faith as Causes of Suicide among New Slaves." *Journal of Negro History* 62(2): 147–59.

Pinguet, Maurice. 1993. *Voluntary Death in Japan.* Translated by Rosemary Morris. Cambridge: Polity.

Plutarch. 1918. "The Life of Brutus." Pp. 127–47 in *The Parallel Lives*, Loeb Classical Library Edition, vol. 6, translated by Bernadotte Perrin. Cambridge, MA: Harvard University Press.

———. 1919. "The Life of Cato the Younger." Pp. 237–409 in *The Parallel Lives*, Loeb Classical Library Edition, vol. 8, translated by Bernadotte Perrin. Cambridge, MA: Harvard University Press.

Poole, Fitz John Porter. 1985. "Among the Boughs of the Hanging Tree: Among the Bimin-Kuskusmin of Papua New Guinea." Pp. 152–81 in *Culture, Youth, and Suicide in the Pacific,* edited by Francis X. Hezel, Donald Rubinstein, and Geoffrey White. Honolulu: Center for Asian and Pacific Studies.

Popper, Karl R. [1934] 2002. *The Logic of Scientific Discovery.* London: Routledge Classics.

———. 1994. *The Myth of the Framework: In Defense of Science and Rationality.* New York: Routledge.

Price, Richard. 1973. "Avenging Spirits and the Structure of Saramaka Lineages." *Bijdragen tot de Taal-, Land- en Volkenkunde* 129(1): 86–107.

———. 1975. *Saramaka Social Structure: An Analysis of a Maroon Society in Surinam.* Rio Piedras: Institute of Caribbean Studies.

Price, Richard, Sally Price, and Ian Skoggard. 1999. "Culture Summary: Saramaka." Human Relations Area Files. New Haven, CT: HRAF. http://ehrafworldcultures .yale.edu/document?id=sr15-000.

Qin, Ping, Preben Bo Mortensen, Esben Agerbo, N. I. E. L. S. Westergard-Nielsen, and T. O. R. Eriksson. 2000. "Gender Differences in Risk Factors for Suicide in Denmark." *British Journal of Psychiatry* 177(6): 546–50.

Rajagopal, Sundararajan. 2004. "Suicide Pacts and the Internet." *BMJ* 329: 1298–99.

Randle, Martha Champion. 1951. "Iroquois Women, Then and Now." Pp. 167–87 in *Symposium on Local Diversity in Iroquois Culture,* edited by William N. Fenton. Washington, DC: Smithsonian Institution.

Rankin, Andrew. 2012. *Seppuku: A History of Samurai Suicide.* New York: Kodansha USA.

Raum, Otto Friedrich. 1973. *The Social Functions of Avoidances and Taboos among the Zulu.* New York: De Gruyter.

Red, Christian. 2013. "Troubled Country Music Star Mindy McCready, 37, Who Had Affair with Ex-Yankee Roger Clemens, Kills Her Dog and Then Commits Suicide." *New York Daily News,* February 18. http://www.nydailynews .com/entertainment/music-arts/mindy-mccready-reportedly-commits-suicide -article-1.1266650.

Red, Christian, and Daniel Beekman. 2013. "'David Was My Soulmate': Country Singer Mindy McCready's Boyfriend David Wilson Commits Suicide." *New York Daily News,* January 15. http://www.nydailynews.com/new-york/country -singer-mindy-mccready-boyfreind-david-wilson-commits-suicide-article-1 .1240171.

Reeves, Aaron, David Stuckler, Martin McKee, David Gunnell, Shu-Sen Chang, and Sanjay Basu. 2012. "Increase in State Suicide Rates in the USA during Economic Recession." *Lancet* 380(9856): 1813–14.

Riedel, Marc. 2010. "Homicide-Suicides in the United States: A Review of the Literature." *Sociology Compass* 4(7): 430–41.

Resick, Patricia A. 1993. "The Psychological Impact of Rape." *Journal of Interpersonal Violence* 8(2): 223–55.

Rich, Charles L., Joanne E. Ricketts, Richard C. Fowler, and Deborah Young. 1988. "Some Differences between Men and Women Who Commit Suicide." *American Journal of Psychiatry* 145(6): 718–22.

Rich, Charles L., Deborah Young, and Richard C. Fowler. 1986. "San Diego Suicide Study: I. Young vs Old Subjects." *Archives of General Psychiatry* 43(6): 577–82.

Robbins, Thomas.1986. "Religious Mass Suicide before Jonestown: The Russian Old Believers." *Sociological Analysis* 47(1): 1–20.

Robinson, Dwight, C. Renshaw, C. Okello, H. Møller, and E. A. Davies. 2009. "Suicide in Cancer Patients in South East England from 1996 to 2005: A Population-Based Study." *British Journal of Cancer* 101(1): 198–201.

Rogers, Everett M. 2003. *The Diffusion of Innovation.* 5th ed. New York: Free Press.

Rogers, Ethan M., Ricard B. Felson, Mark T. Berg, and Andrew Krajewski. 2019. "Taking Sides: Gender and Third-Party Partisanship in Disputes." *Criminology:* 1–24. Published online before print: https://doi.org/10.1111/1745-9125.12215.

Rojas, Yerko, and Sten-Åke Stenberg. 2016. "Evictions and Suicide: A Follow-Up Study of Almost 22,000 Swedish Households in the Wake of the Global Financial Crisis." *Journal of Epidemiology and Community Health* 70(4): 409–13.

Rosellini, Anthony J., Amy E. Street, Robert J. Ursano, Wai Tat Chiu, Steven G. Heeringa, John Monahan, James A. Naifeh, Maria V. Petukhova, Ben Y. Reis, Nancy A. Sampson, Paul D. Bliese, Murray B. Stein, Alan M. Zaslavsky, and Ronald C. Kessler. 2017. "Sexual Assault Victimization and Mental Health Treatment, Suicide Attempts, and Career Outcomes among Women in the US Army." *American Journal of Public Health* 107(5): 732–39.

Rubenowitz, Eva, M. Waern, K. Wilhelmson, and P. Allebeck. 2001. "Life Events and Psychosocial Factors in Elderly Suicides—A Case-Control Study." *Psychological Medicine* 31(7): 1193–1202.

Rubinstein, Donald H. 1983. "Epidemic Suicide among Micronesian Adolescents." *Social Science Medicine* 17(10): 657–65.

———. 1992. "Suicide in Micronesia and Samoa: A Critique of Explanations." *Pacific Studies* 15(1): 51–75.

———. 1995. "Love and Suffering: Adolescent Socialization and Suicide in Micronesia." *Contemporary Pacific* 7(1): 21–53.

———. 2002. "Youth Suicide and Social Change in Micronesia." Occasional Paper No. 36, Kagoshima Prefecture, Japan: Kagoshima University Research Center for the Pacific Islands.

Ryan, D'Arcy. 1973. "Marriage." Pp. 122–41 in *Anthropology in Papua New Guinea: Readings from the Encyclopedia of Papua and New Guinea*, edited by Ian Hogbin. Melbourne: Melbourne University Press.

Ryan, Yasmine. 2011. "The Tragic Life of a Street Vendor." *Al Jazeera*, January 20. https://www.aljazeera.com/indepth/features/2011/01/201111684242518839.html.

Sainsbury, Peter. 1955. *Suicide in London: An Ecological Study*. London: Institute of Psychiatry.

Sainsbury, Peter, and J. S. Jenkins. 1982. "The Accuracy of Officially Reported Suicide Statistics for Purposes of Epidemiological Research." *Journal of Epidemiology and Community Health* 36(1): 43–48.

Sanger, Sandra, and Patricia McCarthy Veach. 2008. "The Interpersonal Nature of Suicide: A Qualitative Investigation of Suicide Notes." *Archives of Suicide Research* 12: 352–65.

Saran, A. B. 1974. *Murder and Suicide among the Munda and the Oraon*. Delhi: National Publishing House.

Schmid, Calvin F. 1928. *Suicides in Seattle, 1914–1925: An Ecological and Behavioristic Study*. Seattle: University of Washington Press.

Schmidtke, A., U. Bille-Brahe, D. DeLeo, A. F. J. M. Kerkhof, T. Bjerke, P. Crepef, C. Haring, K. Hawton, J. Lönnqvist, K. Michel, and X. Pommereau. 1996. "Attempted Suicide in Europe: Rates, Trends, and Sociodemographic Characteristics of Suicide Attempters during the Period 1989–1992. Results of the WHO/EURO Multicentre Study on Parasuicide." *Acta Psychiatrica Scandinavica* 93(5): 327–38.

Schnyder, Ulrich, Ladislav Valach, Kathrin Bichsel, and Konrad Michel. 1999. "Attempted Suicide: Do We Understand the Patients' Reasons?" *General Hospital Psychiatry* 21(1): 62–69.

Schoen, Robert, Nan Marie Astone, Young J. Kim, Kendra Rothert, and Nicola J. Standish. 2002. "Women's Employment, Marital Happiness, and Divorce." *Social Forces* 81(2): 643–62.

Senechal de la Roche, Roberta. 1996. "Collective Violence as Social Control." *Sociological Forum* 11(1): 97–128.

———. 1997. "The Sociogenesis of Lynching." Pp. 48–76 in *Under Sentence of Death: Lynching in the American South*, edited by W. Fitzhugh Brundage. Chapel Hill: University of North Carolina Press.

———. 2001. "Why Is Collective Violence Collective?" *Sociological Theory* 19: 126–44.

Sengupta, Kim. 2011. "Tunisia: 'I Have Lost My Son, but I Am Proud of What He Did.'" *Independent*, January 21. http://www.independent.co.uk/news/world/africa/tunisia-i-have-lost-my-son-but-i-am-proud-of-what-he-did-2190331.html.

Seward, Jack. 1968. *Hara-Kiri: Japanese Ritual Suicide*. Rutland: Charles E. Tuttle.

Shakya, Tsering. 2012. "Self-Immolation, the Changing Language of Protest in Tibet." *Revue d'Études Tibétaines* 25: 19–39.

References

Schmid, Calvin F. 1928. *Suicides in Seattle, 1914–1925: An Ecological and Behavioristic Study*. Seattle: University of Washington Press.

Shneidman, Edwin S. 1996. *The Suicidal Mind*. New York: Oxford University Press.

Shon, Phillip Chong Ho, and Michael A. Roberts. 2008. "An Archival Exploration of Homicide-Suicide and Mass Murder in the Context of 19th-Century American Parricides." *International Journal of Offender Therapy and Comparative Criminology* 54(1): 43–60.

Shotland, R. Lance, and Margret K. Straw. 1976. "Bystander Response to an Assault: When a Man Attacks a Woman." *Journal of Personality and Social Psychology* 34(5): 990.

Shternberg, Lev Iankovlevich. 1933. *The Gilyak, Orochi, Goldi, Negidal, Ainu: Articles and Materials*. Khaborovsk: Dal'giz.

Shugar, Gerald, and Robert Rehaluk.1990. "Continuous Observation for Psychiatric Inpatients: A Critical Evaluation." *Comprehensive Psychiatry* 31(1): 48–55.

Silke, Andrew. 2006. "The Role of Suicide in Politics, Conflict, and Terrorism." *Terrorism and Political Violence* 18(1): 35–46.

Simon, Bob. 2011. "How a Slap Sparked Tunisia's Revolution." *CBS News*, February 22. https://www.cbsnews.com/news/how-a-slap-sparked-tunisias-revolution-22-02-2011/.

Simonton, Dean Keith. 2004. *Creativity in Science: Chance, Logic, Genius, and Zeitgeist*. Cambridge: Cambridge University Press.

Smith, David. 1981–82. "Suicide in a Remote Preliterate Society in the Highlands of Papua New Guinea." *Papua and New Guinea Medical Journal* 24(4): 242–46.

Smith, Jack C., James A. Mercy, and Judith M. Conn. 1988. "Marital Status and the Risk of Suicide." *American Journal of Public Health* 78(1): 78–80.

Sohn, Jie-ae. 2009. "Former S. Korean President Roh Commits Suicide." CNN, May 29. http://www.cnn.com/2009/WORLD/asiapcf/05/23/roh.dead/.

Sorokin, Pitirim A. 1959. "Genesis, Multiplication, Mobility, and Diffusion of Sociocultural Phenomena in Space." Pp. 549–640 in *Social and Cultural Mobility*. London: Free Press of Glencoe.

Stack, Steven. 1980. "The Effects of Marital Dissolution on Suicide." *Journal of Marriage and the Family* 42(1): 83–91.

———. 1990a. "The Effect of Divorce on Suicide in Denmark, 1951–1980." *Sociological Quarterly* 31(3): 359–70.

———. 1990b. "New Micro-Level Data on the Impact of Divorce on Suicide, 1959–1980: A Test of Two Theories." *Journal of Marriage and the Family* 52(1): 119–27.

———. 2000a. "Media Impacts on Suicide: A Quantitative Review of 293 Findings." *Social Science Quarterly* 81(4): 957–71.

———. 2000b. "Suicide: A 15-Year Review of the Sociological Literature Part II: Modernization and Social Integration Perspectives." *Suicide and Life-Threatening Behavior* 30(2): 163–76.

———. 2003. "Media Coverage as a Risk Factor in Suicide." *Journal of Epidemiology and Community Health* 57(4): 238–40.

Stack, Steven, and Jonathan Scourfield. 2015. "Recency of Divorce, Depression, and Suicide Risk." *Journal of Family Issues* 36(6): 695–715.

Stack, Steven, and Ira Wasserman. 2007. "Economic Strain and Suicide Risk: A Qualitative Analysis." *Suicide and Life-Threatening Behavior* 37(1): 103–12.

Stark, Rodney, and William Sims Bainbridge. 1980. "Networks of Faith: Interpersonal Bonds and Recruitment to Cults and Sects." *American Journal of Sociology* 85(6): 1376–95.

Starr, June. 1978. *Dispute and Settlement in Rural Turkey: An Ethnography of Law.* Leiden: E. J. Brill.

Stensman, Richard, and Ulla-Britt Sundqvist-Stensman. 1988. "Physical Disease and Disability Among 416 Suicide Cases in Sweden." *Scandinavian Journal of Social Medicine* 16(3): 149–53.

Stephan, Paula E., and Sharon G. Levin. 1992. *Striking the Mother Lode in Science: The Importance of Age, Place, and Time.* New York: Oxford University Press.

Stewart, Pamela J., and Andrew Strathern. 2003. "The Ultimate Protest Statement: Suicide as a Means of Defining Self-Worth among the Duna of the Southern Highlands of Papua New Guinea." *Journal of Ritual Studies* 17(1): 79–89.

Strathern, Marilyn. 1972. *Women in Between: Female Roles in a Male World Mount Hagen, New Guinea.* New York: Seminar.

Stuckler, David, Christopher Meissner, Price Fishback, Sanjay Basu, and Martin McKee. 2012. "Banking Crises and Mortality during the Great Depression: Evidence from US Urban Populations, 1929–1937." *Journal of Epidemiology and Community Health* 66(5): 410–19.

Subrahmanian, N. 1983. "Self-Immolation in Tamil Society." Pp. 17–50 in *Self-Immolation in Tamil Society,* edited by N. Subrahmanian. Madurai: International Institute of Tamil Historical Studies.

Sverdrup, Harald U. 1939. *Among the Tundra People.* Translated by Molly Sverdrup. La Jolla, CA: Scripps Institute of Oceanography.

Tarde, Gabriel. 1903. *The Laws of Imitation.* Translated by Elsie Clews Parsons. New York: Henry Holt.

Taylor, Anne Christine. 1983. "The Marriage Alliance and Its Structural Variations in Jivaroan Societies." *Information (International Social Science Council)* 22(3): 331–53.

Taylor, Steve. 1982. *Durkheim and the Study of Suicide.* London: Macmillan.

Telegraph. 2001. "South Koreans Sever Fingers in Anti-Japan Protest." August 13. http://www.telegraph.co.uk/news/1337272/South-Koreans-sever-fingers-in-anti -Japan-protest.html.

Thakur, Upendra. 1963. *The History of Suicide in India: An Introduction.* Nai Sarak: Munshi Ram Manohar Lal.

Timmermans, Stefan. 2005. "Suicide Determination and the Professional Authority of Medical Examiners." *American Sociological Review* 70(2): 311–33.

Tsai, Alexander C., Michel Lucas, Ayesha Sania, Daniel Kim, and Ichiro Kawachi. 2014. "Social Integration and Suicide Mortality among Men: 24-Year Cohort Study of US Health Professionals." *Annals of Internal Medicine* 161(2): 85–95.

Tucker, James. 1989. "Employee Theft as Social Control." *Deviant Behavior* 10(4):319–34.

———. 1999. *The Therapeutic Corporation*. New York: Oxford University Press.

———. 2002. "New Age Religion and the Cult of the Self." *Society* 39(2): 46–51.

———. 2015. "The Geometry of Suicide Law." *International Journal of Law, Crime, and Justice* 43(3): 342–65.

Van Hooff, Anton J. L. 1990. *From Autothanasia to Suicide: Self-Killing in Classical Antiquity*. New York: Routledge.

Van Tubergen, Frank, Manfred Te Grotenhuis, and Wout Ultee. 2005. "Denomination, Religious Context, and Suicide: Neo-Durkheimian Multilevel Explanations Tested with Individual and Contextual Data." *American Journal of Sociology* 111(3): 797–823.

Vasavi, A. R. 2009. "Suicides and the Making of India's Agrarian Distress." *South African Review of Sociology* 40(1): 94–108.

Waern, Margda, E. Rubenowitz, B. Runeson, I. Skoog, K. Wilhelmson, and P. Allebeck. 2002. "Burden of Illness and Suicide in Elderly People: Case-Control Study." *BMJ* 324(7350): 1355.

Wagner, Barry M. 2009. *Suicidal Behavior in Children and Adolescents*. New Haven, CT: Yale University Press.

Waismel-Manor, Israel. 2005. "Striking Differences: Hunger Strikes in Israel and the USA." *Social Movement Studies* 4(3): 281–300.

Waller, Altina L. 1988. *Feud: Hatfields, McCoys, and Social Change in Appalachia, 1860–1900*. Chapel Hill: University of North Carolina Press.

Walter, Garry, and Saxby Pridmore. 2012. "Suicide and the Publicly Exposed Pedophile." *Malaysian Journal of Medical Sciences: MJMS* 19(4): 50.Wasserman, Ira M. 1984. "A Longitudinal Analysis of the Linkage between Suicide, Unemployment, and Marital Dissolution." *Journal of Marriage and the Family* 46(4): 853–859.

Watt, Jeffrey R. 2001. *Choosing Death: Suicide and Calvinism in Early Modern Geneva*. Kirksville, MO: Truman State University Press.

Weaver, John, and Doug Munro. 2013. "Austerity, Neo-Liberal Economics, and Youth Suicide: The Case of New Zealand, 1980–2000." *Journal of Social History* 46(3): 757–83.

Websdale, Neil. 1999. *Understanding Domestic Homicide*. Boston: Northeastern University Press.

Wikipedia. 2017a. "Cheng Nan-jung." https://en.wikipedia.org/wiki/Cheng_Nan-jung.

———. 2017b. "Emperor Ai of Tang." https://en.wikipedia.org/wiki/Emperor_Ai_of_Tang.

———. 2017c. "Jan Palach." https://en.wikipedia.org/wiki/Jan_Palach.

———. 2017d. "Junshi." https://en.wikipedia.org/wiki/Junshi.

———. 2017e. "Lawrence Oates." https://en.wikipedia.org/wiki/Lawrence_Oates.

———. 2017f. "Oleksa Hirnyk." https://en.wikipedia.org/wiki/Oleksa_Hirnyk#cite _note-BBCUOH21113-1.

———. 2017g. "Per-Axel Arosenius." https://en.wikipedia.org/wiki/Per-Axel _Arosenius.

Wilbanks, William. 1984. *Murder in Miami: An Analysis of Homicide Patterns and Trends in Dade County (Miami) Florida, 1917–1983.* New York: University of America Press.Williams, Linda S. 1984. "The Classic Rape: When Do Victims Report?" *Social Problems* 31(4): 459–67.

Wilson, Gordon M. 1960. "Homicide and Suicide among the Joluo of Kenya." Pp. 179–213 in *African Homicide and Suicide*, edited by Paul Bohannan. Princeton, NJ: Princeton University Press.

Wilson, Jacque. 2014. "'Suicide Tourism' to Switzerland has Doubled since 2009." CNN, August 20. https://www.cnn.com/2014/08/20/health/suicide-tourism -switzerland/index.html.

Wilson, Margo, and Martin Daly.1993. "Spousal Homicide Risk and Estrangement." *Violence and Victims* 8(1): 3–15.

Wolf, Margery. 1972. *Women and the Family in Rural Taiwan.* Stanford, CA: Stanford University Press.

———. 1975. "Women and Suicide in China." Pp. 111–42 in *Women in Chinese Society*, edited by Margery Wolf and Roxane Witke. Stanford, CA: Stanford University Press.

Wolfgang, Marvin E. 1958. *Patterns in Criminal Homicide.* Philadelphia: University of Pennsylvania.

Woo, Kyung-Sook, SangSoo Shin, Sangjin Shin, and Young-Jeon Shin. 2018. "Marital Status Integration and Suicide: A Meta-Analysis and Meta-Regression." *Social Science & Medicine* 197: 116–26.

World Health Organization. 2002. *World Report on Violence and Health.* Geneva: World Health Organization.

———. 2017. Global Health Observatory Data Repository. http://www.who.int /gho/mental_health/suicide_rates/en/.

Wray, Matt, Cynthia Colen, and Bernice Pescosolido. 2011. "The Sociology of Suicide." *Annual Review of Sociology* 37: 505–28.

Wyder, Marianne, Patrick Ward, and Diego De Leo. 2009. "Separation as a Suicide Risk Factor." *Journal of Affective Disorders* 116(3): 208–13.

Yang, Bijou. 1992. "The Economy and Suicide." *American Journal of Economics and Sociology* 51(1): 87–99.

Yip, Paul S. F., Ying-Yeh Chen, Saman Yousuf, Carmen K. M. Lee, Kenji Kawano, Virginia Routley, B. C. Ben Park, Takashi Yaumachi, Hisateru Tachimori, Angela Clapperton, and Kevin Chen-Chiang Wu. 2012. "Towards a Reassessment of the

Role of Divorce in Suicide Outcomes: Evidence from Five Pacific Rim Populations." *Social Science & Medicine* 75(2): 358–66.

Zadorojnyi, Alexi V. 2007. "Cato's Suicide in Plutarch." *Classical Quarterly* 57(4): 216–30.

Zarghami, Mehran, and Alireza Khalilian. 2002. "Deliberate Self-Burning in Mazandaran, Iran." *Burns* 28(2): 115–19.

Zayas, Luis H. 2011. *Latinas Attempting Suicide: When Cultures, Families, and Daughters Collide*. New York: Oxford University Press.

Zayas, Luis H., Lauren E. Gulbas, Nicole Fedoravicius, and Leopoldo J. Cabassa. 2010. "Patterns of Distress, Precipitating Events, and Reflections on Suicide Attempts by Young Latinas." *Social Science & Medicine* 70(11): 1773–79.

Zeisberger, David. 1910. *David Zeisberger's History of Northern American Indians*, edited by Archer Butler Hulbert and William Nathaniel Schwarze. Columbus: Ohio State Archaeological and Historical Society.

Zhang, Jie, Y. Conwell, L. Zhou, and C. Jiang. 2004. "Culture, Risk Factors and Suicide in Rural China: A Psychological Autopsy Case Control Study." *Acta Psychiatrica Scandinavica* 110(6): 430–37.

Zwillich, Todd. 2006. "Data: Conflict Spurs Suicide, Homicide." *CBS News*, July 6. https://www.cbsnews.com/news/data-conflict-spurs-suicide-homicide/.

Index

Studies in Pure Sociology

Suicide: The Social Causes of Self-Destruction
Jason Manning

The Geometry of Genocide: A Study in Pure Sociology
Bradley Campbell

Is Killing Wrong? A Study in Pure Sociology
Mark Cooney